A. J. Duffield

Recollections of Travels abroad

A. J. Duffield

Recollections of Travels abroad

ISBN/EAN: 9783337211578

Printed in Europe, USA, Canada, Australia, Japan

Cover: Foto ©Andreas Hilbeck / pixelio.de

More available books at **www.hansebooks.com**

RECOLLECTIONS OF
TRAVELS ABROAD

BY

A J DUFFIELD

AUTHOR OF A NEW TRANSLATION OF THE "DON QUIXOTE" "DON QUIXOTE HIS CRITICS AND COMMENTATORS" "THE BEAUTY OF THE WORLD" "THE LAST INCA" "NEEDLESS MISERY" "PERU IN THE GUANO AGE" AND OTHER WORKS

"Magic casements opening on the Foam
Of perilous seas"

"There are in our existence spots of time
That with distinct pre-eminence retain
A renovating virtue whence . . . .
. . . . our minds
Are nourished and invisibly repaired"

WITH MAP SHOWING THE AUTHOR'S OCEAN ROUTES

LONDON
REMINGTON & CO PUBLISHERS
HENRIETTA STREET COVENT GARDEN
1889

TABLE OF CONTENTS.

		PAGE
	Epistle Dedicatory	vii
I.	At Sea with a Dushenka	1
II.	Don Juan Badulaque de Gorduro	24
III.	Santa Fé de Bogota	37
IV.	Baranquilla, United States of Columbia	41
V.	Lima, Peru	51
VI.	Lima (Continued) and Guayaquil	60
VII.	The Peruvian Coast	70
VIII.	From Silvern Potosi to Golden Australia	84
IX.	Silver Lima and Golden Melbourne	117
X.	From New Zealand to Bolivia	128
XI.	Venezuela, Negroes, and Trinidad	155
XII.	More Gold and Silver Comparisons	167
XIII.	Australia	174
XIV.	Chile	182
XV.	Colonial Religion and Morals	195
XVI.	The United States	211
XVII.	Spain	231
XVIII.	Canada	247
XIX.	Still in Canada	280
XX.	Books and Libraries in the Colonies	298

EPISTLE DEDICATORY

TO

CHARLES BROOKFIELD, ESQUIRE.

MY DEAR BROOKFIELD,

It gives me great pleasure to dedicate this book to you, because your name is associated with reminiscences that cannot be made public on account of their private nature, and for affections that would lose their charm if they were shared by others. I shall never forget the extemporized dramas that were played in your youth, in which the *dramatis personæ* were numerous, and the players few, for they included only your brother Arthur and yourself. Those of us who were admitted to the gallery know well enough where the future comedian was born; but I believe I was the only one who prophesied his coming. Of course people in the private boxes had better knowledge, and were therefore not among the prophets.

The other day, as I was dining at a nickel restaurant in a back street off Broadway, in the modern city of New York, a man, who guessed that I was an Englishman, asked me if I knew Mrs. Brookfield. I was greatly surprised by this question; not only on account of the lowliness of the house in which I was, but by the obvious obscurity of the person who put it. These Americans, however, are of a strange nature, and it is impossible for an insular British man to tell in America what manner of man it is who sits next to him at dinner, either by the cut of his clothes, or, to use one of our own unrefined expressions, the cut of his gib; he may be a man of cultivated mind, but of limited means, or a man of many millions and of miserly disposition. He may be a literary man, who frequents out-of-the-way places in search of character— for clever as the American novelist is, he seldom travels in Parnassus—or he may be a genuine man, whose inside spirit is represented by his outside form. Such men are not rare even in New York. This was a genuine man. He kindly and dispassionately informed me that he had been greatly struck by my resemblance to a miniature which he had at home of Michael Angelo, and he had resolved to break through his ordinary reserve in order to have the pleasure of speaking to one who bore so striking a likeness to the greatest artist and one of the greatest men of the old world. I told him with all humility that I was less surprised by his discovery of the likeness to which he had so flatteringly referred than by the question which he had asked me, for the same remark had frequently been made before, and always by persons who were perfect strangers to me; but his question had startled me, for I knew the lady of whom he spoke very well. He assured me that it was entirely owing to my distinguished appearance that he had asked that question: that he had been reading some letters which Thackeray had addressed to the Brookfields, and which were then in course of publication in the foremost of all the monthly magazines of both hemispheres, and it would be only likely that a man of my mien should know the gifted persons of whom Michael Angelo Titmarsh was an intimate friend.. When I told him that you and I were intimate friends he insisted on ordering in two glasses of lager beer, which at that house you get for a nickel a glass. I was glad of this little adventure, for the world then seemed to me not so bad a place for a man to live in, even though he may have a broken nose.

I hope you will read this book; not because I have the vanity to think it will improve your own style, but because it contains something original on a subject about which of late there has been much unoriginal talk. I refer to the colonies, which are not worth talking about unless you can say something that is true about them, or paint something that will wash, and not wash out.

In the first chapter I give you a picture from life of a woman whose husband died in the Indies, and who belongs to the women for whom are expressly written eight hundred novels every year—some of which you may see praised to the skies in newspapers—and for whom are prepared and preached fifty thousand sermons every week; the women who worship in the temple of fashion, and who fashion the manners and morals of English "Society," and are the *beau ideals* of colonial life. I have little doubt about your recognizing the Dushenka.

The second chapter contains a sketch of some of the followers of this class of women, and what they are prepared to do to win their smiles. Also an etching of one who represents many who are masters of the approved way of enlisting the energies of these young bloods.

The third chapter gives you an incident in a silver colony of a people out of whom the gold colonists find it easy to make slaves; also the slightest outline of a man who, though poor, lived like a prince, and about whom I had hoped to say much, but my recollections brought so many tears to my eyes that I could not see to write more than I have. Allusion is also made to the kind of colonist who professes to build his house on the sand.

In chapter four we dive deeper, and bring to light the stuff out of which the atheist is made—a lurid picture—which if I had not remembered it early in the morning I should not have slept at night.

The fifth chapter contains the way by means of which many men and women, by false representations in a good cause, are made credulous and weak. Also what the lazy and voluptuous suffer who are victims of terror and superstition; people who never kneel before the throne of grace except when it thunders, or lightens, or when an earthquake is abroad.

The sixth chapter makes mention of some heroical women whom

I recollect, together with my first experiment with *cuca*, the magical leaf that was not then known to anyone in England save perhaps to Charles Kingsley and myself; or if others did know of it, it was only to laugh at it as a traveller's tale.

In the seventh chapter you have a discursive view of some silver colonists, with some remarks about ourselves.

In chapter eight I give you a translation of the petition of a silver colonist who had, in common parlance, had enough of Peru, and wanted to go in search of New Lands. He had helped to pick the plums out of the Peruvian pudding, and these having disappeared he longed for another pudding. This is what has recently happened in the gold colonies. Forty years after the finding of gold the Australians began to turn their eyes to New Guinea, Fiji, and elsewhere; hence the Australian kidnappings in the South Sea Islands, and slavery on the sugar plantations of Mackay and other parts of North Queensland, where you have a remarkable reappearance of some "old foes with a new face."

In the ninth chapter we have some further comparisons of gold and silver colonists;

And in chapter ten a glimpse of New Zealand, a Presbyterian descendant of Robert Burns; and how I took a skipper into custody on the high seas, together with an adventure, which taught me a lesson on the value of keeping on a straight line when you find yourself lost, and would not be lost for ever. There are also pictures of Potosi, and further adventures, which prove how true it is—in the colonies—that you never know what a day may bring forth, and that the best policy is to be always prepared for the worst.

In chapter eleven there are more pictures of silver colonists.

There is a long extract from an old book in chapter twelve with more comparisons of gold and silver colonies; and novel particulars of certain black fellows.

In chapter thirteen these comparisons are kept up, and you will also find a court of justice conceived in fancy.

A trip to Chile occupies the fourteenth chapter, and the comparison between, or rather likeness of, gold and silver colonists still maintained.

In the fifteenth chapter I make some remarks on a dry, but vital, subject, as you will see.

In chapter sixteen I make certain piebald remarks on the United States, the "biggest colony out," to cull a flower from the ever sparkling rhetoric of our old friend Tapaculo.

In the seventeenth I give you a glimpse of Spain, and still harp on the Don Quixote.

In the eighteenth and nineteenth chapters I warm up a little Canadian broth.

And in the last I show how loth I am to conclude, but finally conclude with an archbishop, which considering that I began with you, is not a bad ending.

I have said little about Canada, although I know it so well, and have so many pleasant recollections of some of its people, of Montreal and the St. Lawrence, and the good old times when you would often dine at mess with some of Her Majesty's officers and discuss the meanness of the Imperial Colonial Office, the futility of the Royal Colonial Institute, which someone calls the Colonial Young Men's Christian Association, and make plans for fishing excursions and shooting wild turkeys. No; Canada is a colony *sui generis*, and does not lend itself to comparison with the gold and silver or shoddy colonies. It never had anything to do with slavery for one thing, but did often get into hot water by giving hospitality to slaves who fled for their lives and freedom from Egypt—or was it South Carolina? All the other colonies of the world—whether Spanish, Dutch, Portuguese, German, French, or English—are represented in the "Federation of Man" by Sancho Panza, the materialist; the man whose eye was always fixed on the main chance—the would-be governor who was consoled for his cudgellings by "finding" gold in the Sierra Morena. Canada has about her some of the charm of heroism, a spice of Don Quixote, and is quite equal to a quarrel over a kettle of fish. I always thought that the name Canada was of Spanish origin; that it was written Cañada, which means a glen or dale, while *Cañada real* means a sheep walk, a passage from the cold uplands to the warm flats. Very pretty, but quite wrong. Canada, I am delighted to find, is an Indian native name, not Spanish, and signifies a collection of wigwams.

I have been further moved to throw together these Recollections of Travel by certain eloquent writers and orators who have lately been making pets of the colonies and ringing rhetorical changes on their favourite Colonial-Institute-word, "Disintegration," which is as high-sounding and meaningless as Mesopotamia, but which does not contain half the comfort. When you hear of Sir Toby Belch or Sir Andrew Aguecheek separating from their titles, then you may possibly hear of the colonies separating from England, and the "disintegration of the Empire" will begin at the Antipodes. The separation of these colonies from each other should be encouraged, for this will be the best means of drawing them closer to their beloved mother. The federation of the Canadas was imperative; the achievement of the Dominion was demanded by Imperial necessity. Even if it were possible to federate the Australias, it is not in the least needful or desirable. Let the colonies first agree on much more simple matters, and then they may agree on greater. Of the influence of the colonies on England I have not spoken. It is a wide and important subject. Here, there is no comparison between the gold and silver colonies. The influence of the silver colonies on Spain was hurtful and disastrous. Cervantes has given us a picture of a returned colonist, who, after spending twenty years in Peru, and gaining thirty thousand pounds in that time (a large sum in 1590), returns to Seville to be mocked, and made a contemptible spectacle of; but Felipé de Carrizales does not represent the returned English colonist, either in his morals or his maudlin end. England has sent many ruffians to Australia, but Australia has sent to England many honourable men. If Philip II. had had the gold of Australia at his command at the time that he had the silver of Potosi, you and I, my dear Brookfield, might now be talking Spanish, and worshipping a doll twelve feet high, which is supposed, in Madrid, to have been painted, or at least varnished, by St. Luke. The colonies have now for several years sent home some admirable cricketers. I was present at the first great cricket match in Melbourne, when H. H. Stephenson's team of Eleven of All England met a team of twenty-two of the United Colonies, and gained an easy victory. This could not now be done. A Colonial Eleven is a fair match for an Eleven of All England. I wonder that a good theatrical company has not been organized in London to make a tour of all the colonies ; not to spend a year starring in the chief ports and returning home, but a tour that would take three years at least, leaving some of the company who would elect to remain behind, as some of H. H. Stephenson's team did. The result to the colonies and players would not fail to be good. But what excites my wonder much more is that so little has been done in the Australias on a grand scale in the way of colonisation. There are many thousands of young men in London alone who could make themselves a name and a position of renown if, for example, they were to establish a fishery in Australian waters, which should include whale fishing. All the large towns are ill off for fish ; the supply is not sufficiently well maintained, while the demand is great. It is a splendid calling, full of adventure, and requiring courage as well as skill and training. There are also many new industries which remain to be introduced into the colonies. There is a fine opening for a Limited Liability Company to undertake the development of useless young men. Will no one start The Industrial Army ? There are many thousands of black fellows in North Queensland who are being hunted down like kangaroos who could be overcome by kindness and enlisted in this army. Is there no spirit in England among the great families whose younger sons are able to discern this, and

"To fulfil
This labour, by slow prudence to make mild
A rugged people, and thro' soft degrees
Subdue them to the useful and the good ? "

Or are the native races which have been committed to our care to remain for ever the victims of greed and a low ambition, or to be restricted to the ineffectual goodness of missionary zeal?

Resta.—Do not wonder at my writing this book. I could not help it. My love to Kemble and all the rest whom we both know.

Always, my dear Brookfield,
Yours faithfully and affectionately,
A. J. DUFFIELD.

P.S.—There is a *Post scriptum* of some magnitude inserted for no other reason than to show what may happen to a man in the Lands of the Golden Fleece.

CHAPTER I.

AT SEA WITH A DUSHENKA.

THESE Recollections are memories which are left clear after a long lapse of time. By waiting, in some cases as long as six-and-thirty years, I find that either the weather has changed or what was foul has died out of mind like the sound of the trumpets of mosquitoes, or the rattles of snakes; and the sea with its rage or its calm, its terrors or its joy, is no longer thought of with disgust, although to me the sea has always been a delight, nor has every long voyage been only so much waste of time. There have been whist parties between England and India which I can never forget, theatres on the way to Australia which are always delightful to think of, and friendships and companionships formed which made the longest voyage too short.

I shall never forget, for example, how on one of the longest journeys I ever made, a woman, who was a charming, youthful widow, made love to me, as I have often made love to little children. She was deliciously stupid, but with liquid brown eyes; and her well-made body was as full of health as a full magnum of Dagonet is of liquid joy. Before joining the ship in which the Dushenka, as I will call this lady, and I were to be together for many days, I had been in the saddle for more than a fortnight, during which time I had ridden something more than a thousand miles, six hundred miles of which were over a desert, under the tropic of Capricorn, and I was very tired when I got on board. How delightful it was to be clean, once more to sleep in a Christian bed, sit on a clean deck, with everything wholesome and sweet about you, and resting! Even now, after the lapse of years, the recollection of those fifteen days of travel over hot sand, with little to eat but raw onions and cheese, and nothing to drink but cold tea, comes back far more vividly than anything which I did last week. Nor can I forget the soothing pipe of tobacco, without which I could not have gone to sleep after the day's hard ride. Let no traveller in the far interior of any foreign land ever be without tea, tobacco, onions, and cheese; if he can add to these cuca and preserved potatoes* he need fear no evil. But the glorious rest which followed the toil of that tropical fortnight is graven on my bones. I wanted nothing else but to sit still in an arm-chair on deck, breathe fresh air, and in imagination travel over again those fifteen days in the saddle.

* *Preserved potatoes*, called in Quichua and Aymará *Chunyo*, or Chuño, according to Spanish orthography. They will keep for years, and it is a wonder to me that Chunyo is so little known among us. The art consists in mechanically taking all the water out of the vegetable and leaving the protein, the fat, carbohydrates, and mineral matter behind. This reduces the potato more than 75 per cent., and is as hard as old mortar when quite ready for use. When required for food a handful of what appear to be small marbles is thrown into hot water for half an hour; the first water is thrown away, and they are then boiled in the usual way. When cooked the potato will have assumed its normal size and taste. Of course, this method of preserving potatoes is only possible under a tropical sun, where there is also much frost.

The only acquaintance I made during the first day or two on board was that of Colonel Lawrence, who had served her Majesty as a warrior in India and was ending his days in her Civil Service, a man of delightful manners and much pride. Dushenka and the Colonel were well acquainted, and he informed me that she was desirous that he should introduce her to me. I begged him not to do anything of the kind; but while we were thus chatting the lady came, brought her chair, and began talking to the dear old Colonel on matters of great triviality. Just as I was in the act of getting up to avoid this youthful, restless woman, Lawrence got up and walked away, saying that he was going to look after his horse, whom some "Jew fellow had been interviewing, and, perhaps, had made him unhappy." I was thus left at the Dushenka's mercy.

"You are a great traveller Colonel Lawrence tells me," she said, turning her brown eyes full on me.

I knew I was in for it, that not again should I as long as that journey lasted know another day of uninterrupted quiet. Without replying to her question, I said —

"You are going to England?"

"Oh, yes," she answered.

"Are you fond of reading?"

"It is my only pleasure. But I have nothing with me that I have not read over and over again," she answered, as if the knowledge she imparted was worth rubies to me.

"What kind of reading do you like best?"

"Oh! poetry. I am fond of all the poets, but I don't like Tennyson; indeed, I may say that I detest Tennyson."

This I was not surprised to hear, for, in spite of her brown eyes and cherry lips, her pretty-dimpled little hands and graceful bust, I was certain that she had no reason to give for her verdict on the author of

> "There lies a vale in Ida, lovelier
> Than all the valleys of Ionian hills."

So I said to her with studied gentleness —

" If we have any luck, you and I will be together for the next thirty days; we shall see each other every day, whether we like it or not. We shall, perhaps, quarrel; or, if not quarrel, we shall hurt one another by some unintentional word or deed. It is the inevitable result of living together under circumstances which do not admit of your going into another neighbourhood, if only for a change. Now, if you do not want to quarrel with me, or me to be ungracious to you —"

" I am sure you could never be anything of the kind," she threw in.

" Let us agree," I continued, without noticing her interruption, " to meet every day at one particular spot in all weathers, at one particular hour, for real work, let us call it. I will read to you, and you shall sew or knit some little thing for me, and this work shall last exactly seventy minutes each day, and no more. In this way we shall get along, and during our thirty days of travel we will make certain of three whole days of pleasure."

" I like the plan ever so much," she answered; " but the worst of it is I can't sew and I can't knit."

" Why!" I retorted, with some mastership, " you are like the lilies of the field. Do you like the comparison?"

" I think it a great compliment," she said.

" I surely thought you would be offended," I said.

" How could you think so?" she asked.

"Do you think it a compliment to be compared to a vegetable?" I inquired.

"Ah! but lilies are not vegetables," she said.

"What are they, then? Are they animals or minerals?" I asked.

"Oh, no. A vegetable is something to eat, like a cabbage or celery. Lilies are to look at and to smell, to give delight."

She said this without the least effort. She neither smiled, nor winked, nor turned a hair. I did not expect her to wink, but I did look for some change in her expression that would guide me to appraise her knowledge. But no, she sat as unmoved as a piece of waxwork in a barber's window, which is used for setting off a style of hair-dressing. What she said was not untrue, but it was not her own.

"What will you do, then," I asked, "while I read to you if you can't sew or knit?"

"I shan't want to do anything," she said, "but to sit still and look at you, and listen, and enjoy your voice, and what you will read."

I confess that I thought it somewhat early for this, but after living in countries where you can eat your green peas for 300 days the year round you get accustomed to anything. Only an earthquake is equal to keeping up a sense of novelty. You get accustomed to the peas, but not to the earthquake. I had never met a woman like this, at least, not an Englishwoman. I never knew an English lady who couldn't sew or knit, and who could dispense flattering remarks without effort to a stranger. I never knew a woman who, after five minutes' talk, and meeting her for the first time, announced that she would enjoy my voice, and look at me while listening to what I might read to her. Here was a well-made, fascinating woman, well groomed, and certainly under thirty, with a musical voice, brown eyes, and a refined row of teeth, surrounded by red velvet, who could neither sew nor knit, and who was prepared to sit and look at me for the space of an hour while I read to her.

I was much puzzled. Spanish women, or rather Colonial Spanish women, will surprise the best travelled man in the world, I don't care who he is, even if he were Gulliver himself, or the new translator of the "Thousand Nights and One Night." But here was an Englishwoman, good looking, well dressed, fresh as a daisy, and of quiet manners, with all her features, as well as her hands, under perfect control, saying things to me which a wife may have said—I believe there are wives in the world who flatter their husbands in private—and even English wives—or as a sister might have said to her brother—but which, to say the least, were somewhat unusual.

No doubt "society" on board ship, especially during a long voyage, is very different to society in a village or in London. It is also likely that Lawrence, who knew something of me, had told the Dushenka a few favourable lies (men will do this sometimes if they wish to gain anything by it for their friends) of one of whom he had heard somewhat. But this was not sufficient to account for the free speech of this woman. I have now little doubt that it all came from the fact that she was a young widow, and had "moved" in military circles in India, and that, unconsciously, she had acquired a familiarity with things which produced carelessness, and had banished all tendency to shyness. How much longer this interesting communion would have lasted it is hard to say, but here the ship's drum beat the *réveille,* and we separated, I with some alacrity, to prepare for dinner.

On the whole I felt much like an invalid who was being nursed into wellness, and no doubt my fifteen days in the saddle had prepared me for such idleness as the Dushenka could make pleasant. I was too tired or too lazy for any other thoughts about the words and ways of this, to me, new sort of woman.

The next day we kept our appointment. It was delicious weather, and we made ourselves snug on deck. Dushenka brought plaids and shawls, and I a handful of manuscript.

After reading for an hour I asked how she liked it.

"I never heard anything so beautiful," she said.

"Oh, you must have heard or read something like it, at any rate."

"Never; all these thoughts are quite new to me, and they are as beautiful as they are new," she said.

"Will you please repeat to me one thought which you noticed?" I said.

"Oh, there are many," she answered. "I shall go and write them down. One is —

"'Tho' I should die, I know
That all about the thorn will blow
In tufts of rosy-tinted snow.'

"The other is —

"'Every cloud that spreads above
And veileth love, itself is love.'

"But this is the one I like best —

"'Oh, to what uses shall we put
The wild-weed flower that simply blows?
And is there any moral shut
Within the bosom of the rose?'"

Away she went, and I confess that I was surprised, for I did not believe she was even equal to the task of remembering the lines, and still less of picking them out as beauties worth storing.

We kept up this kind of reading for nearly a week, at the end of which I wound up by repeating "Œnone," and then I again demanded of her how she liked these poems. Her answer I did not expect. She said—

"They are marvellously sweet. I am quite enchanted. The man who wrote them can write anything."

"Who do you think wrote them?" I inquired.

"You," she answered.

"No," I said; "the man who wrote 'Œnone,' and the rest, is Tennyson."

She was not in the least embarrassed, but said—

"If it had not been for your beautiful reading I should never have understood or liked him."

"Do you now know why you detested Tennyson?" I demanded.

"No, indeed; I feel ashamed of myself for saying what I did of him," she replied. "I suppose I must have been very stupid."

"And arrogant," I added. "When you first tried to read Tennyson you found him, I suppose, to be the fashion. You heard so many people talking of the poet that you found it necessary to know something about one whose name was on everybody's lips. You began to read his works because you wanted to follow the fashion. Is not that so?"

"I suppose it is. You speak very plainly to me," she said.

"Well," I answered, "you can't sew or knit, and I must

have some wage for reading to you. Let me have the pleasure of converting you. I shall be quite satisfied with that. But then you must allow me to speak in plain words, or I shall lose my time and you will not be converted."

"Converted!" she gasped.

"I don't mean," I said, "to make you religious, or to change your religion. I do not even know whether you have any religious convictions or not. I simply want to turn you round; that's what I mean by converting you."

"Pray, what do you mean by that?" she inquired.

"I have turned you or reversed you on Tennyson—you detested him once, and now you love him; and I now want to convert you so that you shall never again make such another blunder with regard to any great man, or great thought, or beautiful object."

"Do you think I am incapable of knowing what is beautiful or great? You are very complimentary," she said.

"And you," I answered, "are hasty; I suppose you always were. What I meant to say was that you must not expect that you are to be supplied with a love of knowledge and good taste, and the means of cultivation, in the same way as you are supplied with gloves, nor will you get new eyes by wishing for them."

"New eyes, indeed!" she said, curling the corners of her mouth.

But I was not to be put off in that way; therefore I said to her—

"The reason why you once detested Tennyson is that you were, shall I say a wild rose, or a wild olive—suppose we say an olive, because it is a Scriptural figure of speech, and we may kill two birds with one stone; the fruit of the wild olive is sour, and its sourness comes from the root. You, I say, were, or are, if you like, a wild olive tree, with a root of your own, with power to bear fruit of yourself—the sour fruit of the wild olive. If you ever bear good olives it will not be as a tree, but as a branch, and that will be when you are grafted into a good olive tree. The source of all beauty, all truth, and love, is God, and until we are brought under His influence or into communication with Him we shall detest all that is beautiful, all that is true, and all that is lovely: 'They are the best for the longest time whom the gods love.'"

"Indeed," she said, raising her eyebrows the sixteenth of an inch, "I thought, on the contrary, 'whom the gods love die young,' but please tell me how I am to get grafted into a good olive tree?" meaning to give me "a facer."

"These metaphors and figures of speech," I said, "you must be as careful of as you are of sugar-plums, or any other sweet things, or they will spoil your stomach; I mean your moral stomach. You will easily get grafted into a good tree and become a branch by first ceasing to be an independent person, and next by cultivating reverence, lowliness of mind, sweetness and reality, or naturalness, and then, then —"

Here, to my great surprise and thankfulness, Dushenka rose to her full height, shook out her dress, and without giving me a look she said, as if speaking to herself —

"I was never so spoken to in all my life," and off she went, and I lit a pipe. If you want to anger a highly respectable or fashionable woman—by which I mean a woman who gets herself up to be looked at by other people—you have only to make mention of the name of God as a real name of a real being, and she will melt into thin air, like the "insubstantial pageant" mentioned in *The Tempest*.

We met again at night and she was my partner in a rubber, and very well she played. When it was over and she was going to bed I told her that she played a very good game, and we shook hands, on which she made me a curtsey, not a mere saucy bob like a float on a fishing line indicating a bite, but a real curtsey, such as you sometimes see in a country village, and it was a very pretty sight.

Our cabins were next to each other; hers being the outside one looking on to the sea, which was so calm one morning that the port windows could be opened. Along the top of the partition which divided us was a perforated metallic plate, and hearing the Dushenka busy in her cabin I filled my hand with toilette vinegar and sent it flying through the ventilator.

She came on deck in a French muslin dress and without a bit of gold about her—except her wedding ring—or precious stone, or fluttering ribbon.

"Good morning," I said, which she responded to by remarking—

"Did you notice how delicious the sea smelt this morning?"

"No," I answered. "What was it like?"

"I hardly know," she said.

"Was it like a druggist's shop?"

"Yes and no."

"Or a glove shop?"

"I never perceived any odour in a glove shop."

"Ah, then you have never been in Cadiz. Was it like Eau de Cologne?"

"A little."

"Or toilette vinegar?"

"Not the least like toilette vinegar, which I hate," she said.

It was Sunday, and I waited to see if she would notice it, or make any reference to our "work."

"Will you read me something, to-day?" she said at length.

"What would you like?" I inquired.

"I will leave it entirely to you," she said, and then we went to breakfast, but I had no appetite. That toilette vinegar was too much for me.

At the usual hour we met, and I read to her Sterne's sermon "On Enthusiasm," of course without telling her who the author was.

On asking her how she liked it, she said —

"It is beautiful."

This was her constant verdict on anything she liked, "It is beautiful." The words were as necessary to her as her gloves were necessary. On the hottest day she must put on gloves or she would not feel dressed, and "It is beautiful" were equally stock words. The sermon is not beautiful, it is, indeed, very plain; the language is not always pure, and the eloquence is not always natural, but it is the work of a man of genius, a man who is a good olive tree, or a true vine, the fruit of which is sweet and wholesome.

"Do you know who wrote that sermon?" I asked her.

"No, indeed, nor can I guess," she answered.

"I suppose not. The author is the Reverend Laurence Sterne, who wrote 'Tristram Shandy,' the 'Sentimental Journey,' and is commonly known in the world of letters as *Yorick*."

"I am very much astonished," she said.

"Why?" I inquired; not because I expected her to tell me the real reason, but I could only learn more of the quality of her mind by this way of catechising.

"I always thought," she answered, "that Sterne was a humourist."

"So he was; but do you attach any definite idea of your own to the term? What is a humourist?"

"Well, I suppose a Punch and Judy sort of man; not exactly a wicked man, nor even a naughty man, but a man who lives by his wits."

"A literary *chevalier d'industrie*," I suggested.

"No, I don't mean quite that," she said, "but certainly something French, something not *comme il faut*."

It is more than likely that she had read either the "Sentimental Journey" or "Uncle Toby," and, regarding both as books only fit for men, did not like to trust herself to make confessions, or to have it known that she had read what some immoral confessor had perhaps condemned.

If she had read "Tristram Shandy" she was, I suppose, quite right in not owning it to one who was quite a stranger to her, although a fellow passenger occupying the next cabin to her own. I do remember a married woman once exclaiming in the innocency of her heart, "I never knew what that meant till now," on the occasion of a certain incident being mentioned by her husband. We all laughed, but then we were all old friends, and she was a gifted woman, and very pretty. She had read the Shandyan philosophy when she could not understand it, and her eyes were opened at a time when it could only move her to wholesome laughter.

Dushenka was a very different woman, and the difference, I think, was in her cultivation. She had been trained in a hot-house, and the other woman had been trained in the fresh air. One was natural, the other was artificial, and sprinkled with toilette vinegar.

I will mention another matter which occurred in the course of our acquaintance on board, because I think it opened my eyes to a new thing, namely, the religion of fashionable English women, the ladies who fill London churches and the grand stands with fashionable bonnets and artificial perfume.

"What church do you go to when you are in town?" I once asked her.

"Oh, we often go to the Chapel Royal—the music is so good. But our own church is St. Elizabeth's, in Moat Lane," she said; and there was a certain gravity in her voice which made me fancy that she was not a mere outsider.

"They have early celebration there, have they not?"

"Oh, yes."

"Do you take the Sacrament yourself?" I asked, with decorum.

Thereupon she closed her eyes, turned away her head, and would, I think, have got up and gone away, but several women were, as usual, watching our "goings on," and she would not give them occasion for supposing that we were having a tiff.

"You pain me," she said, at length.

"I am very sorry; it is the last thing I should dream of doing," I said. "Perhaps you will tell me what I have done?"

"You speak of sacred things in a very improper way,"

she remarked. "I do not think that anything is sacred to you, and this gives me pain."

"I simply asked you if you went to the Sacrament," I said.

"Yes," she replied, "as if it were a dance. I have no patience with you."

"Shall I call it the Lord's Supper?"

"Pray do change the subject."

"Do you call it the Eucharist?"

To this she made no answer, but called my attention to something in the sea. "Was it a sail?"

Sail! There wasn't a sail probably within a thousand miles of us. She wanted to "change the subject," and she didn't want the other women to imagine that we were having a row.

"How brown your eyes look this morning!" I said.

She smiled, shook her head, and said —

"You have no right to look in my eyes," and she closed them.

On which I remarked that I was then looking at something which she had never seen, and never would, or could see.

"What is that?" she exclaimed, with animation.

She knew well enough that I was looking at her eyelids, but this was the kind of make-believe of which she was master, the twaddle she cultivated and practised every day of her life.

After a little space I said to her —

"Have they gone away?" meaning the women who were always watching us.

"Yes," she said, "they have gone. How they hate you!"

"Never mind them, tell me if you go to the Sacrament?"

"I am not good enough," she said, almost naturally.

"Would it make you any better, do you think, if you did go?"

"Indeed, I am afraid not. I did partake when I was confirmed, but it made no difference in me. I was just as ready for a dance, or a horse in the Park, the next day as ever," and she looked quite sad.

She seemed to regard the Sacrament as a balsam, the balsam, perhaps, of Fierabras;* and I was unwilling to say anything that might disturb her superstition. A little superstition in her case could do no harm, and might do her good. No amount of positive instruction that I could give her would have been of any use, and so I let the subject drop for that day. But some time after, when our intercourse had become warmer, she asked me why I drank so much wine at dinner.

"Because I like it, and it is good for me; I can do more work on wine than on anything," I said.

"But what an example you set! Don't you think of that?" she said.

"No. What I think of are the words of our Lord, 'As oft as ye drink, do this in remembrance of Me.' That is the best temperance pledge a man can take."

"You are more profane than I thought," she said.

"And if you had only some legal right in me how miser-

---

* "What balsam is that?" asked Sancho.

"It is a balsam," said Don Quixote, "with which no one need fear dying of any wound; and when I make it and give it to thee, thou hast no more to do, when thou seest me in some battle cloven, than to take deftly that part of the body which has fallen to the ground, and with much subtlety, before the blood has congealed, to place it on the other part which remains in the saddle, taking care to adjust it nicely and fitly. Presently, thou shalt give me to drink but two draughts of this said balsam, and thou shalt see me sounder than an apple."

able as well as profane I should become," I said, on which she was silent; but after a little she said—

"You did not quote that text right. It is, 'As oft as ye drink it,' not as oft as ye drink," and she gave me a superb look.

"Indeed. You have been thinking over this subject of the Sacrament?"

"Yes, a little," she answered.

"I'm glad of it. Do you know why some words in the Bible are printed in italics?"

"Of course I know that."

"Well, why?"

"For the same reason that you underscore a word in a letter," she said.

"To give it emphasis?"

"Yes."

"How clever you are!"

"Do you really think so?"

"You found out all this about the *italics* yourself?"

"Yes."

"No one told you?"

"No one. I have always known that."

"Well, it is all wrong. Those words are put in italics to show you that they are not in the original Greek, and if you look up the text, 1 Cor. xi., 25, you will find that '*it*' is in italics."

"Are you sure?"

"Quite sure."

"You would not deceive me?"

"Not for the world."

It was dark when we held this talk, and we were walking up and down the deck, and because the ship was rolling

c

a little I offered Dushenka my arm; and the ship appeared to roll very much while we were talking about italics.

"Why are they called italics?" she inquired—for she was fond of catechising.

"The type founder," I answered, "who first invented or designed them called them by that name. Some types are called Roman, Egyptian, Gothic, Brevier—"

"What is Brevier?" she interrupted.

"It is the size of the type in which Breviaries were first printed," I said.

"Dear me! how interesting!" she said. "Do you know, I think I am getting quite afraid of you!"

*   *   *   *   *   *

We reached London at the appointed time. A few days afterwards, as Lawrence and I were on our way to the Colonial Office, he asked me—

"How's the widow?"

"I've no idea."

"What! ain't you going to marry her?"

"My dear fellow, I am married," I said.

"I'm devilish glad to hear it."

"Why?" I demanded.

"She is such a fool!" said my fatherly friend.

But how happy some men of my acquaintance might have been if they had married fools such as Dushenka. Some of them, on the contrary, married intellect, others money, others hair, or a foot, or a seat in the saddle, or music, or some poor wretch had the ill luck to catch a glimpse of an ankle, and he married on that, and what a mess they all made of it. My interest in this lady arose from discovering in her the typical woman who reads eight hundred new novels every year, who hates Tennyson, despises Browning, can't abide Charles Reade, and thinks Shakespeare to be a profane writer; the woman who is too ignorant to be honest and sufficiently vicious to follow after priests, superstitious enough to require an Established Church, and with sufficient taste and observation to make a market for the sale of artificial flowers. If the active clergy, the missioners, the archbishops, bishops, and other great and lesser officers of the Church could convert all the Dushenkas in London to a simple knowledge of the Christian faith, it would, I think, do more good than all the other conversions which are reported in the religious newspapers.

Sometimes my residence in foreign countries enabled me to be of unexpected service to friends who, but for information which I could give them, would have been swindled. The story that I am about to tell will not only explain the nature of this service, but it is also full of interest of an unusual kind. With my reader's permission, however, I should for a moment like to return to Dushenka. With all her shallowness and hollowness, I really believe she had some honest desire to find out a method of improving herself. She was fond of reading—and she read much —and carried about with her a great basket full of books, and one day she begged of me to tell her what to read, and how to read to the best advantage.

"You are always reading," she said to me on that particular day; "do you remember what you read, or do you read only to forget?"

"What do you mean by reading to forget?" I inquired.

"I don't know," she said, "it was what a man once said to me when I asked him why he read so much."

"What was he, or, as the Americans say, what did he do?" I asked.

"He was nothing—he was a gentleman," she answered.

"And young, I suppose?"

"No, indeed, he was past middle life."

"You mean by saying that the man 'was nothing' that he had a fixed income, and was of no profession, except the profession of an idler?"

"He was a gentleman," she reiterated.

"Beau Brummell once said that a gentleman is 'one who never perspires;' is that your view?"

"Don't be disagreeable; you know what a gentleman is as well as I do," she said.

"But pray let me hear you say what is a gentleman. My favourite author* says the true Latin word for a gentleman is *ingenuus*—a freeman, and the son of a freeman. Yet there were distinctions. Under the emperors the courtiers were divided into two classes. With respect to the superior class, it was said of the Sovereign that he *saw* them; with respect of the other, that he *was seen*. '*Cæsar is in the habit of seeing me,*' etc., will convey to you a world of meaning. Then, again, one of our most popular religious poets has said, 'He is free whom the Truth makes free, and all are slaves beside,' and another, 'Only a Christian is a gentleman, for a gentleman never hurts the feelings of others.'"

"I like that," she said; "who said that?"

"Never mind who said it. Is it true? Is that your idea?"

"I like it very much," she said. "I suppose it is your own?"

---

* De Quincey. See "The Casuistry of Roman Meals."

"No, indeed," I said; "it is the saying of a man who many years ago wanted to be a missionary to the heathen, and had to give up the wish because he shrank from having to tell them they would go to the place below if they did not believe what he preached, and so he stayed at home in his delightful Devonshire parsonage, and passed his time in fishing and idleness."

"Dear me!" she exclaimed. "Perhaps you knew him; you appear to know a great many clever men."

I kept her chattering away after this fashion because I wanted, if possible, to help her in this matter of desultory reading, a subject on which everybody is so ready to give advice.

"I am not always reading," I began, "as you say, but when I am at sea I carry a book in my pocket that I can open or shut up when I like. Books are the best friends a man can have about him."

"Yes, I know all that," she said. "I mean that is not what I want to know. Can't you tell me some way that is the best way for reading? I know you men have ways of reading that are of great advantage, and I wish you could put me up to some of them."

What would have been the good of giving this chatterbox any of the well-known methods common to reading men? So I promised to give her a hint or two, if she liked, that would be useful.

"What time of day do you go visiting?" I asked her.

"Between four and six in the afternoon," she said.

"And you make a list of the people you are going to see?"

"Of course."

"And there are some people you like better than others,

and you plot and plan to meet them, and do all kinds of things on purpose to make the most of those you care for, and some you don't care to know at all, except by their backs."

"That's the way," she said, with a knowing smile, for, highly connected as I found her to be, she had certain defects that proved she had mixed with inferiors.

"Then, besides these, you have friends whom you see at all times, and are always happy with them, and you don't dress on purpose to receive them, or take care of your mouth while you talk to them, or show off your hands, or your eyes, or your feet to them."

"I have very few of them—some, no doubt," she replied.

"Well," I said, "that is all I can tell you about books and reading."

"What have you told me?" she said, with wide open eyes.

"I have made you go over in your mind your method of seeing people, and what you do with them and for them. You must do the same with books, and then you will become as good a scholar as you are a good fashionable neighbour in society. If you take as much pains to know books as you take to know people, inquiring about them, talking about them, reckoning them up, or even, say, running them down, treasuring up all you hear, and forgetting nothing, and telling all the good things you find in them, you will become as learned as Hypatia without being as disagreeable, and if you don't become very wise you may be witty, and full of sweet thoughts and feelings which never grow old."

"Feelings which never grow old! Do you think so?"

"It requires no thinking about," I said to her with some asperity, for she cared only for herself, and wanted nothing but things that would serve as cosmetics.

"You know I am very stupid; do not be impatient, but tell me plainly what you mean," she pleaded, with much apparent earnestness.

"Did you ever drink at a mountain spring?"

"Yes, often," she said.

"Wasn't it always fresh, exhilarating, even intoxicating?"

"Always."

"Well, 'whosoever drinketh of this water shall thirst again, but whosoever drinketh of the water that I shall give him shall never thirst; but the water that I shall give him shall be in him a well of water springing up unto everlasting life.' Those words, you know, were said to the woman of Samaria, at the time she was living with a man who was not her husband, and you know who said them. What the words mean you must find out for yourself, but I will tell you what they do not mean: They do not mean going to Church, or reading the Bible, or singing Psalms, or giving away money in what you call charity, or being proper, or wearing costly garments, or believing in certain doctrines, or even going to the Sacrament."

She was much astonished. The woman of Samaria was to her as an unsavoury smell, for she quietly opened her little reticule and pulled out a smelling bottle which she used with much grace.

If anything else occurs to me about this lady I will tell it. She engaged my attention a good deal, for she belongs to the unwritten history of England—a "girl" of my own period, who I have the satisfaction of knowing still speaks well of me.

CHAPTER II.

DON JUAN BADULAQUE DE GORDURO.

THE story I was about to tell of being once, as we say by accident, of some use is as follows :—I had strolled into the city one summer morning, probably to get some money, when a kinsman of mine met me in Throgmorton Street, who said —

"Have you ever been in Guayaquil?"

"Certainly; I was there last year," I answered.

"Well, just step into Radaman's chambers over there, and tell him all you know about the place; I promised that he should see you."

"Who is Radaman?"

"Never mind that just now; go and see him."

Radaman, it appears, was a young sporting man who gambled on the Stock Exchange and "made money" sometimes, and sometimes lost, as all—even the best of them—do; "they can't help it," their friends say.

Radaman, when he heard who I was, plunged at once into business.

"You know Guayaquil? Is there a river there? How

close is the river to the town? Can a large ship get up from the Pacific? How long is this river?"

I answered these questions, adding —

"No ship can get up to within twenty miles of the town now, owing to some vessels having been sunk there to prevent the town being bombarded by a hostile fleet."

"The devil!" exclaimed Radaman; "would you have any objection to making that statement in the presence of a—a—a friend of mine?"

"If it will be of any service, I shall be glad."

"It will be of the greatest service; he will be here almost directly."

Indeed, while Radaman was yet speaking in came one who was introduced to me as Señor Don Juan Badulaque de Gorduro.

He was a handsome fat man, like a prize man got up for show; he had a diamond as big as a big raspberry in his shirt-front, a hearty smile on his face, and he spoke excellent English.

When Radaman told him of the sunken ships in the Guayaquil river he said —

"All that is now cleared away, but I will drive to the Foreign Office, and return within an hour with authentic information."

His brougham was at the door and he straightway drove off and returned as he had promised, bringing a note written on Foreign Office paper in a gentleman-like hand, which said:—"The Guayaquil river is quite free for navigation, all the sunken vessels have been removed." The note was not signed—nor did Radaman notice this omission, who then said to Gorduro —

"I wish you to go into this thing with Mr. Duffield, who

knows those countries; explain everything to him, introduce all your friends to him, and omit nothing. If Mr. Duffield makes a satisfactory report to me in the morning the enterprise will go on, if he advises against it you must go to somebody else."

"Very well; then Mr. Duffield, shall we go at once to my hotel?" said Badulaque de Gorduro in an exuberance of politeness.

We drove to the most expensive hotel in London. Radaman had possessed me of all the wondrous tale, and I was to hear from Gorduro his plans, and read his papers, and see his friends, and report.

The enterprise was nothing less than the seizing and holding of the town of Guayaquil and conquering the republic of Ecuador. Once in possession of Guayaquil, nothing and no one could come in, or go out of the republic without the permission of the invaders. There really was no obstacle at all. Ecuadorian stock could then be bought in Capel Court for £8; by skilful management the expenditure of £100,000, and a little daring, a million pounds sterling could be made in less than a year. Some merchants in the city were to be allowed to enter "the swim," and the conquest of Ecuador was to be achieved by young bloods of the English aristocracy. The people of Ecuador were ready, they would join in the movement, it would be a bloodless conquest, the only people who would be killed were those who made any resistance. But no resistance would take place. The President would formally resign to the English gentlemen at their request.

This is the mere outline of the swindle.

Badulaque was delighted to have me to go through his

papers, for I could read them in the original, and Radaman could not.

I spent an hour with Badulaque in listening to a long verbal statement of his magnificent plot, and how he intended to proceed. His object, however, in our first interview was not so much to unfold his plot and plan as to unfold me; and being satisfied, I suppose, with his conclusions, he invited me to dinner that evening when he would have his chief confederates to meet me.

The dinner was excellent. The guests were all fine young fellows, highly connected. One was the son of a foreign European Ambassador, then resident in London. It would not surprise me to be told that some of the youngsters connected with our own Foreign Office were in the conspiracy. Those with whom I dined were obviously in earnest, and had probably given in their names as volunteers. They fired many questions into me during dinner, which I had no difficulty in answering, and from these questions I gathered how deeply they were involved in the scheme. There was abundance of wine of the best kind, but it was moderately drunk. They had obviously all often met previously, for each talked of his command and his preparations in the most business-like way, and with perfect *nonchalance*. One of them came in late, after we had got through the *entrées*. He was a tall, handsome fellow, of striking looks. I knew him, although we had never met before. After dinner, as we rose from table and were grouping ourselves in talking knots, I took this last-comer on one side and said to him —

" Your name is Pendargon."

He started, and asked, with a little fierceness —

" How do you know that ? "

"Never mind. I know some of your people—your brother, who is now in Peru, and your aunt, who is with the Colonel, her husband, in Melbourne—and for their sakes I wish to save you from failure and disgrace. This man, this Badulaque de Gorduro, is a swindler. Meet me in Throgmorton Street to-morrow morning at eleven, and you shall know more."

He was sulky, and only promised to meet me after much hesitation.

"What are you doing here?" he asked me, with waking reason.

"I am here," I replied, "on behalf of Radaman. Gorduro is to show me his credentials after you have all left, and I am to report to-morrow."

"I thought it was all settled," he said.

"No; Radaman cannot read Spanish, and I am to go through the originals."

"That's quite right. Very well, then, at eleven to-morrow. Shall I take these youngsters away now?"

"Let us have a peaceable smoke first, and then, pray, go away not later than eleven."

All that I recollect of this part of the evening was an animated discussion on the manœuvring of cavalry at Guayaquil.

"You can move cavalry about Guayaquil," I said, "as easily as you can on the Dome of St. Paul's."

"Are you a military man?" inquired one of the would-be *conquistadores*.

"No," I answered; "a man doesn't need to be a watchmaker to tell what o'clock it is, nor does he need to be a cavalry officer to know that you can't turn a charger on an upright ladder."

They agreed to this, and then there was a display of Admiralty charts and maps, which showed how far these young would-be heroes were in for it, and how thoroughly the swindler had done his work.

"What is the distance of Quito from Guayaquil?" inquired one.

"It is," I answered, "sometimes a month, now and then a week, or four or five days, and it has been done in one day."

"How is that?"

"It is a matter of weather. For three months in the year—sometimes for more—the rain is wonderful, indescribable. It draws the stones out of the mountains like a dentist will draw your teeth. The roads become rivers, and the mud is simply maddening. Indeed, mud is an inadequate word to express the condition of things."

I noticed the impatience of these youthful military aspirants. They knew well enough all about mud, and did not require definitions; indeed, it was not worth consideration. Some time after this I recollect a puzzle-headed F.R.S. asked me to define mud, and when I replied, "Inorganic matter in a state of liquefaction," he shut up like a knife, for I had seen the thing in oceans, and could speak with authority, which he was bound to recognize.

"You say," continued the youngsters, "that the banks of the Guayaquil river are flat. Is that the case all the way down to the Pacific?"

"Yes, from the town; but those banks are more inaccessible than if they were steep and high."

"Please explain."

"Both sides of the river, except here and there, where are patches of hard ground, are covered with dense forests of mangroves, miles in breadth, which you can see early in the morning by the mist which hangs in dense white clouds over the tops of the trees. This mist is sometimes so thick that not even a whole day's sun pouring down upon it in a straight line from right over head can disperse it."

"Then there is no towing path along the river—no road at all?"

I could not help laughing at this question, which was simple remissness on my part. None of these youngsters, except Pendargon, had ever been in tropical countries. How, then, could they know that a tropical river is as like an English river as a domestic cat is like a jaguar? And certainly no geography that I am acquainted with pretends to make known the difference.

"Are the people quiet and peaceable?"

"As vermin."

This short answer of mine provoked many more questions, which I need not repeat. It was evident to me that they had given much attention to the subject of invading and conquering Guayaquil, and that they knew absolutely nothing about it, nor was it possible to convey to their preoccupied minds any accurate knowledge.

"You have been through the Straits of Magellan?"

"Yes."

"And across the Isthmus of Panama?"

"Many times," I answered.

"Well, suppose you wanted to surprise your friends in Guayaquil, would you go across Panama or through Magellan's Straits?"

"In a case of war," I replied, "with very limited supplies, with all your men and munitions of a select kind, and profound secrecy being of the essence of your success, you would go the round-about way through the Straits. Coaling and watering at Puntas Arenas, and then at Tocapilla, finally at Payta, you would fly the Pacific Steam Navigation Company's flag and get all you want. The captain of the port would come off to you in each place. You would have to take him into your confidence, or take him along with you. In either case you must be prepared with some small change in the current coin of the country. But if you have plenty of funds and secrecy is of no importance, then you would send your steamer through the Straits with the heavy material to meet you at Panama, and take another steamer from hence to Colon, and so cross the Isthmus. If, however, any suspicions were roused, you would be all taken prisoners by the Government of the United States of Colombia, through whose territory the Panama railway passes, and you would be detained until everything about you was known, and then all the fat would be in the fire. Therefore, all things considered, you would doubtless elect to go the longest way about, which, as Lord Bacon says, is sometimes the shortest."

"Oh yes, the Panama route was out of the question," said one; "I always said so."

And so it was, and what with the good wine, the animated talk, the familiar handling of the subject they had in view by conversing with one who, as they said, "knew the ropes," it became well known to me that these ardent young gentlemen, led by a plausible swindler, were resolved on taking Guayaquil and conquering the republic of Ecuador. Before the hour arrived when we should separate, I knew who was to command the cavalry, who the infantry, which should be Chancellor of the Exchequer, and which Prime Minister. But who was to be Commander-in-Chief of the expedition I was not told. At length, soon after eleven, we separated, and I was left alone with El Señor Don Juan Badulaque de Gorduro.

We had all drank well, but the wine was good, and nobody was the worse for it. Gorduro was a teatotaller; at least, he said he was. I am not of a suspicious nature. I have never cultivated suspicion, but no sooner was I alone with this man than an irresistible conviction seized hold of me that he was up to anything and would do anything.

This was not the first time that I had been in the power of a murderer. I was once quietly taken possession of by two mounted murderers, whom I escaped by tempting them with some of the *leche de la Madre de Dios*. They and I dismounted in a solitary part of a mountain pass, and I gave them to drink of the enchanting liquor.

"Have another *trago*," I entreated, and they had another, and another, and between them they emptied a bottle of old French brandy, as soft as milk and potent as laudanum, and in a moment they fell dead asleep, and I rode away.

Now I do not claim any merit for the manner in which I acted on that occasion. Everything was unpremeditated. I knew absolutely nothing against these men, and was guided only by the evil looks of the oldest of the two ruffians. It is true that those looks were enough to frighten the devil himself, and why I was not frightened I do not know. I was, on the contrary, somewhat gay. Perhaps the air of the upper desert entered my brain, and made me for a moment like the desert itself, steadfast and calm. But I do not know. I will tell the whole story at length in its proper place.

"Have another bottle of wine," said Gorduro, when we

were quite alone. As fast as I emptied my glass he filled it. Of course. I partly expected this. But I did not expect the wine to be so fine, or the effect on me so strengthening and refreshing. He showed me all his papers. He talked well, and with much discretion.

"Where did you learn English?" I inquired.

"In Mexico," he answered.

But as Satan, or somebody else, would have it, the way in which he pronounced "Mexico" was as if Ariel had suddenly sounded a Jew's harp. There was a twang about it which was peculiar to Broadway, Wall Street, Fifth Avenue, or Cincinnati.

I complimented him on his English; but he suddenly dropped it, and began talking in the Spanish tongue, the odd thing being that he made more blunders while talking in his native language than when he addressed me in English. He became conscious of this, which was shown by his overbearing affectionateness. At one time I really thought he was going to give me a kiss; Peruvians do this when they are meditating murder.

"Have another bottle of wine."

"Waiter, will you please carry this bottle into my bedroom."

Then, turning to me like a wanton, he said —

"I am going to show you my heart!"

We adjourned from the private dining-room of the hotel to his bedroom, and heartily did I wish that I had never been let into this filthy business. Having now to go through with it, I proceeded to give the man all the benefit I could of all the doubt which hung over him. I began to pity the brute, and thought of the words of Prospero when describing his false brother to Miranda as

> "Like one,
> Who having, unto truth, by telling of it,
> Made such a sinner of his memory,
> To credit his own lie,—he did believe
> He was indeed the duke."

I ought to say that Gorduro had made up his mind to the conviction that I would certainly report favourably of him to Ramadan. He did not once venture to put to me a plain issue, but in answer to one or two little questions which pointed in that direction he had received from me certain nods and winks of the eye, which he interpreted in his own interest.

Before showing me his heart he unlocked a green morocco despatch box, and taking from it a document which he unfolded, handed it to me, and said—

"Read *that*."

It was simply an agreement, or rather a promise, on the part of another native scoundrel, in the event of Gorduro and his friends taking Guayaquil, to hand over to them his right to the Galapagos Islands—of course for a consideration.

This document, by a strange freak of fortune, I had seen in the hands of an Englishman who showed it to me, and who died in Guayaquil some little time before.

Seeing me read it with so much care and interest—for I was much concerned in the history of the man to whom it had once belonged—he said to me—

"Are you satisfied?"

"Perfectly," I answered, and Gorduro was pleased.

"But now," continued the enchanted fool, "prepare for something greater. Read this!" And in handing me what proved to be a piece of parchment he went through the ceremony of symbolically cutting his throat.

The parchment was written in Spanish, and set forth that el Señor Don Juan Badulaque de Gorduro was raised to the dignity and degree of a master mason in the Lodge of Santa Apolonia, in Lima, in the year 5637.

"Have another bottle of wine, Don Alejandro."

I told him an exciting tale—two tales in fact—of men who by means of a similar piece of parchment had been saved from impending death, and subsequently raised to affluence and power. I left him long after midnight, much more drunk than I was, although I had drunk a good deal of wine and he not any.

The next day, in the evening, Badulaque just managed to catch the tidal train to Paris. He never returned, and Guayaquil stands where it did, and so do Ecuatorian Bonds stand where they did in the market quotations.

How near these English youngsters were to doing a big thing! If they had been properly trained, or had contracted some human ideas of human life and human dignity, they might have set a great example. It is quite possible to take Guayaquil, and with it one of the most gorgeous countries in the world, where grow all the fruits and all the flowers, and where are wonders beyond the power of man to tell in the animal, mineral, and vegetable kingdoms. Nor is it necessary to shed blood or to steal. Let a band of gentlemen, with gardeners, builders, blacksmiths, ship-carpenters, and others, go there and do as Abraham did, they shall become as great as Abraham was. But before they try to imitate Abraham they must, I suppose, have a little of Abraham's faith, or something that will stand them in stead. The work can be made more exciting than war; I mean bloody, grim-visaged war, for there is a war in which courage, endurance, skill, knowledge, temperance, self-sacrifice, and manliness in all its forms are needed, and is more full of fun and noble happiness than the other war, and why this kind of warfare has been dropped by English gentlemen is a question that ought to be answered, and will be answered one of these days, perhaps, when Mr. Walter Besant has finished his work on "The Immigration of the Gibeonites to Santa Fé de Bogotá."

My own answer to this question is that the Dushenkas of our time are incapable of inspiring men to do great things; and that as long as the Dushenkas are content to be dressed, and be-bejewelled, and worshipped by men, so long will men prefer idleness, selfishness, and littleness to fighting Philistines, or doing any other hard and noble work.

CHAPTER III.

BOGOTÁ.

BUT Bogotá, like Quito, is too far from the sea. To reach Bogotá you must ascend the River Magdalena, which, in a good steamer, and with no accidents, will take at least ten days, for you have to tie up every day at sundown on account of snags and shifting sand-banks. You can't travel by night in a steamboat on the Magdalena, excepting in very few well-known parts, and these are very short reaches. Then after reaching Honda, which is less than 600 miles up the river, where you disembark before you reach Bogotá, you have seventy miles to go over land. And it is over land, with a vengeance. If it were to be ironed out flat it would be, not seventy miles, but five times seventy miles. You go up and down for three, sometimes for five, days through all kinds of weathers, climates, and temperatures, until at length you reach the pass described by Kingsley in his "Westward Ho," in the chapter "How they took the gold train." Seeing that Kingsley was never there, it is a wonderful piece of accurate description. He only makes one mistake; there is "no ditch" on either side of the pass, "once paved when Cundinamarca was a kingdom." From thence you mount to the plain of Bogotá, which is ten thousand feet above the level of the sea ; a beautiful climate, but, as I have said, it is perhaps too far from the world's highway to be turned to much profit.

On my way up to Bogotá from the sea I had skirted the base of the Quindio Mountains by making a wide detour from Carthagena on my way to Baranquilla, the headquarters of the steamers which navigate the Magdalena. I know of no country so gorgeous in its desolation as this through which I wandered all alone for several days. It had once been densely populated ; there were still to be seen great wide and straight roads running for miles through vast forests, where were numerous orange trees full of golden fruit. I was galloping down one of these roads at a good pace, being well mounted, when an enormous yellow and black striped jaguar sprang over a wall of creepers into the middle of the road, immediately in front of my horse's nose, and in an instant picked himself up and bounded over another vegetable wall on the other side, making a standing jump of some twenty feet in length and at least sixteen feet in height.

On my arrival in Bogotá, which happened to be on a Saturday, I was astonished to see the grand plaza fitted up like a Spanish bull ring, in which on the following Sunday was to be a fight between a wild bull and a jaguar. I told the story of my jaguar to some friends, who made light of it, and disposed of the dimensions I had given of the jaguar's jump in the usual way. The Sunday came, the fight came off ; the bull and the jaguar met in a ring sixty feet wide, made of iron railings twelve feet high. The jaguar crouched close to the railings, the bull put his nose close to the ground and drew stealthily towards him ; and when the bull made his spring the jaguar sprang into the centre of the ring, and then over the railings among the densely-packed crowd, killing many before he was himself killed.

I have often thought since that if I had not been so circumstantial in my account of the jaguar's jump, which I had been careful to note, the friends to whom I told it might have been induced to put a stop to the dangerous exhibition which resulted so fatally to many.

Bogotá is eminently a commercial city, of many thousand inhabitants. When I was there the trade was chiefly in the hands of Englishmen and Jews, and consisted of quinine and tobacco as the chief exports. The tobacco was grown in the valley of Ambalema, on the Magdalena, and the quinine was brought from the forests by the natives on donkeys and mules. In these two trades there was ample room to build up a lasting fame for the English name, but the sole object which the merchants had in view was to make money as quickly as possible for themselves; and some did make it in a way which altered their good looks. Some of these men who went to Bogotá as good-looking young fellows are now coarse and common-looking—not worth looking at in fact; very rich, and living in the best parts of London "town," but with no wholesome ambition, and with no noble example to set or knowledge to impart that is worth listening to. Bogotá is a delightful memory to me and to many. What Bogotá may think of the Englishmen who have left her and the Jews who made themselves rich by her help we shall probably never know.

I have met many men in the course of my travels who towered above the common run of men as the aloe towers above the weeds which creep at its roots; men of all colours—black as well as white, and the intermediate shades of these ; of all conditions, also of all tongues ; men whose lives do as surely hasten the progress of human love and reason as a river hastens in its peaceful progress to the ocean the nearer it approaches it. "These kind of men," says the ancient sage Albupharage, "are the elect of God, His best and most useful servants, who are the torches, the legislators of the world, but for whom mankind would fall into ignorance and barbarism." Such a man was *Patrick Wilson*, of Bogotá, a very human man, despised, yet envied by Dives and his brethren, but loved and adored by Lazarus and his family, which in that region are numerous. He was a most gracious man, of much cultivation and fine presence, who, though poor, lived like a prince, reminding me of the "one event" of Emerson "which never loses its romance," "the encounter with superior persons on terms which allow the happiest intercourse." *Dr. Cheyne* was another similar man, but of less romantic character—he was a man of science. They were both gifted with vast and peculiar influence, and they were men who also had suffered much. Like el Rio Seco, they have disappeared from the face of the earth, leaving behind only a name—but one is Don Patricio el Bueno—Don Patricio the good, and the other the Famous Doctor—both Englishmen, who have left behind them in the memories of men an idea of the greatness and splendour of the nation to which they belonged. If the same could be said of all Englishmen who have lived in foreign parts, the world would now be flocking to England for lessons in greatness.

It would be delightful to tell more of Bogotá, but as this could only be done by mentioning the names of persons who are still living, we will go down the Magdalena, and prepare for a visit to Peru.

CHAPTER IV.

BARANQUILLA.

THERE are men, some of whom I have also met, who look as if they were skulking in corners in hope to hide themselves from merited scorn. There are men who it would seem have their service in this world, men but for whom the greatly good could not so readily work their will if there were not in the same neighbourhood men who were, or had once been, equally great in working evil.

On my way down from Bogotá to Baranquilla I arrived just in time to miss the northward-bound mail, and I had to remain a month in that dismal place for the next ship. There were plenty of mosquitoes, scorpions, caimanes, snakes, vampire bats, stinging spiders, and a great excess of solar heat.

There was also much cotton—the beautiful long stapled perennial cotton which grows without gardening, also fields of tobacco, and forests of caoutchouc and ivory nuts, and where these are, commercial man will not be far off. The day of my arrival in Baranquilla was marked by an event which I shall never forget. It was towards evening, and the sun was red hot, when suddenly there came on us, or we ran into it, a thick fall of snow!

Snow at the mouth of a tropical river only ten degrees north of the equator! Snow falling all around us when everybody was profusely perspiring, and millions of mosquitoes were blowing their trumpets!

A strong north-west wind had been blowing all day and had stripped the trees of their ripe cotton for miles around, carrying it up to heaven. As evening came on, the wind suddenly ceased, and down came the silvery flakes of cotton back to the earth. Could I have been carried direct home on an aëronautic broom-stick without touching at the village or asking for explanation I should have been prepared to swear on reaching London that I had seen a snow-storm in Lat. 10′ N., Long. 75 west, so easy is it for a man with as many eyes in his head as there are in a peacock's tail to be blinded or bamboozled by his pre-occupied senses. This theatrical snow-storm which had delayed us was the cause of my making the acquaintance of a man whose manners and conversation I will describe.

He was not a striking man to look at, although he came from New York. He was, for one thing, very silent; he asked no questions, he did not even guess at anything. He was in the caoutchouc business, that is, he employed as many of the native people as would accept his wage to go into the forests, collect the exudations of india-rubber trees and bring to him. There are hundreds of such men in this masterless part of the world who come from New York, Paris, London, Liverpool, Manchester, and Birmingham, who make it their business to collect bark for extracting quinine from, ivory nuts, cochineal, coarse wool, old silver, orchids, emeralds, old gold, and gold dust, getting these things sometimes for an old song, or even less, exactly as H.M.S. *Challenger* got the art treasures of the South

Sea Islanders by bartering for them Sydney goods or Brummagem trash.* It is not an exciting business; at least, you must not get excited over it. It was in every way suited to the man of whom I am to tell. We ate and drank together at the same comfortable, cool hotel, which was kept by Miss Creighton. Knowing that I had come down the river, I wondered he did not ask me something about gum trees, or ivory nuts. To my surprise he asked me if I played chess?

"A little," I answered, "just enough to make me enjoy a scrimmage."

This brought us together, and every night for several nights we passed away the hot hours in mimic war. But he was a dull dog, and forced me to believe that he cultivated dulness for some commercial reason. He had had enough of chess, and now wanted to talk. This he did in a jargon which for some time engaged my attention; but finding myself going to sleep, and the hot room reeking with stupidity, I roused myself, and said, for pure fun, quoting the well-known words of Hugh Latimer —

"Here now I remember an argument of Master More's, which he bringeth in a book which he made against Bilney; and here, by the way, I will tell you a merry toy. Master More was once sent in Commission into Kent to try out (if it might be) what was the cause of the Goodwin Sands and Shelfs that stop up Sandwich Haven.

"Thither cometh Master More, and calleth the country before him, such as were thought to be men of experience and men that could of likelihood best certify him of that matter concerning the stoppage of Sandwich Haven.

"Among others came in afore him an old man with a

* See Moseley's "Challenger Notes," a valuable book, p. 437, etc.

white head, and one that was thought to be little less than an hundred years old.

"When Mr. More saw this aged man he thought it expedient to hear him say his mind in this matter, for being so old a man it was likely that he knew most of any man in that presence and company. So Mr. More called this old, aged man unto him, and said —

"'Father,' said he, 'tell me, if ye can, what is the cause of this great arising of the sands and shelves here about this haven, the which stop it up that no ships can arrive here? Ye are the eldest man that I can espy in all this company, so that if any man can tell any cause of it, ye of likelihood can say most in it, or, at least wise, more than any other man here assembled.'

"'Yea, forsooth, good master' (quod this old man), 'for I am well nigh an hundred years old, and no man here in this company anything near unto mine age.'

"'Well, then,' quod Master More, 'how say you in this matter? What think you to be the cause of these shelves and flats that stop up Sandwich Haven?'

"'Forsooth, sir,' quoth he, 'I am an old man. I think that Tenterton Steeple is the cause of Goodwin Sands. For I am an old man, sir,' quod he, 'and I may remember the building of Tenterton Steeple, and I may remember when there was no steeple at all there. And before that Tenterton Steeple was in building there was no manner of speaking of any flats or sands that stopped the haven, and therefore I think that Tenterton Steeple is the cause of the destroying and decaying of Sandwich Haven.'"

"What has all that to do with what I said?" demanded my companion.

"Do you not see it?" I inquired.

"No," he answered, with firmness.

I consoled him by saying that many well-to-do persons were often at a loss to know the meaning of many stories. But he would not be consoled, and wanted an explanation. As he knew a little of the Spanish tongue, I said, quoting again—

> "'Dijo á la rana el mosquito
> Desde una tinaja
> Mejor es morir en el vino
> Que vivir en el agua."
>
> Said the frog from his jar
> To the drown'd little fly,
> I would not live in water
> If in wine I could die.

When again he declared that he did not see it, I wished him good-night and went to bed. But I found, as I thought him over, that for some reason he had interested me.

The next morning was cool and fresh, and my india-rubber man, with commercial cordiality, asked me if I would join him in a ride. I could not well refuse, and we set off. On a pair of nimble little ponies, who knew the art of pacing, we were carried into a green world, adorned with glad colours and scented with delightful perfume.

I made some enthusiastic remark in playful words.

"You are a pantheist," he suggested.

I asked him how he could imagine an English gentleman to be a heathen.

This brought out my india-rubber man, and in a little while I discovered that he was a weak-minded atheist. He did not avow himself in any offensive way. He seemed rather to regret that he had taken this disease, as he had once taken the small-pox, and that it was not his fault.

Here my pony got one of her feet into a crab-hole, stumbled, and very nearly surprised me out of the saddle.

It must have surprised me out of myself, for I turned on my india-rubber atheist and asked him a most rude question, namely, if he had ever in his life done any man any great evil which could have brought him to such a pass as being an American and an atheist?

He became silent, and we rode back together without another word, at which I was glad, for it enabled me to give my attention to the marvellous world through which I rode.

We got back in time for a fresh-water bath before breakfast. The breakfast was admirable; there was an excellent *chupé*—good fish, cutlets, and curried eggs, fried bananas, Abocado pears, oranges, and figs, all freshly gathered. There was excellent light wine, and the snow-white tablecloth was adorned with sprigs of red peppers and vessels containing flowers.

The india-rubber atheist looked miserable, nor was I sorry. He was still silent, even surly. I had not the least desire or intention to deliver him from his distress. What right has a man to be an atheist with an Abocado pear in his mouth?

I saw no more of him till night. When we were together alone, he drew his chair close to mine and said, in a voice charged with pain—

"You asked me this morning if I had ever done any man any great evil. No one has ever asked such a question of me before; but I am here to answer you. I have in my time done great evil. I know that it has made me that mean that life is fast becoming odious to me, and I am sure that every kind of evil-doing carries its own punishment in a mysterious way. I've watched it, and it's true. But I didn't intend to do evil; I only thought of doing good.

It's true that I made money by it, and perhaps it's right that I should suffer."

Now, I abhor listening to a man telling his sins. In a woman it is different; I could listen to a woman's tale of her own wickedness if it lasted three days. Therefore I tried to break away from the india-rubber merchant, who I thought was probably a commonplace commercial swindler, who was hiding in these wilds from those whom he had wronged, and that this was what he intended to confide to me.

"You, sir, have been very kind to me, and I feel it." (Here he added some flatteries which I do not intend to repeat; perhaps he did this in order to keep me interested in him.) "I was a medium—a spiritualist; you know what that means," he said, and looked me in the face as if to see if I did know.

"God Almighty forgive you," I said, as if I didn't believe that He would.

Then in a very cruel way I attacked him with much human bitterness, and said with sufficient arrogance that his present denial of God's existence came from his spiritualistic impostures, and that a strong delusion had been sent upon him by God Himself in order that he should believe a lie to his present undoing and his future misery. No Presbyterian or physiologist could have been more unfeeling or high-minded than I was towards this man.

In a passionate cry he swore that he did not know at the time that he was doing wrong, and many times that he did not know what he did at all.

" Did you write on a slate?" I asked.

"No," he said, "that was not in my line."

"What was your line?" I demanded.

"I saw things," he said, with much emotion, "and these I embellished and made interesting on purpose to make people believe in a world of spirits, a future life, and an unseen world. And now I don't believe in spirits, nor an unseen world, nor another life, nor God," and he hung his head in abject misery.

All this was in a new key. There was a dithyrambic tide—if I may so say—in his flood of speech. I began to pity him.

"Would you like to get back your child-like belief in God?" I asked him.

"Like?" he exclaimed. "Would I like to be at home at my own fireside instead of in this howling wilderness, where there is so much beauty that you get sick of it, and so many sweet things that you almost die for a little oatmeal porridge? No, I shall never go home again."

Here he paused, and looked strangely into space as if he were in a trance, having his eyes open.

"And," he added, "I shall never have faith in God again—that's all up."

I could say nothing, but relented towards him. He seemed like one who had slain his father, and did not know it until his mother made it known to him in words of anguish and despair.

I would have cheered him if I could, and did say something to the effect that one need not doubt of God if he retained a human heart—that if a man cultivated a love for his brother whom he could see it might lead him to loving God, who at present was out of sight—and so left him, feeling equal for little in that way.

Not much intercourse passed between us for the next

and following days. It was, perhaps, my fault; I had made another acquaintance.

But my india-rubber friend joined me soon after in my own room.

"I have something to say to you," he began.

"Say on," I said.

"I have seen a thing which I want to tell you," he said. "Last night I was waked up by my wife in the middle of the night. She came into my room and sat on my bed. I rose to take her in my arms, and she vanished out of sight. She is dead—of that I feel quite certain. No letter has come to me by the mail which arrived this morning; the only time that she has missed writing since I have been away from home. Last night was the 25th of August. Next mail I shall get a letter telling me that she died on that night. I hope you will be here."

I was there when the next mail arrived from New York, bringing a black-bordered letter for my friend. It was not in his wife's handwriting.

He opened the letter in my presence. It began: "Dear Joe,—Your wife died suddenly on the 25th of August," etc., etc.

We looked at each other and said nothing, nor do I say anything except to say with Don Quixote, "God hath many ways of bringing His own to heaven."

To me there was something startling in this man, having vulgarized his soul by imposture, in league with money-making spiritualists, waking up in a world of wonders to find that for him there was no God.

Is the present condition of Spain in no manner connected with the way she governed her American Colonies? It is simple folly to deny it, as it would be folly still greater to deny that it is owing to the Spanish inheritance that the Spanish Republics are what they are at this day—a disgrace to human government and human nature.

The present condition of the West Indies and their negro populations cannot be said to be unconnected with their past treatment by English planters.

The hatred with which the Roman Catholic Church is regarded in many parts of the New World springs from the manner in which a spiritual faith was materialized by its teachers.

CHAPTER V.

LIMA.

I ONCE spent the early part of a Good Friday in Lima. At noon I left for Callao, to take the homeward-bound mail, for the manager of the Pacific Steam Navigation Company was not only a Scotsman, but an Aberdonian, and Good Friday was to him a Friday and nothing more. So, amid the unexpressed maledictions of the pious ladies of Lima, we sailed. But the early part of the day in the city was singularly impressive. Christ was dead, and everybody wore the trappings and signs of an immortal woe. All the churches were hung with black. Every house was close shut up; every face hidden away. There was something very expressive in this silence of a great city, more than twelve miles in circumference, and given over to jabbering cheating, chaffering, laughing, fifing, drumming, and dancing for the rest of the year. If anyone had gone about his usual vocation on that day he would have had his ears cut off. Not even the biggest German bully in the place had the temerity to appear in his usual holiday attire of a red beard, lemon-coloured gloves, and a six-inch cigar.

But a priest on the sly was selling a publication. It was only a reprint, but I bought a copy for 2½d. I will translate a portion of this relique of the religious press of Peru. It is called:—

"*The marvellous account of a case which happened in the Church of the Magdalen, in the village of Eten, Diocese of Truxillo, in the Kingdom of Peru, when was seen for a good space a most beautiful Child in the sacred Host, with other marvels, which you shall see.*"

"Seven leagues from the city of Santa, in the village of Eten, whose priest and vicar was El Padre Predicador Fray Geronimo de Sylva Manrique, as noble a religious man as a zealous minister. On a Thursday in the month of June, 1649, which was the vigil of the Most High and August Mystery of the Most Blessed Sacrament of the Altar, at the end of the holy father's oration, it pleased the Most Holy One to descend from His throne in the presence of all the people, and visibly to take up His abode in the consecrated wafer (*hostia*), in the form of a very beautiful Child, in half figure, from the waist upward, which was distinctly seen of the Vicar and by all the people. The Child was dressed in a mulberry-coloured tunic, the rest of the Host being very white, so that it was easy to distinguish one colour from another. The hair of the head was ruddy (*rubio*), and reached to the shoulders, and was curled at the ends most gracefully (*retorcidos las puntas dellos graciosamente*). It was parted in the middle, half falling on one side and half on the other. The face and flesh were human, and plainly distinguished from the wafer, all of which was clearly and distinctly seen by the people, men and women, who were all moved to tears in spiritual joy, praying for the mercy of the Lord, who had, in the most rare and admirable way (*tan admirable y raro*), condescended to manifest Himself so as that they could see and rejoice in Him with their mortal eyes.

"Then the musicians played, these on their clarions, and those on their trumpets, the children ringing bells, and all the villages round about to which the fame of so great a miracle reached were filled with spiritual joy and gladness, and the Indians, both men and women, were moved to great tenderness of heart, and brought wax, fireworks, and sweet scents at great cost to testify their gratitude, which is abundant proof of the marvellous effects which the visitation of the Lord had caused in their souls, and so great was their devotion that they did not stir out of the Church at Eten for eight days."*

It would be easy to multiply extracts of instances of this kind; they may be found in all the remote parts of South America as well as in places not remote, nor are they confined to remote times. The tragedy at Santiago de Chili in connection with the "Virgin's Post Office" is still fresh in our recollection. It is no libel to say that the Romish Church in that part of the New World has proved a dire failure. It has corrupted the national morals, destroyed faith, and debased human reason. Patriotism there means revolution, liberty is not known, but license abounds, showing its strength by prevalent immorality, and I think that much of it, if not all, proceeds from this gross materialization of spiritual things. The priests for very shame, or idleness, have not been able to keep up their impostures, and have become victims of their own delusions; as a body they are utterly degraded and corrupt, and are the corrupters of family life. Happily for human nature, there are some notable exceptions, but they are few. A

* A copy of this "*Relacion*" is now in the British Museum.

priest is seldom or never seen in any respectable house in South America. Like priests, like people. The common people are given up to an insane belief that they will be allowed to work out their passage to heaven by the suffering, poverty, and dirt to which they submit themselves on earth. The governing class, the men in uniform, "the cocked hat and feather gentry," have no notion of influence or power, goodness or greatness, save as existing in something that can be seen, smelt, tasted, or handled. There never has been a single monthly, bi-monthly, or quarterly revolution in Peru, Chili, New Granada, Mexico, or Santo Domingo, or elsewhere that was not begun and ended with English money, the money of English money-makers and dealers in guano, or the monies of Jews and Germans, whose mission in this world has been to propagate the ambition which springs from lust, avarice, and greed. Not a single revolution ever began with the people, nor has there been a revolution out of which the people have not come greater sufferers than ever, until, like their priests, they are left without hope, and with no other god save one which can be made by a baker, or dressed up by a priest's house wife.

Nor can I refrain my eyes from looking at home and asking myself to explain to myself the gross ignorance of some of my own countrymen, to say nothing of their idleness and general sinfulness, their cruelties, and the brutish lives which some of them lead. Are these things in any way connected with English religion and English priests and English merchantmen, manufacturers and traders, and men in uniform, the cocked hat and feather gentry? Are the women who toil night and day in all parts of London, but especially in some parts more than others, only responsible for the misery and crime and the everlasting sorrow by which they are surrounded? Are the toilers in our beautiful black country only to blame for the ruin which may be seen there? Are the sixty thousand, men, women, and children who in Birmingham do not know where they will get their dinner to-morrow, or whether they will get one at all, to be held solely responsible for the plague which will one of these days break out among them?

Having seen the growth of the modern commerce and watched the manner in which the world's markets have been supplied during the time since India and the Australias, New Zealand and the Cape, and elsewhere gave new markets to England, and having been over all the world and seen with my own eyes the goods which have been sent for sale or for barter, I confess that it does not become an Englishman to take up much time at dinner or in the smoking-room in making reflections on the morals or manners of other people.

Still it may be permitted to speculate a little on the time when it will be our turn to be looked at and criticized by the traveller who will, a little later on, sketch the ruins of St. Paul's from London Bridge.

I do not say there is not something to be justly proud of even in Peru and along the whole coast, which bears the image of England, but the little there is to be seen makes one regret that there is not more, while it is impossible to resist the conviction that if there had been less selfishness and vainglory, and more modesty and love of justice, Peru might have been a living country now, and Englishmen its best friends. But Englishmen, as a rule, were too fond of heaping up money, living sumptuously every day, and setting an evil example of extravagance to be atoned for by some of them by endowing London charities or building an occasional church whose foundations are laid in Peruvian guano.

I had my first earthquake in Peru, in Lima, its capital, and Lima for many years was Peru, as Paris used to be France. It was early one morning, and before the sun began to shoot his beams against the back side of St. Bartolo, a hill which rises something less than two miles north-east of the city. I was in bed fast asleep in Maury's Hotel. I was waked by a noise such as I had never heard ; it was like a noise in a dream, and it was penetrating; it shook all my bones, then my bones seemed to be shaking the bed, the bed to be shaking the house, and the house to be shaking the solid earth, and the earth to be rocking the sickly moon, which seemed to grow pale as it looked down upon sinful, half-naked Lima, then running to the great plaza to be out of the way of falling houses and falling churches. When the unearthly noise which waked me from sleep became mingled with frantic human voices squealing for heavenly mercy I thought it time to turn out of bed.

But I could not stand steady. I was drunk, but not with wine. The earth was reeling to and fro. I shall never forget the sight which awaited me in the great square. Long before I reached it, and while yet out of ear-shot of what was going on, my eyes caught the gestures of great numbers of half-dressed women, who were stretching their open hands to the sky, and straining their necks to raise their upturned faces towards the clouds. Here was one of Martin's bad pictures painted to the life, one of the chapters of the Revelation made into a living scene. I never shall see such another tragedy as that, nor do I wish to see a repetition of the scenes of that morning. Being ignorant, I was callous to all fear or danger. I even wanted my breakfast, and asked for it, to the disgust of everybody, who looked upon me as a hardened wretch, who must be either a Protestant or an Englishman, or both. I was both, and am still, but I am no longer fearless in an earthquake, at least, in Spanish towns or South American cities, where the houses are specially built for murdering you when the earthquake is abroad.

The last earthquake I went through was at the Solomon Islands, but as there was nothing to be thrown down there was nothing to fear. I must confess that the priests on that morning in Lima behaved with singular assurance. They went everywhere "as bold as brass," as they say, comforting and exhorting the women, and receiving diamond rings from their fingers and ears as peace offerings, and even begging for money. Nothing brings so great a harvest to the Church in Peru as a violent earthquake. This one of which I am now writing lasted three days; I mean, of course, that the shocks at various intervals, and with more or less force, lasted three days and three nights.

How pious everybody became—how "kind and considerate." They let the thieves out of gaol; everybody fasted and prayed. There was no rubber to be had at the English Club; there was no theatre, no music, not even any cooking; no buying or selling; nothing but calling on the Immaculate and preparing for heaven. It was also very touching to see processions of frightened people coming into Lima from the country, and arriving at each of the four corners of the plaza, for the sake of company, perhaps, or to share the protection of Santa Rosa, the patron saint of the City of Kings. These refugees were invariably led by their village priest, well mounted on a handsome mule, and carrying his niece behind him, or some other connection, the odd thing being that almost in every case the niece was young, good looking, and not at all unaccustomed to be admired.

When the earth became steady, and the tumult and fear had ceased, the great plaza was illuminated. There was a fair show of fireworks, and a well-attended bull fight on the Sunday following. The usual sinning had once more begun.

Sauntering, as was my custom before breakfast, round the shaded side of the plaza, my attention one morning soon after the above was attracted by a table or stall at the corner close to the cathedral church on its south side. It contained a dozen or more flower pots, of varied kinds—a teapot without handle or spout, a porringer, a tea-cup, a blacking bottle, a tin that had once contained oysters, an old boot, a ginger-beer bottle, and a small frying-pan. In each of these was a sufficient amount of earth to support a flower or flower-bearing plant, the flowers having quite as disreputable a look as the "pots" in which they were stuck.

Wondering at such an odd assortment of things, obviously offered for sale, I said to the business-like looking little woman who attended at this stall—

"Pray how much do you ask for this?" pointing to a faded hyacinth.

"An ounce," was the reply, which, in plain English, amounted to some £3 10s. 0d.

"And for this one?"

"Ten dollars."

"Then what is the price of this?" pointing to a rose of little colour, no scent, and hardly any form.

"Fifteen dollars."

"And this one?"

"Oh, that you can have for what you like to give," and the business-like looking little woman treated me, I thought, with the same scant courtesy with which I regarded her and her miserable flowers.

On telling the story to a friend who had lived some time in Lima he burst into a fit of laughter at my ignorance, and continued to laugh as I continued my tale of the faded flowers, the quaint pots in which they were stuck, and the high prices asked for them.

These flowers, if you please, represented so many of the women who a few days before had parted with their ear-rings to the priests of the earthquake god, and who wanted to buy new ones. Where they lived and when you could visit these fair *chuchumecas*—to use an old word, because it is so expressive—the old flower-girl would have told you, with other particulars, on payment of the stipulated price. How well I recollect dear old Colonel Espinosa saying in his dry, fatherly way, as we sat that morning over our breakfast at Maury's, and the laughter of the malicious had cleared away, "Man is the one animal that has most to learn, and who the least learns what he ought to know; hence the need of professors. The greatest teachers of man are Nature, History, and Experience."

CHAPTER VI.

LIMA (*continued*) AND GUAYAQUIL.

THE mention of breakfast reminds me of the market in Lima, and the fruits and vegetables brought there for sale.

In the months of February and March grapes and pears were in abundance, together with *lucumas* and figs; in April and May, apples, quinces, ceruela de frayle (*Spondias dulcis*) and cerasnas (*Malphiga glandulosa*), patillas (*Psidium lineatum*), guavas, and cherimollas; in June, July, and August, and even into September, cherimollas, guanavanas, sweet and sour oranges, apples, limes, sweet and sour lemons, oranges, paltas, and plantains, which are obtained, by-the-bye, all the year round. Besides these there are melons, the musk and water-melon, olives, strawberries, and pine-apples. In vegetables the variety is equally great and attractive. If the human were in equal perfection to the vegetable world in Lima, and, indeed, throughout Peru, no part of the world would have such attractions for the lover, and the student of human nature.

The best part of the human world is beyond all doubt the women part. There are countries where this is not the case; but, on the contrary, the women are vastly inferior to the men in every way. There are countries also where the women only excel man in wickedness; but in Peru it is beyond question that the women surpass the men in intellect, in moral sense, in courage, in honesty, in taste, in loving, in charity, in heroism, in religion—certainly in fidelity and good looks.

The principal cause of this is, perhaps, that in no other part of the world has woman so effectually resisted man in his endeavour to make her merely a beautiful animal. She has a beautiful face, but she knows it quite as well as those who adore her. If the whole of the Peruvian woman were as beautiful as her face she would make her country as famous as any in ancient story. But the food she eats, the liquors she imbibes, the air she breathes, and the general unsanitariness of her surroundings are great obstacles to health; and no woman, however glorious her face, can ever have a beautiful body unless she is in sound health.

Even in my limited acquaintance I have personally known three of these beauties who have done marvellous acts. One was married to a man who was overtaken in time of great trouble by the temptation to forge another man's signature, for which crime he was transported, went raving mad, but happily ultimately soon died. His wife, hearing of his state and condition under confinement, forsook her home, and went and shared her husband's shame—his prison—and nursed him till death brought him and her deliverance; then she returned to look after the education of her children, and became for the rest of her life an example of generosity and compassion to all.

Another case, altogether different, is as follows: There had been a revolution which involved and compromised everybody, including Colonel Belgrano, who was taken prisoner, put in gaol in Cuzco, and who would certainly have been put to death but for his beautiful and heroic wife, Doña Juana. She journeyed all by herself from Lima to Cuzco, and arrived the day before the Colonel was to have been present at a firing party to be held in the plaza. When the guard came to assist the Colonel in his toilette on the fateful morning they found, not the Colonel in his cell, but a comely woman partly dressed in military attire, the Colonel having walked out of durance in his wife's *saya y manto*, and probably was at that moment a hundred miles away. Of course, they could not shoot the beautiful Doña Juana, and the governor of the gaol had the good sense to send her in search of her husband, carrying his uniform with her.

This dress, known as the *saya y manto*, consists of two parts—the *saya,* which is an elastic petticoat, and made to fit so tightly that the form of the limbs is rendered visible; the *manto* is also a petticoat, but instead of hanging about the heels, as all honest petticoats should, it is drawn over the head, breast, and face, and is kept so close by the hands, which it conceals, that no part of the body is perceptible, except one eye, and sometimes only a portion of that, which seems as if it had burnt its way to the surface of things. It is the most perfect of disguises, and I, for one, am not sorry that this bewitching dress is not known out of Lima. That it will become known and adopted at fancy balls in London I have little doubt.

I am not quite sure if I am equal to telling the story of the charming Doña Anita Ysabel de Castellanos. If I make it as short as possible it is because I mistrust myself. She was to all outward seeming as fragile as a champagne glass saucer mounted on one leg. The only sign of strength noticeable was in her spirited riding; she was a daring and skilful horsewoman. She married early, was still young and beautiful, but childless at the time when her husband, a military officer of high rank, was one summer evening, to the astonishment of the whole city, taken prisoner, and shut up in the castle at Callao by the arbitrary will of a Minister of the Republic. No small stir arose, and a revolt appeared imminent. The Minister made an overture to Doña Anita, to which she responded. An appointment was made and kept, and the next morning the apparently fragile Anita was leading a revolutionary army to Callao, mounted on a horse as beautiful, certainly as spirited, as herself, carrying in her right hand a dagger stained with the blood of the Minister, whom she had, for a different reason, like another Judith, slain; she had, in fact, in the words of Don Benito Laso, sent the abominable person, while asleep, to wake up in *el infierno!*

I am not aware of any acceptable theory that explains this singular superiority of the Lima ladies, not only to Peruvian men, which is saying little, but to other women in America, which is saying much. There have been many examples of female heroism from the earliest times in Peru, the most celebrated being, of course, Catalina de Arauso—who, however, was a Spanish nun from her birth —whose story is told by our own De Quincy, and Ricardo Palma gives rare examples, although it is said by Peruvian men that these are fictions of the poet's brain. Doña Isabel Barretto, the wife of Don Alvaro Mendaña de Meyra, whose exploits in the South Seas are matters of history, is a singular case in point, and rests, like the others, upon undoubted authority.

Don Alvaro went from Callao to find the Ophir of Solomon, and got as far as the Marquesas, when they reached a new island which Don Alvaro called Santa Cruz. Soon after he died, and as he had been empowered by the King to appoint his successor, he nominated his wife to the command of the expedition. She went through terrible hardships and failures. Why it has been said of her that "she was lean and ill-favoured"* is hard to understand. She married again and went to Mexico. This was one of the greatest expeditions which set sail from Peru, and was at the time of its sailing—June 16, 1595—the next in importance to that of Columbus. We also hear in the early times of beautiful women being tied naked to trees and shot at by the valiant Spanish soldiery with bows and arrows to make them divulge some secret which would have compromised their kinsmen, and so died rather than confess.

It is beyond all controversy that the record of the Peruvian women for heroism is lengthy, genuine, and well authenticated. That they are full of sparkling wit I know, and I am sorry that the limits of space do not admit of my giving samples of its quality.

There was once a period in the year when these fair and other women were to be seen under peculiar and striking circumstances. This was on St. John's Day, the 24th of June, when all Lima, its wives and concubines, met together on the gentle slopes of the lily-covered hills of Amencaes. The day was given up to festivity and joy. Not only are the hills on that festive occasion covered with St. John's flowers, but so are the men, women, children, horses, asses, and mules. The noise of the *jarana*, or

* See " Cruise of the *Rosario*," Captain A. H. Markham, R.N., p. 15.

carousal, is kept up all through the day without ceasing. It is a noise which penetrates like the bag-pipes, but is more multitudinous in sound, being composed of drummings, pipings, shoutings, harpings, guitarings, songs, laughter, and the rustle of silks in the dance. They are all earthly sounds. The laughter is hearty enough, but there is a twang of wickedness in it, as there is a decided squint in some of the eyes which would dance with mirth were the dance innocent and natural. The laughter, *á carcajadas*, is loud and certainly stimulating.

Don Tomas Hump, an Englishman, as broad as he is long, with a face beaming like a warming-pan, his merry laughter burying his little nose in the circular wrinkles of his corpulent cheeks, has put his arm round the waist of a *chuchumeca*, or *gilflirt*. A ring is instantly formed of the principal visitors, chiefly men; there are some women, but the English ladies have gone into the nooks and clefts of the hills to gather flowers.. It is not a fight; there is no fighting to be seen anywhere. It is a dance called the *samaqueca,* danced only by a single pair, and is supposed to represent the emotion of Adam and Eve when they first met in paradise.

From Callao we proceeded to Guayaquil, where we had the delight of meeting the cargo steamer of the same company going south. It was the only approach to Noah's ark that I had ever seen with my mortal eyes. Besides abundance of the most rare and delicious fruits, which were piled up in glorious heaps on the open deck, there were all kinds of birds, monkeys, alligators, armadillos, wild cats in beautiful furs, young jaguars, black and spotted—rare things innumerable, " more lovely than their names." I was

F

shown among other things a copy of the real kind of apple which our mother Eve was tempted with. It was not a Ribston pippin, a Foxwhelp, or a Hagloe crab, nor even the Friar, nor the Brandy apple, the Duchess of Oldenburgh, the Cornish gilliflower, the white Juneating, much less the delicious Coccagee, or any other respectable Christian apple of my believing childish days, but a thing as big as a big turnip, and quite as homely to look at. I repudiated it with vehemence.

"Ah, señor, have you ever tasted it?" inquired several voices.

"Never," I answered, with energy.

"Then you shall" said this new kind of apple dealer. He took a table knife and cut off a great slice, showing me the inside, which was full of yellow seeds, like a "nutmeg" melon. These he took out with a table spoon. He then poured in a glass of sherry, adding some white sugar, and proceeded to whip the fruit and wine and sugar into a cream.

"*Toma*" (take it) said the enthusiast, giving me the fruit and the spoon, and leaving me while he went to wait on another customer who wanted to buy a parrot.

I certainly never in my life tasted anything so bewitching. I ate the whole of it, never offering to share it with any of those young fellow passengers who were awaiting my verdict. For the first time in my life I approved of my mother's taste; but perhaps Eve's apple was not dressed with sherry and sugar.

"How much have I to pay?"

"Did you like it? Was it fine? Would you like another?"

"I liked it, it was fine, and would like another," I

answered, on which he gave me another, and charged me *un peso*, that is, 3s. 4d.

Guayaquil is a filthy place, sufficient to give an ordinarily constituted human being a permanent fever to look at it. Here, and in the interior, are made the celebrated "Panama" straw hats, some of which cost as much as £10 apiece.

Here, and a hundred miles north inland, is a new world for the Panama Canal to wake up when it is made. It will bring new rivers into use which at present are stagnant with the spoil of an exuberant nature, which man, up to the present, has been unable to subdue. Many of the villages, and some towns, have no coin circulating among them, but pay for their tools, hatchets, and clothing in cocoa, gold dust, and tortoise-shell. The mode of travelling is different. Here, especially in Macuchimina, rich in mines, the country is intersected by so many rivers and precipices, principally by the Yana, Yacu, and Pilalo, that the only mode of travelling is on the shoulders of Indians. Probably there are no people so poor as those who live in these parts, where nature does everything for man except make roads, build bridges, and keep things clean; and because man does not, or will not, do any of these things, nature kills him with kindness, holding up to his foolish eyes in the rays of the morning sun some of the finest gold, which foolish man goes after and finds it all his own. But the sun goes to bed early, and foolish man, left in the dark, burdened with a weight he cannot carry, goes to sleep in a forest hung round with poisoned curtains, and never wakes up from his dream.

We left Guayaquil in time to see the sun set in the sea. If the glorious colours which he then threw into the sky were only to be seen once in a lifetime, how we should love them, talk of them, doing everything to keep up our remembrance of them; but because they are common to all, and occur nearly every day, we regard them as we regard women, or bread, or salt, the sweetness and delight of which things we only know at their right value when we cannot have either one or the other.

Here the Pacific sea began to trouble some of our passengers, among whom were Peruvian priests, poets, and women. I was the only seafarer who was not sick, and some were so very sick that it was heartrending to see and hear them. I had brought with me from the south some fresh-gathered leaves of the Erythroxylan cuca. Of some of these I made an infusion in a teapot, and sweetened it so as to hide the characteristic flavour which it carries. All the priests, poets, and women were comforted; they all went to sleep and slept all night!

To my great delight, on arriving at Colon—the Atlantic end of the Panama railway—I found my dear old friend, Captain Hole, in command of the steamer which was to carry us as far as St. Thomas, but such a wreck of a man that I hardly knew him. He had just sufficient strength to crawl from his cabin on to the bridge, take his ship out of port, give her her course, and crawl back to his bunk exhausted. He was suffering from a malignant dysentery, which robbed him of all sleep and strength.

"You shall sleep to-night, old fellow," I said; but he was unbelieving.

"You shall sleep now and sleep on till nine o'clock," I reiterated; but he was hopeless and incredulous.

I gave him a large teacup of cuca tea, weak, and only of a light straw colour.

He slept three hours, and awoke with an appetite; we supped together. At midnight I gave him another cup of tea, a little weaker than the first; he slept all night. On the third morning after this Captain Hole appeared at breakfast as usual, in his white waistcoat, clothed, and in his right body. This he had not done for three months before.

As the leaf of this shrub has now come into such remarkable use, let me say that every care should be taken to bring these leaves, hermetically sealed, from the west coast of Peru to England; but I trust that before long we may see the shrub growing in Jamaica, Ceylon, and India, like the cinchonæ. It will not grow in tropical Queensland, to my disappointment and grief. I made several experiments, but the south-east monsoon came and killed the young suckers with its icy breath.

CHAPTER VII.

THE PERUVIAN COAST.

THE coast of Peru extends from the River Loa, lat. 21, 30 south, to the River Tumbez, lat. 3, 30 south. It is one continuous desert, intersected here and there by several rivers, some—perhaps the most—of which have not sufficient strength or volume to reach the Pacific sea, but are wasted in the sand or licked up by the sun before they reach the bourne from which no travelled river e'er returns. The coast is dotted with a few towns, which, like the intersecting rivers, are of various sizes, shapes, and importance. They all look well at a distance, but, like many things in Peru, none are pleasing on a close acquaintance.

Along the whole coast the soul of the traveller is wearied by passing in front of interminable sand plains and hills which are covered with sand—sand, and nothing but sand, all of the same colour; Nature there, to all outward seeming, having turned Quaker, and, discarding the vanity of bright colours, the sinfulness of beauty, and the dangers which come from joy and gladness, hath assumed an everlasting monotony of drab. The only time when this dulness is broken is when the south wind holds a controversy with the sand, knocking it about in a thousand ways and lashing it into a picturesque fury, like as the same wind tosses the sea sometimes in foam on to the outlying rocks, or sends it running in angry force among the chattering pebbles of a wreck-strewn beach. It is a wonderful sight, well worth seeing from the deck of a British ship, but infinitely miserable to be in the midst of. There is a pleasing excitement in being caught in a storm of wind and rain if you are not far away from shelter, but if caught in a storm of sand you can't get out of it; all your five senses are turned against you. It is better to be a log than a man in a storm of wind and sand on the Peruvian coast; there is no torment that can be likened to it.

But once out of the rainless zone, and you reach the other side of the Tumbez river, Nature is found in her right mind. She is once more beautiful, busy making love to careless man, even to bird and beast; busy in finding daily work for the sun, who in that region puts on his paint, not with a dainty brush, but with a broad palette knife throws about his belts and robes of green, red, and blue in mighty grandeur. The birds are decked in the gayest, brightest waistcoats, impossible to name or to number. Even in stockings there is an infinite variety of speckled, blue, red, yellow, black, gold, and silver; so in bills. These gaudy creatures, however, have nothing else to boast of save their clothes. They do not sing; fine feathers do not always make fine birds. Who would give the song of a throstle for the chorus of a wilderness of peacocks, or for a grey parrot with a topknot as "killing" as any in Regent Street, or even a forest full of humming birds! Yet is that a hard saying, for I have seen humming birds which outshone in lustre and wondrous strange beauty any confection of emerald and diamond, diamonds and rubies, diamonds and sapphires, or all these bossed together and hung round a maiden's throat. The humming bird does not sing, but it is, if one may so say, clothed in music. The butterflies also compete with the flowers in beauty of form and colour. There are trees —notably the cinchona when in bloom, and the purple jagaranda—which suggest that neither men nor architects have even yet begun to know how colour can give an ineffable grace to some structural changes found in complicated forms. One remarkable characteristic of the jagaranda, as I have seen it in the open air, is that it apparently sheds its first blossoms to make a magnificent show of itself. When its second bloom appears, which soon follows after the first, the blossoms on the ground seem to be a lake reflecting the purple glories above.

Few quadrupeds are seen in the landscape. The monkeys are a great population, but they keep out of sight. They are, however, of much use, especially in certain parts, where very precious fruits grow, which only ripen on the tops of tall trees, which no man can climb, or shake. I forget the name of the fruit, but its form and flavour I can never forget. It has a hard rind. Monkeys are fond of these fruits, climb the trees, and throw them down to the ground, when large families assemble to hold a great feast of fruits, unless they are disturbed by the coming of some powder-smelling enemy. One monkey, or rather sloth, which goes by the name of *Perico ligero,* doubtless because of its slow movement, as the bird without covering for its shame is called *Tapaculo,* is beautifully clothed in silver-grey. The chinchilla is beautiful, but that little animal is confined to the rocks of the upper desert. The jaguar can put on, and does, very handsome apparel, but it is a wild beast, and will never be anything else. The puma, which is a Quichua name, signifying lion, is beautiful, so is the vicuña; but these occupy the snowy Andes, six hundred miles away from the coast. The llama and alpaca, the domesticated congeners of the guanaco, and wild vicuña, having been long in business, chiefly the carrying and wool trades, seem, from the look of their large pensive eyes, to find life full of anxiety and care, and would give up commerce if they could only find a place of rest.

The ass and mule are also in trade, and travel much, and are seen everywhere in all parts of Spanish America. So is the horse, but he is an aristocrat among quadrupeds, with Spanish manners, and a good conceit of himself. He is never a drudge. The mule is the most sagacious animal in all that vast and varied world of beasts, of heat and trouble. There are sagacious men in Peru, but they are not so numerous as mules. The ass keeps up his universal character for patience, but my opinion of him has been modified since I saw him feeding on old newspapers in the public streets. The ass, so far as I know, has never shown any sign that he prefers death to dishonour. I have heard him bray in all parts of the world, but never with so loud and dreadful a voice as in Peru, perhaps for the same reason that some men blow on their unmusical noses louder in church or in the high-domed reading-room of the British Museum than anywhere else, and this may be the unconscious betrayal of a family connection.

Of the climate of this coast it is difficult to convey the truth concerning it. The best way for a traveller to enjoy such scenery, air, sea, and sky, as are to be found in some parts of the coast of Peru—if time is no object to him, and earthly peace is—is to select a spot, and there are many such spots, where no Peruvian has ever been. Then he can rely, at least, on being clean. The worst of it is that he can find nothing growing, not even a fig leaf, nor will anything grow on that coast, forsaken, it seems to be, of God, who there never sends the "useful trouble of the rain." There is, however, a never-failing mist, which hangs like a pall for a thousand miles. This waterless belt of sand varies in width along the entire coast as far as it goes. Sometimes it is not more than a mile in width from the sea shore to the frontier hills, which run north and south in almost an unbroken line of varying altitude from the comparative low soft floating lines above Lima to the forbidding monotony further south, where the line is almost level at a height of from three thousand to four thousand feet above the sea.

Of the villages, Chorillos, a fashionable watering-place, is the largest, and is about nine miles south of Lima, by railway. When I first knew it, it was a delightful place to go to for a change; what it is now, since it was overrun by the Chilian army, and the Peruvian army ran away, I do not know. The rise and fall of Chorillos represents, in little, the rise and fall of Peru, and the rise and fall of all those who have ever partaken of the ways and manners of Peru. The village was once occupied by simple native fishermen, who lived in what are called *ranchos*. It became a favourite resort to some few of the merchants and British residents of Lima, who would ride down on a Saturday night and stay till Monday, to get a sea change. Then some of the best native families began to build houses. The gamblers followed speedily afterwards. The place became a fashionable pigstye, and as unhealthy and insalubrious as Lima. Extravagance and vulgar show took the place of wholesome living, filthiness made even occasional cleanliness impossible, and the sea itself became polluted with the offal and foulness of the shore. Many men and women have lost all they had in this world in Chorillos, including themselves. Many women, who combined beauty with wickedness, lived in Chorillos. Certainly, some notorious men also, for where one of this class goes the other is sure to follow. Chorillos was a product of the guano age in Peru, as Saratoga, Longbranch, and other well-known places in North America were products of shoddy railway speculations, patent medicines, petroleum, and English books. There were, alas! so many other products of guano besides Chorillos, such as revolutions and general, social and political corruption, that now the guano has "given out" almost everything has given out, and Peru itself has become a country that is only worth talking about for the parable which it holds for other countries to read.

What will happen when the ship canal through the Isthmus of Panama is open, few, if any, living men may say. That the vast undeveloped wealth of Peru will then come in for some of the world's attention there can be little doubt. Whether Peru herself will share in the impetus which this great work, if it is ever finished, may give to commerce, depends, I suppose, on the kind of stuff which she may send to market. It may also depend on other things, certainly on other men. It is not unlikely that the Chinaman, by the time the ship canal is open, will be the first to profit by it in Peru. Thirty years ago this multitudinous heathen was merely a domestic cook and bottle-washer in Lima and guano lumper at the Chincha

Islands; then he became a slave on the sugar plantations, but he is now a merchant of considerable importance. Shrewd, thrifty, and possessed of much personal dignity, he may restore the ancient water courses, build again the ruins of the ancient reservoirs, and the desert of Peru would then blossom as the rose, not in figure, but in fact. There is ample room for twenty millions of industrious people along this coast, and plenty of work, with most abundant harvest, for all who know how to make the water—which is at present man's master—his slave and obedient servant. What the Peruvian "Indian," as he has ever been called, will do, or how he will fare, is not easy to predict; he has always been a superior being to his masters, but, unfortunately, has always followed his masters' vices and shared their fate. The Indian of Peru is one of the superior aboriginal races remaining on the face of the earth. He is much the same in Cundinamarca as he is in Atacama, in Potosi as in Bogotá, on the Magdalena as on the Desaguadero, that is, in the north and in the south.* It is worth while hearing what one of the most illustrious Peruvians has to say on the Indian, who knew him intimately:—

"As conquered by the Spaniards," says Colonel Juan Espinosa in his "Diccionario para el Pueblo," p. 608, "the Peruvian Indian was more civilized, more moral, less fanatical, and better governed than were his conquerors; he professed a worship more pure than had ever been known of any people before the Christian era.

* I make exception to the Indians of the Gran Chaco, who belong to a world distinct in itself. These Indians were, while under the rule of Jesuit missionaries, docile, and as harmless as creeping vegetables. They are now as ferocious as jaguars; and if a man in the garb of a priest ventures among them he is taken, mutilated, and finally killed outright. The explanation of this inhuman conduct is easy to give, but it would not be pleasant to read.

"He was certainly more civilized, if civilization consists in good manners, and living a life conformable to the laws imposed for the well-being of all."

The Peruvian Indián, distinguished as he was in civilization and morals, was also famous in architecture, astronomy, navigation, and in the fine arts; he was one of the greatest of agriculturists, and he was very religious. He was much given to hospitality, was industrious, trusting, loving, patient, a worshipper of nature, a botanist, one of the first of goldsmiths, a splendid gardener, an excellent shepherd, a famous builder and road maker, a fine potter, weaver, painter, and bridge builder. Nor does this list exhaust all his fine qualities, accomplishments, and virtues. He lived to a great age; he lived most in the open air, for he knew how and where to live to the best advantage.* It is difficult to ascertain how great were his numbers; the indigenous population of Peru has always been difficult to find out. It was very great. Fray Antonio Calancha, speaking of one particular province once rich in gold and silver, says: "All the people have been worn out—*gastado*—in mines. You may now see some fifteen or twenty persons where there used to be thirty or forty thousand!"†

These were they whom the Spaniards "conquered," carrying a crucifix in one hand and a sword in the other. To complete their barbarity, these precious conquerors brought dogs, whom they trained to catch Indians in Peru as they were trained to hunt boars in Spain. What is worthy of consideration is that the Spaniard at the time of the Conquest was one of the most civilized beings in the world, and the most fanatical in the spreading, defending, and believing the religion of the lowly Christ, or what they

---

* Espinosa. † Calancha, lib. i., 1, cap. xv., fol. 99.

believed to be His religion. What is remarkable is that the Indian of to-day is a greater fanatic for the religion of the Crucified than the Spaniards themselves who taught him.

The odd thing is that the Peruvian Indian is still a slave in the Peruvian Republic, while the negro is free. When they were both slaves together the condition of the Indian was not less hard than that of the negro, but the Indian's peculiar nature has always been, as it is now, his greatest curse. It is well known that the white people steal the children of the Indian of the *sierra* in order to make presents of them to their friends on the sea coast—and if they do not steal them they get them by deceit and lies—where they are brought up in houses and serve without wage. Priests, prefects, sub-prefects, and planters, with other *caballeros,* are all engaged in this infamous traffic in human beings, not now as a commercial speculation, as was once the case, with the negroes, but from pure pleasure—snatching the very child from its mother's breast solely for its good! *Valgame Dios.**

It is still the general opinion in Christian Peru that the pure Indian ought to pay a sufficient poll tax, for the simple reason that if he is not made to do so he will not work. By all means; but as there are a considerable number of people who are not Indians, but impure-blooded Spaniards, in Peru, who do not and will not work, should it not be seen what effect a poll tax will have on them first of all? It is also the general Peruvian Christian belief that the Indian cannot understand anything through the medium of goodness, but only of evil, and should be treated accordingly. There are many other things which

* Espinosa.

may be said of the manner in which the Indians are held by Spanish Peruvian guano-dealers, but they are unfit for publication.

It must, in fairness to the old aristocratic Christian Spaniard of Peru, be said that if under him the Indian suffered all that can make life miserable, all that makes it detestable as well was added under the military despotism which was set up on the fall of the Spanish monarchy. Yet, strange to tell, the patience of the Indian continues. The traveller has his temper often tried by the amazing contrariness of the Indian, and in a fit of despair or disgust cannot help coming to the conclusion that the Indian of Peru is a human being whose soul is wrapped up in a napkin or a piece of Halifax baize and hidden somewhere away in the earth. And yet what an unerring guide he is across the pathless sand of the desert, over barren, rocky mountains or through the forest, day and night, through sunshine or storm, and as trustworthy and temperate as he is sure-footed and quick-sighted at all times, while on the way and on duty.

Dios mio! would that I had strength to handle this subject as it deserves; but I am unequal to the task. Only may I live to see the day when the Indian shall again be free, and his forehead wiped of that stain of slavitude which it at present carries. When that comes to pass I shall know of a truth that there is for all men a resurrection of the dead.*

Of the conquerors, discoverers, soldiers, sugar-planters, miners, priests, and general ruffians who have ill-treated this singular human family and changed them into a herd of dumb animals, the priest, I think, comes out the worst.

* Espinosa, p. 621.

As I do not prove what I say, perhaps I ought not to make this charge against a body of men who have many friends in the world; but when I explain that my inability to bring this proof arises solely from the indelicacy, obscenity, and general satanic quality of the evidence which I have in my possession, I may induce a credence which I am unable to command in the truth of my statement. The Indian could, and often did, emancipate himself from the torments which he suffered at the hands of his secular masters, either by hanging, poisoning, or sharpening a stake and ripping himself open;* but he could not emancipate himself from the soul-destroying priest.† The Indian had always been a religious being, long before he made the acquaintance of the Spanish miracle-monger and dealer in revelations; but when the Spaniard substituted the Jewish maiden-mother for Mama Ocllo—purgatory and hell for the sun and moon, a wooden cross and a dead Christ for the southern constellation of that name, and Pachacamac the divine spirit—the Indian became subject to a bondage more awful and degrading than ever suffered heathen Roman, or theocratic Jew.

The old Spaniard, who, although he was a technical Christian, was a gentleman, confessed and published his sins done against the Indian; but your modern Spaniard, born and baptized in Peru, is not conscious of having committed any sins against anyone, certainly not against the Indian, nor even against any of the English, if they happen to be holders of Peruvian bonds. The Peruvian Republican Spaniard has been as grinding in collecting

---

* See " Peregrenaciones de Alpha," M. Ancizar; Bogatá, 1853.

† I need only refer the learned reader for confirmation of this to the numerous *Confessionarios* drawn up for confessing Indians in their native tongues.

his patriotic poll tax from the Indian as the Royalist Spaniard was in exacting the Royal fifths; but the infamous exactions of the Spanish-Peruvian priest in the way of sacramental fees and keeping up the honour of tutelar village saints, with other ludicrous and cruel exactions, exceed both.

There is one thing worthy of remembrance, namely, that poor a thing as an Indian is in himself—I have had these people come to me in the distant interior, go down on their knees, kiss my feet as I sat in the saddle, and beg in piteous tones for a cigarette—yet when roused in combination they are very swift and terrible in the vengeance they can take. The old massacre in Castilla de Oro, and the later one of our own day in La Paz, bear testimony to the truth of this.

The principal industry of the Peruvian Indian is now that of agriculture; he is also a flockmaster, but on a very limited scale. The cultivation of the cinchona in India, Java, Ceylon, and Jamaica has deprived him of one of his chief occupations, as it has deprived the merchant of the coast of some of his gains; but the cultivation of the alpaca remains to him, and this industry is capable of great, almost indefinite, extension. It has always been a source of wonder to me that while men of intelligence should have sunk their capital, and sometimes their credit, in copper, tin, and silver mines in the far distant parts of Peru, few, if any, have taken pains to cultivate the alpaca on a large scale, or on any scale. I have never heard of a single European owning a flock of these useful and remunerative animals in that country.*

Although Peruvian bark, as we know, is now no longer

---

* I have an impression that the laws of the Republic now prohibit anyone not of Indian birth to own alpacas.

G

confined to Peru, it is successfully cultivated elsewhere, but not so alpaca wool. There is no alpaca wool in the world but that which is grown in Peru and Bolivia. Attempts have been made to transport the alpaca to Australia and acclimatize it there, and other where, but these attempts all failed.

How far we English have contributed to the decadence of man in South America, as a moral, religious, intellectual, and social being, is not difficult to say. We, more than any, helped him to achieve his independence, and he did achieve it, before he knew how to turn it to the best account. We lent him as much money as he asked for, and the amount still owing may be taken as the measure of the evil progress man has made in those miserable lands since he abolished the names of King and Crown. We set him a vile example in leading an extravagant, luxurious life; in our love of money, in our pride and insolence, and in our tyranny over the weak. In Peru, perhaps, more than in other parts of the world we fomented revolutions in order to feather our own commercial nest, and we taught Peruvian sinners the art and mystery of adulteration, and of selling false goods, which have been as hurtful to them as false gods ever were to the children of Israel. The results are everywhere plain to be seen—at least, by those who care to use their eyes.

There are other natural disadvantages under which the Peruvian lives which help him to live a debased national and social life. The climate of the coast, for the most part, is detestable, and sundry diseases are common—phthisis, dysentery, intermittent fevers, or agues, called *tercianas,* and typhus are endemic. In Lima asthma and disorders of the heart, visceral obstructions and intestinal hæmorrhage, as well as consumption, are very general, besides a variety of cutaneous eruptions and nervous diseases of too frequent occurrence. In consumption, says my medical informant,* which in all its various forms is a common disease on the coast of Peru, a portion of the lungs becoming by degrees ulcerated and destroyed, there is an interruption to the proper discharge of the pulmonary functions, accompanied with nocturnal increase of fever and excessive perspiration.

What, therefore, is to be expected from a people thus physically handicapped? But this is not all the trouble which the Peruvian has to bear, or all the payment he must make for living in a climate which, although he knows it to be destructive to human health, is a climate which, nevertheless, he prefers to any other. It is a climate which excites the passion in which he most delights to indulge, and for which he lives, though it reduces him to the mere shadow of a man.

* I am indebted to my late friend Dr. Archibald Smith for much information on this and kindred subjects. He attended me through an attack of yellow fever in Lima, but from the effects of which I was a long time in recovering. One of these effects was a total loss of memory, which loss continued for a long time, and which I regained in Australia during a succession of hot wind days, which lasted for nearly a week. Dr. Archibald Smith was the first European physician who recommended the still mountain air of the Andes, at a level of five thousand feet above the sea, as a cure of consumption. He sent his patients to Jauja, and their cure was, after a residence of some two years, absolutely certain and permanent.

CHAPTER VIII.

FROM SILVERN POTOSI TO GOLDEN AUSTRALIA.

THE most memorable journey I ever made for its duration and variety was from the silver mines of Potosi to the gold fields of Australia. Nothing belonging to either engaged my attention so much as the way in which these deposits of the precious metals have shaped the destinies of many human lives.

With the reader's permission, I will here translate from its original Spanish a remarkable document which contains one of the earliest references on record to the South Sea Islands. It is the petition of Captain de Quiros to His Catholic Majesty Philip III. of Spain, and is as follows :—

"SEÑOR,*—I, Captain Pedro Fernandez de Quiros, say: This is the eighth memorial that I have sent to your Majesty setting forth what ought to be done to people the land which your Majesty commanded me to discover in Australia, the Unknown, without having received any answer or assurance of despatch, although I have been fourteen months in this Court, and fourteen years engaged in this cause, without pay, not minding mine own profit, and also

* Relacion de un memorial presentado á su Majestad por el Capitan Pedro Fernandez de Quiros sobre la poblacion, y descubrimiento de la quarta parte del mundo, Austrialia incognita, su gran riqueza y fertilidad. Pamplona, 1610.

without obtaining a judgment of my cause. Amid infinite controversies, I have travelled twenty thousand leagues by sea and land, wasted all my substance, destitute of the necessities of life, suffering so many and such terrible things that even to myself they seem incredible. All this have I undergone that I might not abandon a work of so much piety and mercy, and, for God's love, I most humbly pray your Majesty not to allow your servant to be deprived of the fruits of so many labours and watchings, and of such a notable perseverance. I claim these fruits with so much earnestness, because if I gain them it will be to the honour and glory of God, the service of your Majesty, and immeasurable good while the world stands, and afterwards for all eternity.

"The extent of the newly-discovered lands is in length as great as the whole of Europe, and as far as the Caspian Sea and Persia, with all the isles of the Mediterranean, and the ocean within that boundary, including England and Ireland. That part hides a fourth part of the globe. It is not in the neighbourhood of Turks or Moors, or other nations who are given to disturb their neighbours. All the islands we sighted fall within the torrid zone, and those which touch the equator some have a latitude of 90°, others a little less, and if their extent prove as great as it promises to be, these countries will be the antipodes of a great part of Africa, the whole of Europe, and the half of Asia Minor.

"The population of these countries is great. They are of various colours—white, yellow, mulatto, and black, with mixtures of these. The hair of some is black, straight and loose, of others it is crisp and curled, and of others, again, it is ruddy and thin; which variety shows how great is the commerce amongst them, for which reason and because of the goodness of the lands, and because they have no firearms with which to kill each other, and *because they do not work any silver mines the population is great.* [Philip must have winced at this.] They know no arts, greater or less, have no walls or strongholds, no king, no law, but are pagans divided into tribes. Their arms are bows, arrows, wooden swords, clubs, spears, and darts also of wood. The people are partly clothed, are cleanly, vivacious, and rational, and as full of gratitude as any of which I have had experience; from all which it may be hoped that under Divine Providence, and by gentle means, it will be easy to subdue them to the useful and the good *(pasificar, doctrinar, y contentar)*, which things are necessary at the beginning, for afterwards they may be conducted to the holiest ends, advancing to great things from small, till they arrive at the knowledge of the greatest good. Their houses are of wood, covered with palm leaves; they use earthenware pots, make nets of various kinds, they work in marble, make pipes, drums, and wooden spoons, varnished; they have oratories and grave-yards, large properties in land, enclosed and palisaded. They use much mother-of-pearl, and of the shells they make chisels, gouges, hooks, and ornaments, and round plates, which they hang on their necks. They have well-built vessels to convey them from one island to another, and they are built so as to indicate the existence of a race of greater and better government. Not a little noteworthy is their practice of castrating hogs and making capons.

"Their bread is made from three different roots, which are collected in great abundance. The fruits are plentiful; there are six sorts of plantains, four sorts of almonds, and large strawberries of extreme sweetness. There are many ground nuts, oranges, and lemons. There are many large sugar canes, and an infinitude of palms, from which sugar, wine, and vinegar can be obtained, as well as honey; the dates are good. They also bear cocos. When these are green they look like thistles, and have a marrow-like cream; when ripe the nuts contain a liquid like milk. When old they produce an oil of great value for lighting, and which cures like a balsam. The shells make excellent cups and bottles. The fibre is used for spinning all sorts of cables, rigging tackle, and other ropes. The fruit of these palms is gathered all the year round; they require no manure, or cost of any kind in money or time. The garden herbs are pumpkins, beet, and many kinds of purslain, as well as beans. Their meat is that of pigs—tame, like our own—hens, partridges, capons, geese, turtles, pigeons, goats, and the natives led us to believe that there were animals, which we supposed to be cows or buffaloes. The fishes are numerous. Besides which there are many dainties.

"There are pearls, silver and gold, mace, pepper, and ginger, cinnamon, cloves, and other spices. There is much and excellent wood for building. The coast for three leagues and more consists of black pebbles, very good for ship's ballast. The coast contains neither ruins nor rocks; the herbage on its banks is green. There is no sound of the tide to be heard, and as the trees are tall and straight, and not torn, I gather that there are no great storms in that land. These lands will bear comparison with Peru, Chile, Panama, Nicaragua, Guatemala, New Spain, Terrinate, and the Philippines, of all which lands your Majesty is lord. They are sufficient to sustain 200,000 Spaniards. He will be lord of the world who shall unite these countries in one, with Spain for their centre.

"The temperature and purity of the air are such as must be evident from all that I have said; none of our people fell sick from ordinary labour, by sweating, or drinking the water, or while fasting, or by eating all that the earth produces, or by the dew, moon, and sun, which is not very hot during the day. We saw no sands, nor any kind of thistles or thorny trees whose roots appear above the ground, nor plains liable to be flooded, nor snow on the high mountains, nor crocodiles in the rivers, nor poisonous reptiles, nor white ants, nor those that destroy fruit, nor worms, nor ticks, nor mosquitoes, an excellency above all others, and so much to be esteemed, if we consider that many of the lands in the Indies are uninhabitable for these insects, as I have myself witnessed.

"Such, señor, are the greatness and goodness of the lands which I have discovered, and of which I have taken possession in your Majesty's name and under your Royal standard; and I may here mention the acts which I performed. In the first place, I set up a cross and a church of Our Lady of Loretto, in which twenty masses were said. I won the jubilee given on the Day of Pentecost, and formed a solemn procession on Corpus Christi Day, in which I walked, preceded by the Holy Sacrament and your Majesty's standard. I also hoisted three field ensigns, and your Majesty's Royal arms were exhibited between two columns. Furthermore, as a loyal vassal of your Majesty, I confide in your at once annexing this great continent to your dominions under the title of Austrialia of the Holy Ghost.

"I have a firm belief in the wisdom, greatness of soul, and Christian piety of your Majesty, the abounding care you take to know certainly what is necessary; the population of those countries now discovered being the principal cause why those lands should not be left uncultivated. I hope, therefore, to be the means of the Lord Our God being known, believed, worshipped, and served by them, and the devil overcome; and, through the energy of the Roman Church, of preventing others from sowing false doctrine and of converting all the good things I have made known into evils of greater magnitude, calling themselves lords of the Indies, and ruining everything. I believe also that your Majesty will be well advised that a loss so pernicious, whether arising from neglect or misfortune, is such that to remedy it in the future might cost millions of gold and thousands of men. Your Majesty then can by means of a little silver spent in Peru gain at once heaven, eternal fame, and the new world, with all else that I have promised. The vessels are prepared, but there is much to be done before they can be made ready to sail, very much, both of a spiritual and temporal nature, and every hour lost can never be regained.

"If Christopher Columbus, under a belief that he could

discover something, was so persevering, shall I not persevere and be importunate with regard to that which I have seen and felt?

"Señor, this is a great work; by it you may make mortal war on the devil. There is no good to be done that can equal it, your Majesty being its protector.

"(Signed)   P. F. QUIROS."

Had Quiros happened to visit these parts of the South Seas, as I did, in January, instead of in June, July, and August, his experience of the climate would have modified his enthusiasm. Still, his contribution to our knowledge is considerable, and it enables us to see the temper of the men of those early times. With the exception of the weather and the plagues, the account remains substantially the same now as in 1605. We may be thankful that Philip III. was not moved by the eloquence of Quiros, and that no Spaniard set his foot in Australia before it had been annexed by ourselves.*

But what will be said of the Spanish cruelties and kidnappings of the sixteenth century being imitated by Australian British colonists in the nineteenth? We shall be assured that the thing is incredible.

It is, alas! too true. The same murders which the Spaniards committed on hapless Indians in the silver mines of Potosi were perpetrated in a certain legal way by British colonists on South Sea Islanders, not a century ago, but only two or three years ago, on the sugar plantations of golden North Queensland.

The greed to which Don Gorduro de Badulaque appealed in the City of London exists in an exasperated form at the

* The lands mentioned in the petition of Quiros were not Australia, but the New Hebrides and the south-eastern part of New Guinea, afterwards named Lousiade by French navigators.

Antipodes; and the enterprise by which he sought to captivate the professional capitalists of Capel Court is but a mild example of schemes which are constantly hatched among the wits of the "Lands of the Golden Fleece"— schemes which are dressed up, not only with scholarly rhetoric and the tropes of poetry, but with figures that might be envied by a Chancellor of the Exchequer in Downing Street.

On the margin of one of these Australian schemes (a prospectus of some Pastoral Land Company) someone had written these lines —

> "If ye buy heav'n with your blood
> In hell's hard market, when the bargain's through
> The toil begins again."

My first visit to Australia was in 1861, my last was in 1885.

One remarkable difference which struck me as between Australia a quarter of a century ago and the same colonies of to-day, was the interest which many rich and titled Englishmen have in Australian things. Lords and dukes are now as common in Australia as they are in New York, while the number of titled Australians is remarkable. Men who were mere barristers, grocers, top-sawyers, teamsters, Irish rebels, Irish adventurers, Scotch shepherds, merchants of low degree, and plumbers, are now baronets and knights of the realm, and the number of untitled Australian men who own racehorses and live in London in the grand style is very great.

We have now an Australian question. The question twenty-five years ago was transportation and the convict system; that was only temporary, but the federation of the Colonial Empire is an idea which is fast becoming a stock subject with politicians. It is as safe a subject for an editor to have an article in type upon as the biography of an aged man of letters, science, or politics.

Less than a quarter of a century ago every Australian and New Zealand colony imported its bread stuffs from Chile, California, or the United States. Now all these colonies export wheat to England as well as beef and mutton.

They had no fish in their waters worth eating except a few possible herrings, some bream, snapper, barakouta, trumpeter, or Murray cod. They have now salmon and trout. Kangaroos and sand-pipers, wood pigeons, and bush turkeys were the only things to chase or to shoot. Now they have partridges, deer, pheasants, hares, a few rabbits, some say many, quail, and the game birds of India.

But I have no wish to draw minute comparisons between New Zealand and Australia between the time when I first saw those lands, and when I left them, as it maybe, only the other day. I am content with general and large interests, and to note chiefly how once, not so very long ago, men cared not if they died out there, and now they

"Lust so to live they dare not love their life."

Death has been made terrible even in the Australian Bush to men who left England with their lives in their hands. It is this spirit which is at the bottom of the new cry for federation, colonial defences, and so forth. Some Australians have made their garden so sweet to live in that they do not want to leave it, nay, they are becoming afraid that an enemy will come and spoil it, take it from them, or drive them out of it, and this garden is, moreover, a quotable article in the market-place, at least those vast portions of it that constitute what may be called the kitchen garden—where the vegetables grow, the sheep nibble, and the cattle graze.

Let us roam a little. We need not stray. I was one night in the Lower House of Assembly in Brisbane, the House of Commons of Queensland. The everlasting subject of land was being debated, and a more absorbing debate I never heard. One of the Members for North Brisbane addressed the House, and in the course of his speech he said —

"The land of this colony is not held by the people. It is held by money-lenders, Jews, dukes, and speculators.

"The Bank of New South Wales holds seventy-six large stations.

"The Commercial Banking Company of Sydney holds one hundred and seventy-six stations, equally large.

"The Queensland National Bank, one hundred and three.

"The Mercantile Bank of Sydney, fifty-two.

"The Union Bank of Australia, sixty-two.

"The English, Scottish, and Australian Chartered Bank, forty-nine.

"The Australian Joint Stock Bank, forty-six.

"The London Chartered Bank of Australia, eighteen."

Or, in popular phraseology, these powerful money corporations lord it over forty-seven thousand nine hundred and thirteen square miles, or thirty millions six hundred thousand acres of the colony of Queensland. "There are other corporations which together with the banks own between them more than twenty thousand square miles of the pick of the land, swelling the grand total to sixty-eight thousand square miles, or nearly forty-four millions of acres!"

The speech made a deep impression. The figures were not disputed, they were simply resented by the squatterocracy, the bankers, Jews, and speculators, syndics and land agents. When the speech appeared in the daily papers it created a still deeper impression throughout the colony. People began to realize what the country was to them who had adopted it as their home. There was a general feeling of dissatisfaction, disgust, and ill-blood.

Hence the present cry for federation among the capitalists. It is not a national cry. It is the cry of dukes and syndics, as well as Messrs. Dives and Co., who want to keep up or raise the marketable value of land in London.

The revelations which I have given above moved the Queensland people to the very depths of their feelings. Sir Thomas McIlwraith was, I think, still in power. He was generally liked. He had a large-hearted way, and a practical mind that attracted the bulk of men. He had done some admirable things. He solved one of the questions of the day—the immigration question. Labourers were now not ninety-nine or a hundred-and-twenty days coming from England in a sailing ship at considerable cost, but the journey was made in the finest steamers that are built, that came, not round the Cape of Good Hope, but through the French ditch, called the Suez Canal. A splendid sea trip of more than thirteen thousand miles for £10, done in forty days! That was what Sir Thomas McIlwraith did. It was not an original idea. It was first done by the French; the author of the daring scheme being my old friend, M. Quesnell, formerly banker and merchant at Havre, now a humble imitator of Cincinnatus at Carupano. But Sir Thomas was the first to carry out the idea on a large scale, and " on strictly commercial principles."

He was full of large ideas. He planned a railway that was to unite Melbourne with Sydney, both these with Brisbane, and all with the Gulph of Carpentaria. The surveys were all made, the money found, all things were ready for this marriage with an iron ring of all the Australian Colonies, when, lo! the people of Queensland rose up and said: "There must be an end of this land grabbing." For Sir Thomas had been very liberal—perhaps not too liberal—in his grants of land to the Great Trans-Continental Railway Syndicate.

That speech of one of the Members for North Brisbane had opened people's eyes. "We will build this railway ourselves," they said. They would not be dependent on any cocked-hat and feather gentry, or bankers, or a mob of titled men.

And they dethroned Sir Thomas, and there was mourning in Judea, and the bankers mourned, and the dukes, and ornamental people who were rich and would increase their riches, and could only dream of the federation of the Empire or the federation of the Colonies.

The railway would have been a great work; but it was a greater work for the people of Queensland to resolve as they did. In this we shall find no parallel in the Spanish silver colonies, and so long as this spirit is kept up in the British gold colonies there need be no fear of their coming into the Spanish heritage of corruption and decay. So long as this national spirit is recognized men do not waste the time in talking about Imperial federation.

But there was another question which occupied the attention of Queensland at the time of Sir Thomas McIlwraith's fall, which may be referred to in this connection. This was the coloured labour question.

SILVERN POTOSI TO GOLDEN AUSTRALIA. 95

The traffic in human beings had assumed alarming proportions under the McIlwraith administration.

This abominable trade sprang out of the activities of the great land-owning companies, the Colonial Sugar Company being one of the most powerful of these. All kinds of persons had "put money" into this Company. Ladies and gentlemen, priests and politicians, professional men of all kinds who had any spare money put it into this great dividend-paying Sugar Company, which had branches in every Australasian colony and every large town. Men who denounced the murder and kidnapping of Kanakas became rich on the profits of the trade.

As late as 1884 there were some thirty ships, carrying the British flag, and licensed by the Queensland Government to go to the South Seas to bring islanders to the sugar plantations of Mackay and elsewhere.

The number of islands from which their inhabitants were beguiled would be between thirty-five and fifty, ranging from the Admiralty Islands, in the north, down south to Fiji. Some of the vessels in the trade were owned by pious grocers and merchants; a few belonged to private men who were not pious. Several well-known brigantines were the properties of the skippers who commanded them. They all were licensed by Sir Thomas McIlwraith. His department was responsible for the number of men and women that were from time to time packed in these ships, for the sufficiency and quality of the provisions put on board for the sustenance of the islanders during the voyage, for the character of the commander and his crew, and for the character of the Government Agent, who went in each ship, licensed by the Queensland Government, to see that fair play and never foul was observed on board. For everything done in connection with obtaining islanders—the way of obtaining them—and conveying them to the sugar plantations of North Queensland, the Government of Sir Thomas McIlwraith was responsible. The planters had nothing whatever to do with obtaining islanders. The Government regulated, or professed to regulate, everything. Even the "trade," as it was called, by means of which the men and women were bought, was settled by the Immigration Department, of which Sir Thomas McIlwraith was the head.

The planters paid a good price for their slaves. The highest ever paid up to 1884 was £25 10s. per head—all to be warranted in sound health, "without encumbrances," and with not more than twenty-five or thirty women to one hundred men. This proportion, however, was seldom observed, and sometimes the women were as numerous as the other sex. Women were more easily obtained than men, and cost much less. No young children were allowed to be taken.

Out of every thirty women brought on board the slaver, not less than ten would leave newly-born children behind them. It was very pitiful to see women, big with milk, milking themselves for several days after the ship had put to sea. The amount of unconscious infanticide which this form of slavery brought about has never been reckoned up. It must have been very great.

I am aware that "slaver," "slavery," and "slaves" are offensive terms—that some of the good people of Queensland resent their use, and deny their correctness. I, who have seen the real thing, know that these are the correct terms to use, and shall use no other.

I believe that I am correct in saying that no medical man

ever accompanied a slave vessel, except in the case of the *Karl*, when the doctor was one of the owners of the ship, and who, if he had not turned Queen's evidence, would certainly have been hanged.

The "trade" which a labour or slave vessel carried, to buy men and women with, consisted, in Sir Thomas McIlwraith's time, of fish-hooks, looking-glasses, lucifer matches, glass beads (small and very common), mouth organs, Jew's harps, gaudy-coloured handkerchiefs, red calico, tobacco, pipes, butchers' knives, glass beads (large), gunpowder, muskets, round iron in 10-inch lengths.

All these things, except the small glass beads, I could understand as having attractions for uncivilized human beings. But why naked people should care for such ornaments as beads no bigger than pin's heads, I could not understand for some time.*

* This matter of the small coloured glass bead remained a mystery to me for a long time. Here were full-grown men willing to sell themselves for a thimblefull of glass beads! What could it mean? Here were women parting with all control over their own souls and bodies for as many glass beads as you could hold between thumb and finger; you could buy a splendid *ummôn* or canoe capable of holding 20 men for six penn'orth of glass beads; you could get 10,000 cocoa nuts f.o.b. for eighteenpence in the form of glass beads.

What could be the meaning of folly so obvious to the commercial mind? I will answer that question.

One day when the weather was unpropitious, the heat excessive, and life dull and heavy, the captain gave our women a present of those beautiful glass beads, 10,000 of which you can buy for 2s. 3d. Instantly the face of all creation was changed; joy took the place of deadly dulness, every woman was happy; and when women are glad men cannot be sorrowful. On another occasion we took on board a youthful naked woman, without the least speck of ornament or cicatrization or tattooing, and she was so melancholy for the first day or two that I began to suspect that she had been carried away against her will. I made strict inquiry, and found that she had come for love; she had climbed out of the sea into the boat of her own free accord, and would not be turned out of it. What, therefore, was the matter? She found herself miserable, poor and naked amongst some of her own sisters, whose necks and arms and loins were covered with the precious glass bead, and she was shy, demure, lonely, and full of woe. She was quite pretty, and the captain, who was not insensible to the

H

When a slaver arrived at an island it was generally met by the natives coming off in their canoes, bringing with them fresh provisions, fruits, and vegetables, poultry, pigs, and opossums, fish, shells, clubs, spears, and masks for sale or barter, but no men or women for sale. These could only, or generally, be bought from the "king," chief, or head man of the tribe or village by going on shore.

Having an overmastering desire to see the South Sea Islands and above all the mysteries of the slave trade, I applied for the berth of Government Agent on one of the crack ships in the business, owned by some Presbyterian provision merchants, commanded by one of the most unique scoundrels it was ever my lot to know, and licensed by the successor of Sir Thomas McIlwraith in the Queensland Government, to go to the islands to fish, not for cod, but for men.

The first island at which we called was New Ireland, and it took us from the 19th of December to the 21st of January

charms of female beauty, gave her a small match box full of beads. As if by magic she was a changed being; it was soon found that she had a peculiarly sweet voice, and five minutes later she was leaning against this one, then against that, giving opinions, and in the most familiar way taking an interest in your welfare, and criticizing everything and everybody all round. Moreover, she was married a few days after she had come into her kingdom of glass beads.

The explanation of this mystery is as follows :—The natives of those Islands are great artists in shells. They make lovely bracelets out of shells, which they call "*altiltol ambulot.*" Earrings, nose and finger rings, all out of shells, which they call kabón. Kabón is a generic word for wealth. The man or woman with the longest string of kabón is the most important person in the village; it is equivalent to the family diamonds of our own aristocracy. An ample necklace of real kabón takes a life-time to make, and these children of the Coral Sea regard our Brummagem moulded glass beads (coloured) as of equal value. This is the solution of the small bead mystery, which, in all probability, will be a mystery for some time yet, but may not last quite so long as some mysteries of less importance to the families of men, which hold them in as deep a spell, and give as deep a tone and tint to their lives.—*From a Lecture delivered by me in Queensland.*— A. J. D.

to reach it from Townsville. This was owing to contrary winds, hurricanes, and calms which we encountered in the Coral Sea.

How I wish that I could throw on to this page for the reader to see as plainly as he reads these words some of the glories which "Nature, the Vicar of the Almighty Lord," there pours upon earth and sea and sky. The Vicar often made his evening dress to consist of heavenly scarlet robes. Not such imitation scarlet as that other Vicar wears now and then in Rome, or the woman in the Apocalypse, but a scarlet that reminds us not of sin, or blood, or shame, but of sweet flowers. Beneath this imperial robe of red danced a sapphire sea, and to the north of us ran a range of hills, of which Mount Huxley was one, whose quick and rapid outlines were picked out with ruby fire.

We saw some very strange fishes, of more colours than are seen in rainbows, and quite as vivid. One seemed to be of solid gold, in shape like an eel—a foot in length—with power to telescope itself to a length of not more than four or five inches. There were few birds, but many flying fishes of unusual strength and length of "wing." The day was warm, but the cold at night was very sharp.

At length, quite early in the morning, we ran close up to New Ireland or Tumbara as it is called by the natives. It is situated some 300 miles south of the equator, and separated by a strait 50 miles wide from the south-east coast of New Guinea. The island is at least 250 miles long—a rough guess would make it 30 miles broad. As viewed from seaward, it is densely wooded and well watered. Cocoa and areca nut palms, stand out against the sky along the summits, and also grow in immense numbers along the shore. Great patches on the hill-sides are under cultivation, fenced in with wickerwork two yards high. Yams and taro are the roots mainly cultivated. The food of the natives is chiefly vegetable, and consists of cocoa-nuts, yams, taro, bread-fruit, arrowroot, nutmegs, haricot beans, the sweet potato, bananas, Chile peppers, oranges, the delicious mangostine, and other dainties. There was abundance of domestic poultry and plenty of good fish, also some fine plump pigeons.

The climate is humid, the vegetation a dark green, and every tree appeared to be overrun with parasitic plants. Although food was abundant, the natives were poor in flesh, lanky, short in stature, slight in weight. Their usual colour is a dark brown, but many are much lighter. The hair of the head is crisp and glossy. Many of the black men had abundance of hair on their bodies. They were not negroes. The lighter coloured had little or no hair.

The tattooings or "cuttings on the flesh," as the Hebrew prophet calls them, were entirely confine dto women and the head men; no ordinary private man carried any, while the finer the woman, or the better looking, the more elaborate were these cuttings; they are abundant on the face, especially at the corners of the eyes, as if to hide the crow's feet, and at the corners of the mouth, as if to secure a permanent expression. The navel—*ambuling*—was always adorned; sometimes in a large diamond, or broken circle. Each breast—*susung*—carried a well-cut ornament, much like a Maltese cross. The tattooings on the buttocks —*putputungé*—and back—*ampocktán*—were always well done. The cheek—*tataan*—generally carried a large diamond figure. The tattooings were darkened by rubbing in the powdered oxide of manganese, which they call *labán.* The septum of the nose in both sexes is always pierced to carry a ring or polished bone. The men go absolutely naked, but the women wear "aprons" of grass behind as well as before, suspended from cinctures made of beads, strung on fibre threads drawn from the great leaves of the aloe. The women make an excellent bonnet from palm leaves, also a cloak, which is used in great heats and against rain. They are more careful to avoid rain than is a well-dressed London woman on her way to church. They stick feathers and bright flowers in their hair. Their feather work is beautiful. Some wear garters under the knee, finely knitted—not to keep up stockings, but for pure ornament. The women do not paint, but the men daub their faces and bodies with red and yellow earths; both men and women bleach their hair with coral lime. They are singularly cleanly in their habits, and in their persons if not made to wear clothing. They are fond of bathing in the sea, of singing and dancing, and telling stories. They easily learn to smoke tobacco, and many like it. Some it makes deadly sick. Give them any kind of food which is new to them, such as rice with treacle, they begin to investigate it, not by tasting, but by smelling it. They became very fond of tea all at once. They are singularly kind and polite to each other so long as they keep in bodily health, but if any fall sick, or come into any kind of disgrace, they pass them by without the least regard, as if they were priests and Levites journeying on the Jericho road and passing by a fellow-sinner in evil case. They would rather die than take physic.

The are full of fun as kittens, and play with each other in the same frank and graceful way. Thieving is a great delight to them, and they evince no shame on being found out. Their laughter is hearty and musical, and their smile is very pretty. They will do anything to please you except work for any length of time, or in a systematic way. All the old-fashioned emotions, tempers, airs, graces, vices, virtues, and personal charms, which are to be seen in parts of the polite world, are to be found among them. Some are full of natural dignity and self-respect, as others are of childlike naughtiness. They bear physical pain with composure, are very patient in privation, and care nothing about other people's opinions.

The women are much less modest than the men. They are grateful, but not confiding. They are not curious, and it takes much to rouse a genuine surprise. For many of them with whom I was in close fellowship for more than six months I retain a delightful feeling of affection. They soon learnt when on board ship to wash decks, and this work was always done to songs of their own making. Both men and women screamed with delight in drawing water from the sea, throwing it over the decks and washing down. They submitted without murmur to occupy different parts of the ship, both during meal times and at night, but their love of talking was incessant.

"Melagót!" I once shouted down the ladies' cabin one midnight to their infinite amazement, for they thought the voice came out of the sky, and this shut them up for that time; but no repetition of the word, which means "silence" in their tongue, in the imperative mood, ever again produced the same effect. As my tent on deck was immediately above their cabin, I was much troubled to find out a way that should bring about a permanent reform of this everlasting female talking nuisance. So, knowing their horror of cold water, I made a little watering pot out of an oyster tin, and went down among them one night of turbulent jabbering, and sprinkled them in the name of *melagót*. This cured them, and I had no more trouble or sleepless nights. They were baptized into silence.

Another reform which I was bent on making was of a more serious kind. Hitherto the women had waited upon the men at breakfast and dinner, carrying the food from the galley where it was cooked, and placing it before the lords of creation. One day, to their great astonishment, I made the women sit down and the men wait upon them. The men at first refused to do this, but as they got no food themselves until they obeyed my order the new reform was adopted—not however until I took my part in waiting on the ladies myself. At first the women did not like it; afterwards they exacted this service with rigour. Then the men abjured the society of woman altogether, and for more than a week kept themselves apart in the forward part of the ship. As the women got on very happily without the men, the men gave up sulking and took to the new way of life with cheerfulness, the women making rapid strides in learning how to make the most of this radical change in their manners. How much would I have given to know the full meaning of some of the women's remarks to the men when they brought in dinner. The shrill screams of laughter with which these were received by the younger women together with the cowed looks of the men, and the hurry with which they would get out of ear-shot, were sufficient to convince me that woman had found a new weapon with which to fight her tyrant and conquer.

Oh! how did these sinful beings revel in this new form of wickedness. Is there any happiness so great in the world to a woman as being able to make a man smart with pain by no other exertion than that of wagging her tongue?

They all went to bed at a fixed hour, cooked their own food, cleansed their own vessels, chopped fire-wood, and learnt to sew and mend clothes. The women took readily to wearing gowns, but much preferred to tear their petticoats into ribbons to adorn their heads than to cover their limbs withal. The thing which, I think, most attracted my notice was their quick and accurate eye-sight. They could, and did, discover land by the naked eye which we were unable to pick out by the aid of good glasses. They could detect a small boat six or seven miles off in bad weather when we were unable to do so with the telescope. They also made minute beads out of shells, and were fond of carving* and engraving on wood, pearl, and tortoiseshell. I think I may safely say that I never had the least thought, wish, or desire to "convert" these people. They did not want any conversion. Much rather would I like to convert some of the religious women of Brisbane into South Sea Islanders.

The way of kidnapping these people was as follows :†—

---

* Their principal graver was a shark's tooth, and bits of obsidian mounted in a wood handle.

† The method of recruiting is exactly like the old method of the recruiting sergeant in the country towns at home. All the lies that can be conveyed to an islander's fancy are palmed off on him, and no mortal mixture of earth's mould is so easily deceived as he; he is an adept in deceiving himself, and he indulges in it as some lower natures indulge in ardent spirits; but when he is helped in his self-deception by one who is an artist in lying, then the islander falls easily into the snare which is laid before his open eyes. Nothing has astonished me so much as the little that is known of the natural history of these people, and apparently no one cares to know anything about them.

Let me remind you that these islanders have never been conquered by a superior race. They have never come under the discipline of military rule; have never known what it is to obey orders, even when these are given by a man in a language they do not know, who thinks he will be understood if he speaks

There are two lifeboats attached to each slaver. Early in the morning these are manned with a mixed crew of old "boys" who had been kidnapped at Fiji, or the New Hebrides. Each carries a rifle and five rounds of cartridges. The recruiter goes in one boat—the Government Agent in the other. There is a box of "trade" in each boat. As the boats reach the shore the natives swarm down to the beach, and many swim off to the boats, men and women, hoping to have a chance of stealing something. The recruiter soon finds out if the natives are friendly or not. He opens his shop, so to speak, begins playing on a Jew's-harp, or talking in broken English, hoping the natives will understand him. After a tedious while it becomes known that the recruiter will give two knives, a thimbleful of beads, two tobacco pipes, some figs of tobacco, three fish hooks, a Jew's-harp, a looking-glass, and a gawdy pocket-handkerchief, for one man. This is too little, or it is sufficient, according to the plenty or scarcity of men. The largest amount of "trade" I ever saw paid for one hand-

sufficiently loud. They have not been trained to continuous effort, they have never felt the insolence or the graciousness of correction; save the little moral influence which may be said to be induced in them by being ruled in a limited degree by their kings or head men, they know little or nothing of restraint. The physic of the doctor, the rod of the schoolmaster, or the rousing voice of the gangman are all odious to them. They die as willingly under the influence of a little authority as they do on a meat diet or a reduction of the temperature. They would give the world to know English, or that the English knew New Irish. Having the frailty of all human beings, they are fond of sympathy and an exchange of ideas; nothing is so sweet to them as beads and a clear understanding of what is wanted from them, what they want themselves, and what they are going to receive for what they are willing to part with. But from this they are at present debarred, and in a manner that is absolutely appalling to behold; men get angry if these summer children do not apprehend the meaning of an inarticulate thundering noise or some unhuman pantomime. Up to the present your South Sea Islander has been an expensive failure, and I cannot help saying it, you who have suffered much are most to blame.—*From a Lecture delivered by me in Queensland.—A. J. D.*

some islander cost the slave hunter seven shillings and five-pence. The property is divided among the man's friends, whom he leaves behind, a portion of it goes to the "King" or head man. A man will sell himself to give his friends a few beads, some bad cutlery, a few pipes, a Jew's-harp, and some fish-hooks. It is the recruiter's duty to tell all the people who are thus bought that they are going to work on a sugar plantation in Queensland for three years; that they will be well fed, and clothed, and lodged, and at the end of three years they will all come back again with the sum of £18 in their pockets, or as many beads and pipes as this money will buy.

Great numbers of men and women were thus obtained in these islands—minus the information which it was the duty of the recruiter to give to the islander. It was the duty of the Government Agent to see that this was done. It never was done. The whole thing was a solemn farce. I will venture to say that no islander ever came to Queensland from those islands who knew what he was coming for—the work he was expected to do, the hours he was to work, or the years he was to stay. The native language is not known by anyone out of the islands. The recruiter was a very ignorant, cruel, malignant wild beast. The language in which the recruiter generally talks to the people whom he is going to enlist, or kidnap, or beguile, is the limited language of sign or pantomime. The Government Agent is absolutely and entirely at the mercy of the skipper when in those waters. It is not a question of fear, lack of courage, or power to exert authority; the skipper knows that he is out of the jurisdiction of the Queensland Government at the time that he is filling up his ship with slaves; the skipper takes no notice of the

Government Agent, nor need he.* I have made the acquaintance of several of these gentlemen, each of whom I believe did all that he could, and did it well, in protecting the natives to the best of his ability against injustice. But not one of them could ever satisfy me that the islander knew what he was about in coming to serve as a slave on the sugar plantations of Mackay, and elsewhere.

What I did in my own case was to inform the authorities immediately on our arrival in port that every one of the islanders we had on board had been illegally obtained, and they were all sent back at the expense of the owners of the ship in which they had been carried. Every effort was made to induce the Premier to allow this ship load to pass, but without avail. Every effort was made to obtain an interpreter by which to communicate with the poor people whom we had brought, and to ascertain if they would not like to go and dig and dung in the sugar garden of Mackay from early morn till dewy eve for three years for ten shillings a month and the run of their teeth.

But no interpreter could be found.

Had Sir Thomas McIlwraith's Government been in power at the time, that ship-load of New Irelanders would have been discharged on to the great blackguard sugar station of Mackay. Had the attempt been made under the Government which superseded Sir Thomas to pass those

* In many cases when a Government Agent has reported to his Government the misconduct of a slave skipper a local court has been ordered to be held by the Premier to inquire into the matter. The skipper and his crew are allowed to give evidence, which is always overwhelming and unanimous. The Commissioners who form this local court consist of sugar planters and others interested in the trade. Probably there is nothing so conclusive of the corruption of some of these Colonial Governments as the ready manner in which they are prepared to sacrifice the men whom they appointed to be their agents or representatives.

islanders, that Government would have been discredited for ever.

Up to the time, for a period of twelve years, that this same ship left Townsville to go to New Ireland and other South Sea islands the only instructions which the executive Government issued to a Government Agent consisted of an obsolete Act of Parliament and a revolver, and my opinion is that if the Government of Sir Thomas McIlwraith had not fallen as it did the slave trade in Queensland would have assumed alarming proportions. New Guinea would have opened up new fields for kidnappers, and kidnapping under the sanction of Government would have gone on at an increasing speed.

At the same time, I am also of opinion that no man is more glad at what bids fair to be the total suppression of this hateful trade than Sir Thomas McIlwraith. The sugar trade, the banking trade, and syndicates of great power had become too strong for him. Queensland will be a far sweeter place to live in when he returns to office than it was when he left it; if it be only from the fact that he will never again have the power of licensing a ship to go to the South Seas to exchange men and women for Sydney "goods" and Brummagem trumpery.

To the credit of the colonists—at least, those of South Queensland, where some of the details of the slave trade were made known—they showed even more spirit than when they discovered how the Land Act had been administered. In North Queensland the spirit displayed was the spirit of the Ephesians, who made silver shrines for Diana, and got their living thereby when they discovered that their craft was in danger by the preaching of St. Paul.

Not only were the planters angry with South Queensland and full of a spirit of hatred, but the townspeople, the great and small shopkeepers, and general traders in the north lashed themselves into a madness equal to that of the priests of Baal on a particular occasion when the planters discovered what were the intentions of the new Government with regard to them.

The reason of the planters' rage was the same as that of the rage of the planters' camp followers. Close to all sugar plantations there is sure to be a village, and the village will contain many little shops for the sale of imitation jewellery, imitation cutlery, imitation meerschaum pipes, beads, bracelets, glass emeralds, glass rubies, glass diamonds, and other Christian rubbish. If there was no village there would not fail to be a general store at which the kanaka would spend his money. In three years a thousand South Sea islanders would spend eighteen thousand pounds sterling in the village in buying detestable trash, such as only a Jew or a colonial scoundrel would sell. I have no hesitation in saying that this rubbish sold for £18,000 would not cost the traders £100. Of course, when there threatened to be no more kanaka simpletons to spend their earnings in toys, the shopkeepers of North Queensland cried out with a loud voice.

Will it be believed that never once among the Presbyterians, the Methodists, or other missionary bodies in North Queensland was one poor effort ever made, I do not say to save the souls of the South Sea islanders, who were living with them under the same sky, but to save them from the rapacity of the despicable shopkeepers who robbed and cheated them?

By all means let the children deck themselves with

trinkets, and spend their pocket money at the fair. But if you discover that one of your own children has been swindled by a villainous hawker you communicate with the police or take other steps. Nothing was ever done to protect the children from the South Seas against the swindling practised on them in Mackay and other sugar towns. Mackay had a representative in the Queensland Parliament, but to my certain knowledge he never denounced the iniquities of the town in this matter.

Here do we come on an old foe with a new face. The old Spanish aristocrats, who received a license from the King to trade in the colonies, the governors of Provinces, and all who had dealings with Peruvian Indians, always carried with them from Seville, when they took ship for Callao, a large, wondrous, and mixed assortment of "goods" to sell to the people in the distant *Repartimientos*, such as gold and silver brocade somewhat tarnished, satins, silk stockings, false hair, waistcoatings, spectacles, playing cards, pictures, rosaries, gold crosses made of brass, tin images, tin suns, tin moons, dolls, crucifixes of varied dimensions, buttons, beads—in short, the sweepings of Seville shops, all damaged, but which would be "sold" at enormous prices to the Indians of Chayanta, Puno, Charcas, Caupolicán, and elsewhere. There is no more pitiful chapter in Spanish colonial history than this, told, as it is, with great minuteness.* The parish priest frequently helped in selling this trumpery, and lent his chapel for the occasion. One of these worthies managed to get a large parcel of common spectacles at a very low price. What could be done with these articles among a

---

* "Noticias Secretas," por Don Jorge Juan y Juan de Ulloa, the only authentic work on the social condition of the Spanish colonies in the last century.

people noted for their excellent eye-sight, whose eyes were never dim except with tears? Priests can do much under certain conditions. This speculator in spectacles stuck a notice on his church door to the effect that all who appeared at mass on the coming Sunday in a pair of spectacles would receive a remission of the last week's sins! "Spectacles can be bought from El R. P. Fray Oscuras Segundo for eight shillings a pair—*muy barato.*" There was a large congregation. The price of spectacles rose in the market, etc., etc. Several of these colonial aristocrats "made" by this form of trading two hundred thousand dollars each within less time than three years. As in kidnapping the Spaniards led the way, so in this infamous form of trading, and North Queensland imitated their example.

I have said that the Executive Government of Queensland was responsible for all the iniquities of the labour traffic. But the planters of the north—notably those of Mackay, represented in the Brisbane Parliament by a planter—were responsible for much. These men were not so foolish as to pay £25 a head for kanakas, and then amuse themselves by killing them as quickly as possible. That charge has been made against them by silly editors and small local preachers. The charge is obviously beneath contempt. The mortality, especially in Mackay, among the South Sea Island sugar slaves was always very great. It was so astounding at the time I was there that the Government of Mr. Griffith[*] was afraid to publish particulars. A medical man was sent from Brisbane by the Premier to Mackay to report, and he did, and received a quieting fee. The document was never published. It would have damned the colony at home, and perhaps inter-

---

[*] Now Sir Samuel Griffith.

fered with the floating of the next loan—at least, the Government may have so thought—for, although the planters and their agents were blameworthy, the principal blame for the fearful mortality, which at one time ran as high as 60 per cent., must fall on the Government and their local officers. The planters supplied all sufficient funds for the building of hospitals, for medical men, for medicines, and all remedial means and measures. The Government received these funds, but disbursed them in the most inadequate way.

The truth of the matter is that the climate was fatal to the islanders; it was too cold and too variable. Frequently a day of broiling sun would be followed by a night of sharp frost. This of itself was sufficient to kill large numbers of the feeble children of the South Seas. The labour was too continuous, the monotony too awful and depressing. These South Sea heathens were from their childhood brought up to dance on their own sun-warmed, yellow sands, to gambol in the sea, to sing and laugh, and subsist on fruits and roasted yams, the delicious cream of the cocoa-nut, the delicate flesh of the banana, and other refined things of exquisite taste. They soon had the song knocked out of them when they came to Mackay. Their limbs soon became too stiff for the dance, and their blood soon too poor for laughter. They were put on a meat diet. Salt pork, and flour made into unwholesome bread, did not suit them, and numbers died because life was hideous to them, many went mad, others ran away thinking—poor children—that they might reach home that night, but night coming and bringing for them nothing but cold and hunger, they would crawl into a field of sugar cane and lie down and die. They died as easily as you could quench smoking flax.

The main blame of the planters was in employing such feeble labourers to cultivate their fields.

Had the conveying of islanders from the South Seas not degenerated, as it was meant to degenerate, into a real slave trade, it would have occurred to someone to set up model plantations in one or more of the islands, where the islanders would have been gradually taught systematic labour, and so be prepared for profitable work. But the truth must be told; the planter thought only of his sugar, and how much he could squeeze out of the cane; the one and only labourer that would suit the planter was a being who would be content with a low wage, and who had no mind capable of hatching a strike at an inconvenient time.

It is, perhaps, an infinite pity that the planters did not press their claims at an earlier time on Sir Thomas McIlwraith in the matter of obtaining coolies from India. Had this been done the colony of Queensland would probably be more flourishing than it is, a great scandal might have been averted, a great good might have been achieved.

If Queensland does not grow sugar, she will not get as much out of her soil as she ought to get. The cultivation of sugar promotes many other industries. For any politician to have it in his power to bar the cultivation of sugar in that colony is a deep disgrace to society; it is a stain on character, and indicates a low, narrow, sectarian mind that should be got rid of. The attitude of that mind, so to say, is not only narrow, it is insolent towards a question of this magnitude and importance, and if some modification does not soon show itself a grave disaster may happen in Queensland.

I cannot close this part of my reminiscences without referring to a matter that is at once painful and startling.

Of the number of kidnapping skippers, who carried on the Queensland slave trade during the past twelve years, thirty died young; they were murdered, shipwrecked, died while drunk, died in consequence of excessive drinking, or they cut their own throats. Not one was hanged, although one was condemned to die in that way, but his sentence was commuted to transportation for life. Had the miscreants who were connected with the massacres done on board the *Karl* been hanged we should not probably have heard of the later atrocities. But how could a jury of men who had been concerned in indiscriminately slaughtering Australian black fellows bring in an English skipper guilty of murder for slaying kanakas?

Doubtless the manner in which the Australians have stained their hands with the blood of the aborigines must have not a little to do with the readiness with which they entered into the murdering of South Sea Islanders.

We read "Las Casas" with horror. The histories by Sir Arthur Helps of the Conquerors of the New World and their Bondsmen and the Spanish Conquest in America make our flesh creep as we read of the massacres of Indians. If the Australian blacks had had a history anything like the history of the Incas, the Astecs, the Muyscas, and the Mexicans, the deeds of our own Australian colonists would have been seen to be precisely the same as those of the Spanish colonists in South America.

Travellers of literary distinction, who visit the Colonies and travel swiftly, and in railway carriages lined with blue satin, and are entertained like princes, write of the coldness of the Colonial Office and British Secretaries of State towards Australians. It so happens that there are men among these great officers of State who have memories, men who have had to regard with pain the meanness, selfishness, and grasping sordidness of colonial politicians and the agitators of the great colonial towns.

Of all the millions of pounds sterling dug out of the earth in Australian lands, or New Zealand, during the past generation, has a single shilling been paid in the form of royalties to the Crown ?

Not a single shilling.

Are we to forget the cruelties, the degrading inhumanities and murders done to the Chinese on Australian Gold Fields ?

Have not the selfishness, the avarice, and greed of the Australian colonists kept pace with their increasing wealth ? These things are forgotten by illustrious writers, or, perhaps, were never known to them ; and when they visit Melbourne and Sydney, Brisbane and Adelaide, Hobart Town and Auckland, and see the splendid streets of these towns, the glorious parks, the magnificent public buildings, the rolling grass plains, the railways and shipping, they are annoyed at the ignorance and rudeness which British Ministers of State almost invariably display towards the colonies.

If such travellers would know the truth about life in Australia, its trials and sufferings, as well as its aspirations, they must not make their inquiries from privileged persons who have settled in those colonies, and who occasionally run home for a year's holiday. The facts of Australian life can only be gathered from people who never leave the colonies, and never dream of being able to leave them. I once came on a curious gravestone with the following lines cut in it. It was in Sydney —

> " Beneath this stone Sam Boden lies,
> No one laughs and no one cries ;
> Where he's gone, and how he fares,
> No one knows and no one cares."

There never was a more sad or truthful epitaph ever written. Of course, it is not true in any but a local sense. I, for one, would give a good deal to know where Sam is and how he fares; but at the time of his death, and in the place where he died, I have no doubt about this being a veracious statement. If there be a real desire in England to know the exact truth about Colonial or Imperial Federation, the witnesses to be examined must be sought among the survivors of Sam Boden, including the man who wrote the doggerel lines which are carved on Sam's tombstone.

The Australians are making of themselves a nation. What it will be like, or what form it will take, no one can forecast.

The likeness and the unlikeness to other colonies, Spanish or other, may be seen with distinctness now and then.

The fact which most vividly brings out the unlikeness is to be seen only at night.

Within less than thirty years the Australian coast has been dotted with lighthouses by the colonists themselves. Not a single lighthouse was erected in South America twenty years ago! That is to say, the Spanish colonists held twenty thousand miles of coast in America for three hundred years, and never built a single lighthouse.

What new developments are in store for Australia and New Zealand, especially when the Panama Canal shall bring them in closer contact with the United States, neither Australia nor New Zealand at present know. What form the question of Federation will then assume, who may say? Of one thing we may be sure, that no form of slavery will be possible under any name that the ingenuity of Ministers or millionaires may suggest.

CHAPTER IX.

SILVER LIMA AND GOLDEN MELBOURNE.

THE humanity of the Spanish colonists has been too much hidden from sight. We have been so occupied with the history of their religious wickedness and general selfishness that we are ignorant of the natural qualities which many possessed, and the great and noble things which some of them did. Let it never be forgotten that there was at one time in Lima a college for the instruction of the aboriginal population in the Christian religion. Not a mere elementary school, but a college—not of children, but of men. There was also a hospital for the poor who were recovering from sickness, another for incurables, one for sick Indians, and nine other hospitals were appropriated to some peculiar charities:—For poor ecclesiastics, for sailors, for negroes, three for women, for lepers, also a retreat for women who wanted to be separated from their husbands, and another for women whose only infirmity consisted in their being poor, and probably not very good-looking; an orphanage; a foundling hospital conducted by lady nuns. I have seen authentic descriptions of these religious houses, and of the riches of the churches, which are very striking. The gold and silver candlesticks, all of solid metal, were marvellous; many of these being high, and well proportioned. The paintings were highly valuable. Some altar pieces were works of the great masters.

Lima, no doubt, was first in all the cities of South America for the splendour of its churches and religious houses. But there were many towns and cities that vied with Lima in this particular. They were a very religious people, and boasted of it.

Within fifty years after its foundation Lima was the largest city in the whole of South America.* It was famous for its orchards and gardens; the splendour of its shops, as well as its churches, the beauty of its women, and the extent of its private wealth. Its public and private libraries are spoken of with admiration in the works of learned men and travellers.

Lima, to repeat what has already been said, is now one of the filthiest towns in the world. Its solid splendours have given way to wretched tinsel; many of its hospitals have been razed to the ground. Earthquakes and revolutions have torn the city to pieces. It has been conquered in war by one of its republican neighbours. Some of the scenes which have taken place in it are an everlasting disgrace to the people and race, or races, who took part in them.

In less than twenty years from the time that Peru separated from the mother country, and Lima ceased to belong to Spain, it became as celebrated for its misery and squalor as it had been for its prosperity and riches.

* We have recently been told by eminent writers who have visited Australia that no ancient or modern city ever grew so rapidly in opulence and power as the city of Melbourne, Victoria. The statement is quite untrue; and it is always made in forgetfulness of the city of Lima, whose magnificence was the talk of the world less than fifty years after it was founded.

Lima never represented the whole of Peru until it became a republican pigstye. It is fifty-three years ago from the present year since the ground on which Melbourne now stands was first trodden by an Englishman, or a white man —at least, so far as we know—and he was an escaped convict. The founder of Lima was the illegitimate son of a Spanish soldier, who, when he was born, was indebted for shelter to a church porch, and for sustenance to a sow. The rise of both towns in size, riches, and splendour within a like period of time is remarkable. But it is of little profit to seek any further similarity between them, except to say that the rapid growth of both was due to the accidental finding of vast wealth, one in silver, the other in gold.

In Melbourne, of provision made for the poor there was none for many years. Five-and-twenty years ago there were nine hundred prisoners in one stockade, all ablebodied scoundrels, as many women elsewhere, and still more insane shut up in a mad-house. Presently, as the colony of Victoria became peopled, churches were built, hotels, clubs, and shops, especially in Melbourne, but the churches remained for a long time far behind in outward appearance. They are fast becoming very handsome. Perhaps the largest and handsomest Wesleyan Methodist Chapel in any part of the world is in Melbourne. There is an admirable University, a truly great Public Library, a Post Office, and Town Hall, which without exaggeration may be called grand. Just as certainly as if you went on board ship in the Firth of Clyde in sight of the Duke of Argyll's Bowling Green the Holy Loch and other sweet waters of Scotland, went to sleep and waked up in Blue Skin Bay, Dunedin, New Zealand, you would fancy that you were still in Scotland. In like manner, if you saw many parts of Melbourne, the chief parts, without being conscious of the space intervening between them and England, you would not doubt that you were in England still. The language is the same, the women are the same, clothed in the same beautiful, expensive, foolish way as they are in London, and almost everything is the same, except the gutters which run down the sides of the streets. The newspapers are the same, with a difference, so are the cabs, omnibuses, clubs, railways, and railway stations. Melbourne is thoroughly an English edition of an English town, revised and enlarged.

If a man were inclined to say that the one abiding and absorbing spirit of the Australian colonies was a spirit of selfishness, an hour's drive through the chief streets of Melbourne would drive that idea out of his mind. There is a look of generosity about the place that is unmistakable. As for the people who are mad or miserable, " it's their own fault;" "they have no business to be miserable out there, under the Southern Cross; certainly they ought not to go mad." " Let people drink less, and drink only good liquor when they do drink, they will then be all right." If they do not follow these golden rules "they ought to come to grief," and there is possibly some beneficence in this brutality.

"Oh, yes, of course, there are heaps of women even in Melbourne who want to be separated from their husbands, but they must grin and bear it. We are not going to build refuges for these. Besides, let people wash their dirty linen at home."

"Niggers? Certainly, there are plenty of them; more useless than dogs, and not half so cleanly."

It is almost worth while to go to Melbourne to hear a real Australian burst of laughter. It is more of a storm, or a heavy windy shower of laughter, that you get in response to the question —

" Do you teach the negroes the Christian religion ? "

By negroes of course I mean the aboriginal black fellows. Now little as I think of the Spanish Peruvian, I am sure that even he would deem it everlasting infamy and disgrace to have walking in the streets of his chief cities such striking scarecrows, such hideously ugly wretches, such a loathsome " eclipse of a manhood divine " as the Australian black fellow and his gin.

It is only the lowest type of Englishman, no matter what may be his wealth in gold-dust or tallow and wool, that consents to keep in his house a human being who is distinguished only for his bad habits, his offensive smell, his dirty nose, and his disagreeable grin. What would our feelings be on reading an Australian edition of *The Tempest* to find that Prospero is no longer master of Caliban, that Caliban no longer fears Prospero, not only steadfastly refuses to carry logs, but boasts of his multitudinous wickedness ?

The last time that I visited the Port of Bowen, in North Queensland, I saw early in the morning three or four cockle-shell canoes paddle up to the starboard side of the English commercial steamer on which I was a passenger. Each canoe contained what seemingly were three or four bundles of rags. I was quite unprepared for what followed, but some of my companions in travel had visited Bowen before, and knew what to expect.

Presently the rags fell from half-a-dozen full-grown naked women, who proceeded to cover themselves up with the transparent waters of the sea. Some ardent Australian-born English youths began to waste their substance by riotously throwing half-crowns, florins, shillings, and six-pences into the great laughing water. Down went the bronze mermaids, head first, into the deep, out of sight, bringing up the shining coin which they had caught, and showing it in gleeful triumph. This submarine exhibition of Australian art was open for more than an hour, and those Australian women paddled to their camp, each with a mouthful of silver coins that would presently be spent in rum and tobacco.

I had seen men and boys diving for silver sixpences on heathen coasts, but it was reserved for me to see full-grown naked women do the like within sound of the English Church bell. Each of these women had a little baby, and I for one should like to ask if those babies are to be allowed to grow up as irresponsible as kangaroos, and to have free warren over the Australian vineyard without being taught to take their share in the art of dressing and keeping it?

The Australian Caliban ought to be kept at Australian work. But the Australian Prospero has not proved himself equal to the task of taming the Australian Caliban. There may be seen in every large town an Australian Stephano and an Australian Trinculo, and Caliban has been allowed to become the friends of these, and has learnt to imitate the drunkenness and wit of both. This is a deep disgrace to the Australian colonists.

Dreadful as it is to read the cold-blooded murders of the aboriginal Peruvians by the Spaniards, it is still more dreadful to see the manner in which the English treat the aboriginal Australians.

In Tasmania the black fellow was mercifully put to death;

it was becoming, in a colony of convicts, to murder the original owners of the soil on which they were to work for a living. In the other Australian colonies the black fellow was almost as plentiful as the kangaroo. The fate of the kangaroos is supposed by many to be identical with that of the blacks.

That the Australian aboriginal is a much more degraded human being than any other aboriginal in any part of the world may be true, although even on this opinions differ; but I shall never, I trust, come into the belief that it is impossible for an Englishman to teach the black fellow how to work and how to live.

Immediately before leaving Brisbane this last time, a white man—an Irishman—was hanged between two aboriginals from the same gallows, all three for the same offence, namely, murdering women, etc. I confess that I should not like to have been the judge who sentenced these two wretched blacks to that death. Identification must have been next to impossible.

But if black fellows are worth hanging they are worth teaching. If the black is not teachable, if it is certain that he is in nothing better than a dog, to hang him is degrading to the community in which he was allowed to live.

There are in Melbourne two separate and distinct quarters, the Irish quarter and the Chinese quarter; they are distinct from the other quarters of the town chiefly in squalor and misery. These quarters were founded and grew just as another quarter was founded and has grown —not in Melbourne, but in another part of Australia—I mean the black fellows' quarter, which is Queensland.

Melbourne was founded on gold, as the strength and glory of Lima was founded on silver and the glory of

Republican Peru was founded on guano; as Birmingham was founded on brass, buttons, and beads, Yarmouth on herrings, the Roman Catholic religion in China on Jesuits' bark, called in their day *quina-quina,* the bark of barks; and the Imperial town of Potosi was certainly founded on silver.

The principal railways in Peru, notably the Callao and Oroya railway, were all built on guano; its Army and Navy were all sustained by guano. The glory and strength of Peru, its Army and Navy and its great railway, are over and gone, simply because the Peruvian guano is no longer sent to market, and is, as the Peruvians believe, all over and gone. It lasted little more than a generation, and Peru is irretrievably fallen. If it ever be set up on its legs again it will be by a people who have something better to trust in than guano.

Melbourne was founded on gold, as every school-boy knows, and all the large towns in Victoria were in like manner so founded; and all the external greatness of that magnificent British colony may be said to have a similar foundation.

What will become of Melbourne when the gold gives out? What effect will it have on the Chinese quarter or the Irish quarter of that magnificent town?

Will the black fellows return to their old quarters? What will become of my old quarters at the Melbourne Club, or the Club itself, where I lived for a year in great comfort and at much expense? And the Melbourne Cup, is that institution not going to last for ever?

Is there in all the world a desolation so terrible to behold as the fenceless desolation of a forsaken, worked-out gold field, unless it be that part of Peru where once were piled up a million tons of guano, and now there is nothing to occupy it but the viewless winds?

It looks like treason to one's own nature to ask these questions. Is there any comparison between an Englishman and a Spaniard, or between an Australian colonist and a Peruvian? or any comparison between the religion of the Papist and the Presbyterian? Is there the slightest reason to imagine that a similar fate is in store for golden Victoria as the fate which has overtaken the Spanish colony of silvern Peru? Shall Melbourne ever bite the dust as Lima has bitten it? Did not Spain and her colonies mainly come to grief because they worshipped a woman and kissed the Pope's toe, or believed in transubstantiation, purgatory, the seven sacraments, and the infallibility of the Church?

Let the Presbyterians of Australia plume themselves on the purity of their faith, the sweetness of their morals, the exuberant bounty of their hospitality, the Melbourne Club and Cup, the Chinese and Irish quarters, not omitting the black fellows' quarters in Queensland. The only difference I see at present between the miners of Peru and the miners of Australia is that the first found silver in marvellous abundance and mined it with little trouble, and the second found gold under like conditions; both have used these metals in precisely a similar way, and for the same ends. There is no difference in the magnificence of the hospitality which both dispensed to strangers. Both may equally boast of their beautiful women; both have killed off vast numbers of aboriginals; and in the acclimatization of birds, beasts, and fishes, fruits, and vegetables there is little to choose between them; and in so far as both these miners use their wealth in the same way and from the same motive, there is little reason to doubt that the same fate will overtake the one as overtook the other.

Happily, there is no reason why the golden Australians should continue to imitate the silver men; and there is evidence to prove that the Australian will not be so selfish and self-indulgent, so lazy and revolutionary, as the Peruvian has been. Those lighthouses along the Australian coast are one guarantee, the Australian prisons are another; and there is an enormous difference in the form and nature of the government of both countries. The Australian colonies are quite as republican or democratic as the South American Republics. But there is this peculiar difference between them : the Australian colonies have the distinguished privilege of very often making the acquaintance of English gentlemen, not only in the form and character of a sailor, but of a Governor, who represents the Queen of England and is the colonial fount of honour. Colonial Governors have not been, as a rule, brilliant men. Some have even been very stupid men; but the cases have been rare when they have not been gentlemen, and the influence which these and their families have exerted on colonial life has been most gracious, fine, and good. English ships of war also pay frequent visits to all the chief Australian ports, and these convey to the colonial mind more distinctly than Governors and their suites do the real greatness of England, the greatness which it is within the reach of every Englishman to achieve for himself; the greatness which springs from self-abnegation, from a sweet courtesy, from obedience, order, rule, and the ever-present readiness to die when duty requires it.

These excellent models of greatness were seldom or never known to Spanish colonists, even under the Crown of Spain, and certainly never under the Republic, and this, no doubt, was a great drawback. So long as England supplies Governors to English colonies there will always follow them English men-of-war, and in the presence of these, vulgarity, selfishness, meanness, cowardice, and their subordinates will skulk out of sight, or become permanently ashamed of themselves and be afraid to appear. At least that is our general hope and belief. No gold colonist from Melbourne, or sugar colonist from Queensland, or mutton colonist from Sydney and New Zealand, can be asked to contemplate a silver Spanish colonist from Peru or Ecuador, Bolivia or the United States of Colombia, and be required to take warning by his example without the gold man indignantly exclaiming, "Is thy servant a dog that he should become like unto this thing?"

Alas! there is a likeness, if not a relationship, between them which a colonist may very naturally ignore, but which no thoughtful man who is not a colonist will fail to recognize.

There is one unlikeness for which we may be thankful. The British gold colonist was never required or even asked by the mother country to give any of his gold for the purposes of war. The Spaniard only cared for his colonies because of the silver they supplied for carrying on great wars, and it is certain that but for the mines of Potosi, Motley's prose epic of the Dutch Republic would never have been written.

CHAPTER X.

FROM NEW ZEALAND TO BOLIVIA.

The most weary of all the long journeys I ever made was from Melbourne, the chief port of Victoria, to Callao, the chief port of Peru. We called on our way at Dunedin, where we remained for a week. Blueskin Bay was beautiful, and very impressive was the sight of the doctor's boat which came out to meet us, manned by eight Maoris, young and handsome, dressed like a man-of-war's men. I also well remember a young Maori girl who stood over a fruit stall in the market-place who had cuttings round her eyes and on the chin, similar in all respects to the young girls of New Ireland. In less than three months afterwards I was carefully examining the tatooings of young women whom I encountered in the market-place of Chuquisaca, eight hundred miles inland from the Pacific shore. They were not natives of Chuquisaca, but "Indians" from Cochabamba, very like in figure to the South Sea girls, and their cuttings in the flesh were precisely the same.

Dunedin was then up to its eyes in mud. The post-office was a wooden shanty made of unplaned boards. It was the age of crinoline. On my remarking at dinner, which was at the house of Mr. Reynolds, the pleasure it gave me to see English women dressed in graceful garments instead of being stuck up in balloons, there was a general laugh at my expense. The women in Dunedin, it appears, did not wear crinoline, solely on account of the uncertain temper of the wind, which came down the gullies and round the hills in sudden, wanton tricks that made walking very slow work and sometimes hazardous. On the Sunday morning I went to church, which was a little Scotch Presbyterian building, delightfully situated at the head of Blueskin Bay. The preacher was the Reverend Doctor Burns, an old man with a fine red face and flowing silvery white hair. Very striking. During the sermon the reverend gentleman took the opportunity of telling us that the name he bore was odious to him, and that he bore not only the name of Burns, but the blood of ROBERT BURNS ran in his veins, and he would spend the rest of his days in repudiating the connection, and doing something to vindicate the honour of his God, whom his relative had always insulted by his words and by his deeds.

This is a sample of that cruel Presbyterianism with which the colonies are cursed a statement that will seem incredible to many. A religion that allows of an exhibition of hatred and ignorance such as this, if not as bitter and hateful as the religion of the Holy Inquisition, is at least liable to become so. I made some inquiries about Dr. Burns, and found that he was from Kincardineshire originally, and a veritable descendant of the poet. I think this Dr. Burns a disgrace to Scotland and a scourge to the cause of pure religion. But he is now dead, *y basta*.

We left Dunedin for Callao with a fair wind, which promised to carry us across the Pacific in good time.

The fair wind left us, or we left the fair wind, in less than a week. There was plenty of wind, but it was foul. The skipper was new to these waters. He had an idea that if he ran south we might reach the coast of Chile, pick up the well-known trade wind which blows there, and so make up for lost time. We ran south, into the coldest and most forbidding sea it was ever my lot to look upon. The clouds hung so low that sea and sky seemed no further apart than the shells of an oyster half-opened.

I was the only passenger. The skipper, to drown his sorrow, took to drinking rum. He became so drunk that he did not know what he was about. I consulted the chief officer, who was an American. I proposed to take the skipper into custody and give the mate command of the ship, but the mate was not inclined to follow my advice. I then demanded of the mate that if I locked up the skipper he would take command. This he promised to do. So I locked up the skipper, who was dead drunk, in his cabin, and awaited with some anxiety the time when he would wake up and ask questions. I had to wait more than twenty-four hours. He at length got up and called for me. I appeared at his cabin window, which looked on to the quarter-deck. He was singularly subdued, and to my great delight handed me the key of the locker in which he kept his liquor. He wished me to hear him swear that he would "never again taste another drop." This I refused to do, but stuck to the key of the locker.

The captain knew nothing of currents or winds except such as blow in the English Channel. Why we were not wrecked is a mystery to me. Starting from latitude 48 south, longitude 160 west, we ran down to latitude 60, longitude 120 west, in order to reach latitude 12 south, longitude 80 east! We were two months at sea, and must have sailed more than eight thousand miles. This skipper is a fair example of the politicians who are navigating the constitutional ship of the Australian colonies—with this difference, that when they get drunk there is no one by to lock them up, or lock up the liquor.

From Callao I took steamer to Cobija, and remained there a month waiting for the coming of mules. It is a small place, but with many pleasant recollections for me. The name of ARTOLA will remain one of the pleasantest memories of my life, connected, as it is, with all that remains of good in South America. I was very anxious to get to the native home of the alpaca, but this could not be done without mules. While thus waiting I observed one afternoon a small crowd gathered round a man in the market-place, who appeared to be preaching. It was on this account, I suppose, that I joined the crowd. It turned out to be an auction. Some spiteful creditor was selling up the Consul for Chile. All his things were put up in one lot, and the lot consisted of ten thousand fire-bricks, thirty barrels of gunpowder, many tons of copper ore, a machine for condensing water, several carts, miners' tools, chains, rope, candles, and I know not what. Merely for the purpose of giving a start to the bidding I bid three thousand dollars, and to my amazement the lot was knocked down to me. The ore alone was worth double the money. A few days afterwards El Señor Osa, who had been thus victimized, came and asked me to let him buy back all the things as they stood, and inquired my price.

"Three thousand dollars," I said.

Knowing me to be an Englishman, and supposing that I had made a mistake, he put the matter in another shape, but

I told him that I thoroughly understood how he had been served, that I was very sorry for having started the bidding at so high a figure; but I did it for the best, intending to serve him, and that if he wanted his things back, and had three thousand dollars at hand he could have them at that price, that I had not used any of them, and that it was a habit of mine if I found anything in the street and knew the owner, to return it without asking for a reward.

He was thunderstruck. He called me an angel; he said I should be laughed at, that they had given him the name of *demonio*, and would not fail to call me *loco*. However, I had my way. Osa still thinks me to be an angel, and many others think me a fool. But it doesn't matter. Here come the mules.

I left Cobija at sundown one Sunday in company of fifty of these sagacious creatures heavily laden with merchandise for the far interior of Bolivia, and ten muleteers heavily laden with ardent spirits. My mule and I were laden also. Attached to the pommel of my saddle were the saddle-bags, containing a bottle of old brandy, three bottles of Vino de Pasto, a goodly number of small meat pies (all made by la Señora Artola), some ham from Estramadura, some cheese, tea, onions from Lisbon, and garlic from Chile, a hundred cigars, each five inches long, from the Havannah, and other comforts. From the croup hung a pair of great horns, which went round the barrel of the mule, containing four quarts of sweet water, all that could be allowed the mule and me until we should cross the river Loa at Mescanti, that is some four days.

We travelled all through the night, which was cooled by the south wind. We breakfasted at Culupo, having climbed five thousand feet above the sea in sixteen hours, and travelled about forty miles. Here I committed one of the greatest follies of my life, and here also began an adventure which I never shall forget. The folly consisted in separating myself from my companions, and setting off alone across a desert where there are no permanent tracks, no landmarks or guide-posts, except such as are known to Indians, who keep their own counsel. It is true that in this desert there are to be seen the blanched remains of many thousands of mules that have perished of hunger, thirst, or weariness, and for six hundred miles you can in the day time trace a certain course that will not fail you; but they are unsafe guides to an Englishman who sees them for the first time, and has heard nothing of them beforehand. It was from no love of adventure that I started off alone from Culupo; it was simply to escape from the torment of clouds of dust raised by the fifty mules. My companions and the captain of the troop assured me that I could not miss my way. So on I went on level ground at an easy pace of five miles an hour.

Before me lay a motionless sea of sand, and above hung the sun pouring down heavy rays of heat. But the air was sweet; it penetrated my bones, and I went on mindless of all things save the bliss of being. This uncommon feeling lasted for some five hours, when I waked as if from a happy dream to find myself all alone.

I had no sense of danger, but pulled up the mule to get a steady view of things. In front there was nothing to be seen but the mule's ears, behind nothing but its tail. I knew enough of mules to tell me that this would not have carried me so willingly had it not known what it was about, and where it was going to. After an hour's steady pacing in the direction which the mule of its own will elected to take, we came up to what I conceived must be my own troop of mules.

"How far are we from Mescanti?" I inquired, in a confident tone.

"This," said the courteous Indian, in cultivated Spanish, "is not the trail that leads to Mescanti."

"Where, then, lies the trail?" I inquired.

"Yonder," was the reply, the dark-faced child of the sun pointing indefinitely with his chin to a part of the world at right angles to that over which we were then passing.

Being in haste, for the day was now wearing, I bolted off and came on not one track, but three tracks. After trying them each in turn, I discovered that they all ran in the same direction.

It was now six o'clock. In less time than it takes a maid to close the shutters, the sun would roll over the side of the world, and I should be left in the dark. Still, I had no fear. But, before deciding upon anything, I thought it good to dine, give the mule a roll in the sand, and otherwise prepare to meet the unmistakable difficulty in which I then found myself, of being lost. On taking a steady survey of the round world, I discovered a dip in the distant hills, then fast becoming clothed in blue. So remarkable was this appearance that I could come to no other conclusion than that there, if anywhere, I might find water, and if water, something else which the mule would be glad to crunch and get into its stomach. I further resolved that if no way of escape was possible, rather than lie down and die I would kill the mule, make *charqui* of her flesh, and live in the strength of that food as long as I could, or till rescue came to me.

I kept my resolution, and we sped on our way to the

space in the hills, which looked as if one of the great pyramids had been cut out of them, peak downwards, the mule still going as fresh as when we first left Cobija. The sun at last did roll over, as I expected, and we two were left in the dark. There was no moon. Soon I caught sight of what seemed to be a torch. It hung over the dip in the hills, making it visible. I pulled up my companion to get a steady gaze at the friendly light, the finger of fire which beckoned me on. It proved to be a star, which was magnified into a blaze of brightness by being seen through the reverberating heat of the hills. It was a long way off.

The night became very cold, but soon the stars came out in emerald, ruby, sapphire, and diamond light. I forgot all about being lost. I wanted all the world to come and see this glory of the heavens, the "vicar of the Almighty Lord" in his richest robes.

It was now midnight, the cold very great. We reached what seemed to be a deep, yawning pit, which lay in a direct line with the star. Down went the mule into what turned out to be an extinct volcano—a crater of pumice. We climbed the other side with difficulty, making a great cloud of blinding dust, and on reaching the solid earth I proposed to give the mule a drink of water. But to my horror there was no water to be had. The strap which had fastened the horns containing the water to the croup had given way. To my actual thirst was now added an imaginary thirst, which became intolerable. In my distress I had no heart to mount the mule, and walked at its side, picking up one or two pebbles to roll them under my burning tongue, which began to swell, or I imagined it did, and my thirst increased. As I walked along, carrying the reins over my left arm, the mule appeared to be in a dismal plight; its tail was pressed between its legs, and its ears hung all awry. The colour of my thoughts changed; the stars lost their beauty. I would have given them all to hear the barking of a dog or the crowing of a cock. But the star, although not a bit nearer, still hung steadily over the dip in the hills. I got into the saddle. The mule cheered up and began a cheery trot, its ears standing straight against the sky like two spikes. The horrible thirst became bearable by this good conduct of my companion. Soon my attention was called to a mysterious stretch of darkness, over which hung the friendly star, and as I was peering into this strange thing the mule turned with a swiftness which nearly hurled me from the saddle. I pulled up, and, listening and looking, heard the sound of rippling water!

We had reached the precipitous banks of the Mescanti river. If the mule had not started back as it did we should have fallen down a deep place and been killed. The mule had found the river; it was now my place to find the ford. This did not take more than an hour. We reached the river's brink, and I gave the first drink to the mule. After half-an-hour's rest I was again in the saddle. We swam the river, and in less than five minutes we were in front of a roaring fire in an Indian's hut at Mescanti—saved!

It is good for a man to be tried in a desert. I was once lost in a tropical forest at the foot of the Quindio Mountains, and felt as helpless as a land crab up a tree. But no man need be lost in a wilderness of sand if the atmosphere is as sweet and inspiring as I found it. No despair is possible when your very bones are full of the power which is supplied by the Queen of the Air.

I had only twenty miles to go before reaching the place

where I was to rest and prepare for what remained of the way. I suppose it was in an insolence of triumph over the troubles of the previous night that I set off still alone for Calama. The Indians of the hut told me that I should not fail to overtake two men, adding some other word of which I took no notice at the time. I quickly made up to them, as they were loitering along.

" Buenas dias, caballeros," I sang out in cheerful voice, as I drew nigh to the two horsemen.

" Buen dia," responded the oldest of the two, who was of saturnine complexion.

There was no expression of human love in his face or voice. I became painfully suspicious that these two men were murderers.

Our talk became as polite as it was reserved. It was nearly all on my side. I could only learn what my fellow-travellers were made of by making remarks which compelled them to look at me. I had never seen such ill-looking men.

" Have you any fresh water?" I inquired.

" Oh, yes, we have two bottles of sweet water."

" And have you, perchance, any good things on which to breakfast?"

" No."

They had nothing of that sort, as I knew full well.

" Then, if it will please your worships to join me at breakfast I shall be happy to entertain you. I have some delicious meat pies, onions from Lisbon, garlic from Chile, cheese and ham from Estramadura, the finest cognac from France, and the choicest cigars from the Havannah. On these we will refresh ourselves under the first rock we come to that gives any shade."

We reached a great rock, under the tropic of Capricorn, which the reader perhaps knows is very hot, take it when you will.

I spread a white diaper napkin on the sand, and began to make an ostentatious display of rare delicacies. Before inviting them to eat I offered the ruffians a thimbleful of the old French brandy. They both praised the liquor.

"Well," I said, "I will give you this bottle of old brandy for your two bottles of water."

They jumped at the chance, and the exchange was made.

They drank freely of the smooth, milky, mild liquor, but very soon they fell fast asleep—all their senses were locked up like pawns in a chest. Fast asleep they lay in the sand, and I could have cut their throats as easily as I sliced an onion. I finished breakfast, leaving the ruffians still sleeping, and off I rode, laughing till I reached Calama, where I learnt further particulars of them.*

And my desert life of seventeen days was over, with its glorious freedom, its pure enjoyment, its unexampled simplicity, its magnificent abundance of all that makes life a blessed endowment.

My travelling expenses on the road amounted to three shillings. This, however, did not include my supper at Ascotán. I arrived there very late at night, having wasted much time in examining some deposits of borax, which I discovered on the way. The keeper of the hut, in answer to my question, said in a surly way that he had nothing much for supper.

"Have you anything good to drink?" I asked him.

He had a large bottle of veritable Bass.

---

* They were subsequently shot in the market-place for murder and highway robbery, by order of the authorities.

"How much silver coin will induce your worship to part with this one bottle of Pally-Ally?"

"Eight dollars," he answered.

"Very well. Get me something warm for supper, and make a good fire. I will give you the eight dollars."

Within an hour I sat in front of a dish of stewed guinea pigs, the brown sort, and did not reflect on the extravagance of paying twenty-four shillings for a bottle of beer. The Bolivian dollar is, or was then, only worth three shillings.

I arrived in Potosi in the afternoon in time to see a revolution, which however was a tame affair, it being winter time. For three months in the year all the four seasons are represented in one day in Potosi. This was the season of my arrival. A heavy fall of snow began at five o'clock, and lasted for three hours. Then it began to freeze hard and fast until sunrise. When the sun got up it began to thaw. Before noon the city was under water. By three o'clock in the afternoon all the waters were dried up and the straws were blown about the windy streets. At five o'clock all nature went again to bed under cover of the wondrous strange snow. A very trying climate.

"Potosi!" exclaims Pedro de Angelis,* "the famous city of the world, whose history is ciphered in its hill. It was the great guerdon of the Conquest of America in the streams of silver which it poured upon the monarchy of Spain, and which raised it to a grade of prosperity unique, to precipitate it by-and-bye into an abyss of disgrace. How many despots, how many wars, how much crime had been saved to Spain, and through her to Europe, if she had not had at her disposal the mines of Potosi." Angelis says

* "Coleccion de obras y documentos," Buenos Ayres, 1836, p. 68.

further that they were discovered by an Indian of Porcos, January 1st, 1546, and since then they have been so ill directed, so tyrannically sustained, that they have cost the lives of millions of aboriginals. "So foolishly and wrongly have these mines been developed that they have had to be abandoned, although only a third part has been worked. Potosi, or *P'potocsi*, in Quichua, signifies "a thing which bursts,"* according to some, but no reliance at present can be placed on any translation from this language.

The town of Potosi, as seen from the heights above, is a striking sight. In the clear light which prevails you can almost count the stones in the street from a height of five thousand feet. It is a sweet innocent-looking place, a picture of order and cleanliness, but a closer contact reveals the exact opposite of these. Every street bears a sinister aspect, as almost every human face is clad in sorrow or pain. It is a town where probably more murders have been committed than any town in the world noted for similar wickedness. Potosi is as much noted for its crimes as for its thousands of millions of pounds sterling. If you did not know this you would not fail to inquire why it is that it carries such a hang-dog look. A sensitive eye has no difficulty in perceiving a likeness between Potosi and Jerusalem in its present condition, or as it was rather, a quarter of a century ago. Are not the crimes done against the poor done against all reason, common sense, and decency in the infamous Black Country, in Staffordshire Warwickshire and Worcestershire, written on the face of all those towns, as well as on the miserable, sorrowful, suffering faces of their people?

* The hill is 16,150 feet above the level of the sea, in shape like a sugar loaf, which it resembles when covered with snow. In it are, or were, 5,000 different openings. Lat. 19° 36' S. and 65° 46' W. long.

Where ever I have been in the new world, or the old, where the landscape has been murdered, and sweet Nature put to death, the marks of violence remain in graphic force for all to read. There is nothing so painfully hideous as the aspect of mining towns, whether in Chile, Bolivia, and Peru, in Staffordshire or Yorkshire, in North America or South, round Lake Superior or Lake Titicaca, in New Zealand or Australia.

The devastation caused by earthquakes is not displeasing; there is a picturesque disordered orderliness about it, a certain beauty, as in icicles torn by the wind, but man's devastation conveys no idea but that of corruption or decay, destruction or death. The ruins of human dwellings in Potosi are hateful to behold, alike for their number, as for the desolation which hangs over them. This is not idle fancy. Some of my readers have, perhaps, been through the vale of Daroka in Castile. It was once famous for its vineyards and its innumerable, happy people, who made a garden of it, from which there went up daily songs of joy and gladness. Behold it now, and you shall see a desolation that is precisely the same as that which I am trying to depict as existing in Potosi.

How came it to pass?

The same people who murdered the Indians in Potosi banished the Moors from Daroka, where there are now more empty houses than inhabitants, and more ruins than both put together. The Spanish colonists in the one case were consumed with avarice and greed and the lusts which come from selfishness, and the Spaniards of the mother country, believing that God had forsaken them because trade was slack and no silver came now from Potosi, thought to appease Him by sweeping their house clean of misbelieving dogs, hoping that He would send them back the good old days of joy and plenty. He has never taken the bribe; certainly joy and plenty for Spain seem farther off than ever.

Would that I could see no likeness between the avarice and greed, coupled with ferocious cruelty, which once prevailed in Spanish silver colonies, and the avarice, greed, and cruelty to be found in some of our gold colonies. The likeness could not be more perfect if it were taken by the sun.

Given a sordid religion at home, we shall not fail to find a debased morality in the dependencies. As a proof of this, let me call attention to the following announcement, which appeared in the London daily papers of March 11th, 1886:—

" Letters received yesterday from the Australian Station state that her Majesty's ship *Diamond* recently returned to Sydney after an absence of three months, during which she was busily employed punishing natives in various parts for murders committed by them on British subjects.

" At Normanby, where Captain Miller had been murdered, the natives refused to surrender the murderers. A number of sailors were accordingly landed from the *Diamond*, and they burnt the villages, drove the natives out, and destroyed their nets and canoes.

" At Hoopiron Bay, Moresby Island, where Captain Frier and one of his sailors were murdered, the skulls of the murdered men were discovered, but the natives disappeared into the interior directly the *Diamond* hove in sight.

" The same thing occurred at Millport Bay, where Captain Webb and his crew were massacred, and here again men were landed, and destroyed all the canoes and nets, and the villages were shelled from the ship.

"The *Diamond* next proceeded to the Solomon Islands to punish the murderers of Mr. Childe. Boats' crews were sent ashore, and not only were the villages destroyed and the cocoanut plantations laid waste, but an armed party marched through the island and destroyed all the cocoanut trees and villages that were met with.

"At San Christóval the natives refused to give up the murderers of Captain Howie and his companions, and they were punished by the entire destruction of their villages, plantations, and nets."

These details are similar to those which took place in 1868, when Commodore Sir William Wiseman, in H.M.S. *Curaçoa,* bombarded the island of Tanna, totally destroying all its villages. He then continued his cruise, Bishop Patteson in his yacht, the *Southern Cross,* being in his company. On the 25th of September, *in consequence of a report* which the Commodore had received, he fired twenty shells and four rockets into a native island village. It was said that frightful damage was done by the bursting of a shell in a cave in which the people had probably taken shelter.*

I must remind the reader that kidnapping in English ships from the South Sea Islands began in 1861. The largest ship load of kanakas which had then been made was carried to Peru by one Byrne, Birne, or Bergne, a notorious scoundrel whom I saw in Lima at the time that he made his bargain with the Peruvian Government. He was an Australian colonist. By the time that inquiries had been set on foot into Byrne's doings, and efforts were being made to compel the Peruvian Government to return the kidnapped people to their homes, they had all died.

* "Cruise of the *Rosario,*" Captain A. H. Markham, p. 47.

The late Sir John O'Shannassy told me that Byrne had asked him to join in this kidnapping speculation, but that he refused.

I may be allowed to add that Bishop Patteson was in the habit of cruising in and out of these same waters, from whence these people were taken, with the object of inducing some of them to go to his school in Norfolk Island. The intentions of the good, let me say saintly, bishop were admirable, but he could not explain them to the natives because he could not speak their language. The natives were unable to distinguish the bishop from a recruiter; while I know of my own knowledge that some of these inhuman recruiters, in order the better to beguile the natives, dressed themselves up to look as much like the bishop as they could.

Bishop Patteson was murdered because the natives believed that he was in the sugar business, or in some way connected with plantations and kidnapping.

Whatever their mistaken beliefs, or their reasonable convictions, no one knows better than Captain A. H. Markham, late commander of the *Rosario,* that the wives and daughters, sisters and mothers of South Sea Islanders, were by cunning devices conveyed to the sugar plantations of Queensland—that they never returned, that many were murdered on board the slave ships, and others died of improper treatment on the plantations.

When the husbands, fathers, and brothers of these women got the chance they murdered in just revenge the murderers of their women.

Blood revenge is the only religion which exists among these people; and for us to send our sailors and men-of-war to cut down the cocoa palms and burn the villages of these people is an everlasting disgrace to those who ordered it to be done.

If any persons deserved punishment it was they who formed the Queensland Government, who licensed the ships to go to the South Sea Islands to fish for men and women—even the men who licensed well-known cut-throats to command those ships, and winked at the abominations that were done on board.

Kidnapping led the way to the passing of the "Queensland Labour Act of 1868," and the Imperial Act for the " Prevention and Punishment of Criminal Outrages upon Natives of the Islands in the Pacific Ocean, 1872."

It was absolutely necessary for the Colonial Government to interfere, or to make a show of interference, not only because murder and kidnapping were being done in the name of commerce, but also to send people to sleep whose business it was to be wide awake, namely, the respectable people of Queensland, and the people of the Imperial Colonial Office. If the interference had been effective all would have been well; as it was, it was the most ineffective interference ever made by Government.

Here I will again quote from a lecture which I delivered in the School of Arts at Mackay, the Capital of the Sugar Industry in North Queensland.

" Under the organized interference of Government, islanders have been brought from their homes who never understood the nature of the 'contract' into which they were beguiled.

" Under the organized interference of Government, labour vessels have been made into dens of infamy, where the grossest sensuality and obscene living have been rampant, in which some representatives of Government took part,

L

and were as conspicuous for their treachery to the Executive as for their loathsome immoralities.

"Under the organized interference of Government, labour vessels have been fraudulently measured, whereby the responsible Minister has licensed a ship to carry more islanders than the Statute allowed.

"Under the same organized interference, many thousands of islanders have, by a legal figment, been enthralled in Queensland after having been illegally beguiled from their homes by the very men whom Government had selected to represent it, and whose duty it was to hinder the doing of these things.

"Under the organized interference of Government, the Government submitted complacently to insult and outrage in the persons of some of its representatives, to which only a Government conscious of its own corruption could have submitted itself.

"There never was any other reason than the apathy of the Queensland authorities for the labour traffic so speedily developing itself, as it did, into a slave trade, except that there is for sinful man some diabolical fascination in manhunting that exceeds fox-hunting, fishing, or shooting birds as much as real war exceeds a sham fight. It has always been so under all the dynasties of recorded time. Manhunting in all probability achieved the acme of its infamy under Charles V., and was carried on by all the Christian monarchies until a very recent date. How it was abolished in the United States we all know full well. How the Southern States are at the present moment yielding a fuller increase under their changed conditions than they yielded under the reign of the slavemonger has been made obvious to the meanest capacity. But that we, at this hour, should, on trying to found an English colony within the tropics, have got hampered and embarrassed with the question of labour is one of those accidents in our history that cannot possibly assume a permanent influence in any shape or form."

The worst thing in connection with the destruction of South Sea villages by British men-of-war is that it has done more harm than good. It is certain that the exploits of the *Diamond* will lead to fresh assaults when the chances occur for committing them on Europeans, whether they be bishops, or captains, or botanists, or other harmless travellers. This has proved to be the case since the foregoing was written.

The little time I had in Potosi for social intercourse I passed in the company of the Archbishop of Charcas and his *familiares,* who were on a visit there. The archbishop always appeared at dinner in a purple cassock, with a large gold cross hanging round his neck, and lace ruffles on his wrists. He was a very handsome man, of delightful manners, full of good stories, which he told with real delight. Everybody listened in silent pleasure, especially our host's wife, a charming woman, *una hija del pais*, dressed all in white lace, looking like a snowball with a red posy stuck in it. After dinner we adjourned to a large, well-adorned room to smoke and tell tales. On one of these occasions I experienced the disagreeable sensation of a priest trying to convert me to the worship of the Virgin Mary. He was a good enough fellow, and fond of wine and fine cigars.

I remained as long as I cared to remain in Potosi, and left it on a somewhat curious mission. I had hoped to return to the Pacific by way of La Paz, but accident, fate, or luck led me back across the same desert over which I had come.

I was made conductor of a remittance of 100,000 dollars from Potosi to Cobija.

This required twenty-two mules, ten Indians, and a capataz, or head muleteer. The Indians went on foot. We had not, among us all, a single weapon of any sort. Leaño, the capataz, was the only one who carried a knife of any use for stabbing. My duties consisted in counting the hide-bound dollars every time we halted for the night, and taking such precautions as circumstances seemed to require for the safety of the lucre. There were forty hide parcels, each parcel containing 2,500 silver dollars. We marched about forty miles a day, always sleeping at night at some well-known hut. We lived well, had always a hot supper, and we were ever ready for our beds after smoking a pipe or a cigar. The Indians, who chewed cuca all day, never cared for tobacco in any other form than that of a cigarette. I never once heard one Indian address another. They were the most silent human beings I ever knew. Trudging along attending to the mules, and looking after the trappings which kept the hide-bound dollars in their places, they seemed in intelligence no higher than the mules themselves, as patient and as silent.

One night we arrived somewhat early at the snuggest quarters of the whole way, after a day of comparatively easy travel—*Canchas Blancas* the place was called. The *puchero*, or stew, was very good, and we spent a quiet, pleasant night, smoking tobacco and drinking home-made *chicha*, or *aguadiente*, and telling tales; our host and his wife listening with much interest and attention.

"Leaño," I said, "how long have you been occupied in carrying money in this way across the desert?"

"More than twenty years," he said.

"And you never had any trouble and were never robbed?" I inquired, hoping to get some knowledge of this kind of life from one who had followed it so long.

"*I* was never robbed, and never had any trouble. Only once, when we arrived at Cobija, there were two *zurrones* missing, but that was not my fault. It was the *remesero's* place to look after every *zurron,* and he was responsible."

"What did you do?" I naturally inquired.

He said —

"We returned very sorrowful to Potosi, for each *zurron* then, as now, contained 2,500 dollars, and we prayed all the way to the Most Blessed Maria that she would find the *zurrones* for us. And now, mark, señor, when we got to Potosi, there were the two *zurrones!*"

"You had never taken them away," I suggested.

I meant no harm, but found that I had greatly hurt Leaño's feelings, and the listeners were annoyed, so I had to remark —

"How kind it was of the Blessed Virgin to bring back the *zurrones;*" on which the sky became once more clear, and we drank together in peace and good fellowship.

I had noticed the emphasis which Leaño placed on the personal pronoun when he said that he had never been robbed, so I inquired if he had ever known of any robbery of or from the remittance during his twenty years of service.

"Ah! Señor Don Alejandro, have you never heard?"

"No, never; let me hear."

"It was the largest remittance ever sent down—it was

250,000 dollars, and it is a long time ago. It arrived at Puquios, and there it was met by French pirates, who shot the Indians, killed the capataz, and after that they bound the *postero* and his wife (*i.e.*, keepers of the post-house) back to back, taking them a good distance away, and so left them, and they had well-nigh perished, but an Indian shepherd with his llamas passed that way some days afterwards, and saved them from starvation. The post-master at once set off for Potosi, told the truth, and the authorities sent out mounted scouts, who overtook the Frenchmen with the remittance and overcame them, and brought them into Potosi, and they were shot in the Plaza."

"Which way had the Frenchmen taken?" I inquired.

"The way to Buenos Ayres."

Leaño's story took a long time to tell, but it was full of incident and was well listened to. We all then went to bed. The best bed was in the room where we had sat drinking and yarning, and belonged to the post-master and his wife. In the most good-natured way they asked me to sleep with them. I excused myself, and said that I must go and count the remittance and look after the mules. They assured me that Leaño was to be trusted in all things; but I was not to be beguiled, and I slept outside in the fresh air.

The climate of the desert after passing Canchas Blancas was singularly benign, and every step now brought us into warmer weather. We did not meet a single mule or man till we got to Puquios, and the post-house being in sight I rode ahead, and arrived in the corral at about five o'clock in the afternoon. Judge of my feelings when I saw sitting outside on the door step of the principal room two French sailors busily engaged in cleaning firearms. They were good-looking, fair-spoken men, well clothed, and wearing

Panama hats, having the name *Hyacinthe* printed in gold letters on a black ribbon running round the crown.

I addressed them cheerily, and they responded in like manner, asked me whence I had come, and on my naming Potosi they further inquired if I seen the remittance on my way.

I kept up a careless talk, remaining in the saddle and taking stock of their firearms. There were two breech-loading rifles, two muzzle-loaders of heavier metal, four horse-pistols, and two handsome revolvers, all of which had been beautifully cleaned and were now ready for use.

I called several times for the post-master, who did not appear. On calling again one of the Frenchmen kindly told me that the post-master had disappeared somewhere.

I said that I would go and hunt him up. My real intention was to communicate with Leaño. This I did. We held a council of war, and, after I had instructed him in what he should do, I rode back to the post-house, dismounted, went inside, and found the Indian post-master hiding in a corner.

"Come and make a fire at once," I said to him. "Do you know that Leaño is close at hand, and do you know that I am the *remesero*?"

"Si, mi amo," said the Indian, but did not budge an inch.

He knew Leaño was at hand with the remittance, and it became obvious to me that the Frenchmen had been working on the Indian's fears, perhaps his loyalty.

In rode Leaño at the head of his mules, filling the corral, and making an imposing appearance. I said, in a low, calm voice, although I did not feel at all calm—

"Leaño, you will make a barricade of the *zurrones*, place all the arms inside, and cover all with your *tolda*. The

Indians will sleep underneath. How many revolvers have you?"

"Ten."

"How many rifles?"

"Two."

"And knives?"

"We are all pretty well knived, blessed be God."

"Place all these arms for my inspection."

Which Leaño said he would do, as was always done.

The Indian post-master still refused to stir. Leaño, however, made a good fire, and we made ourselves comfortable with such things as we had. I brewed a good brew of tea, which I invited the Frenchmen to share, which they did. At nine o'clock Leaño went to bed behind the wall of *zurrones*, under the *tolda*, with the Indians. "I will keep the first watch," I said to him as we shook hands, all of which was observed by the French with marked attention. They also soon went to bed in the one room set apart for travellers. They took their arms inside, placed them handy, left a light burning and the door open, I remaining outside walking up and down like a sentinel smoking cigars, not at all happy although the night was bright with moon and stars, singularly peaceful, and but for those suspicious-looking Frenchmen everything would have been delightful.

About midnight one of the Frenchmen came out of the room with a gun in his hand, walked hurriedly across the corral, got over the *adobe* wall, and disappeared in the desert.

On this I called Leaño, told him that one of the French highwaymen had gone evidently to call his companions, and that the other French highwayman was inside fast asleep; that the thing for us to do was there and then to secure the sleeper—if necessary, to kill him—but at all hazard to get hold of the arms. I particularly wanted Leaño to kill the sleeping Frenchman, for I had no heart to do it myself. My imagination began to work all of its own accord, and so pictured things to me that I could no more have committed that murder than I could jump over the moon. Leaño seemed also to have misgivings.

" Yo no quiero matar á nadie," he said, in good Spanish: which in English is, " I don't want to kill anybody."

I then asked him if he would like anyone to murder him, on which he very properly reminded me that I was the conductor of the remittance, and responsible for its safe arrival, and not he.

This was true, but for the life of me, although I saw that it was necessary to get hold of those arms, and that this could not be done without disabling, or overpowering, or killing the sleeping Frenchman, yet I could not compel my mind to entertain the bloody business.

Some time after this the Frenchman who had got over the wall with his naked gun returned in like manner, carrying by the hind legs a white rabbit, a yard long! This was a vizcatcha—a description of which animal the reader will find in Darwin's charming book.*

Leaño went to bed without giving me a look, or saying a word. The Frenchman went to his bed, and so did I to mine, not in the least sorry for the sight of the rabbit, and the conclusions which it suggested. I had nothing to be ashamed of excepting in proposing to Leaño to kill the Frenchman—a thing which I did not like doing myself; but as I found that I really could not commit that murder I had no compunction of conscience for having proposed

* " A Naturalist's Voyage Round the World."

that it should be done by someone else, it seeming to me so necessary for our own preservation and the safety of that large sum of money that the Frenchman should be killed.

Early in the morning we saddled up. The Indians had a fine hot stew, the Frenchmen skinned their rabbit, and stewed it, I providing some delightful onions and another pot of tea; and while they and I continued to converse together, discussing these and other good things for a couple of hours, the remittance went on its way unmolested to Cobija.

"What may your worships be looking for in the desert, and with such an arsenal?" I inquired in Spanish, which language they spoke very well.

"We are looking," was their reply, "for twenty thousand dollars."

Expressing with great cordiality my wish that they would succeed in finding that small sum, and having begged the favour of their accepting from me a packet of tea, I took my leave, and have neither heard of nor seen them since.

When the gold remittance used to be sent down from the gold fields to Melbourne, well escorted, it did not always arrive, and there are men still living who went through experiences very similar to mine, except that they did not always, if ever, end with a breakfast of stewed vizcatha, or *bizcacha*, as I believe it should be spelt, with other good things.

Of the gold and silver remittances much could be said of how and with what success they were conducted in the gold and silver colonies, but this would be a mere catalogue of crime, and of these catalogues there are quite enough in the world already.

CHAPTER XI.

VENEZUELA—NEGROES—TRINIDAD.

THE last silver deposit I visited was in Carupano, that part of the north-east end of Venezuela, in the Carribean Sea, which is immediately in front of Trinidad.

The climate is superb. I remained there a month, making excursions to Cumaná, the Bays of Paria and Santa, the roads of New Barcelona, and the offing of La Guayra, visiting Caracas, and finally spending a month in Trinidad; all renowned and famous places, blessed with uncommon beauty and abounding wealth, and all except Trinity, or Trinidad, cursed with silver fame. Carupano is the most favoured spot of earth that I know of. I never saw such caoutchouc, or india-rubber trees, such sugar cane, such cacao, and I am almost quite sure that I never saw such miserable men and poor women as are to be seen there.

Where there are silver mines the sweeter and more endurable sources of wealth are always neglected by the foolish people who there spend their days " in misery and iron."

Why the vegetation should be so rich and all growths so fine, why the sugar cane should have a girth of thirteen inches, and the theobroma, shrub or tree, be so vigorous I could not tell, much less did I dream of ever being able to find out. But one day as I was walking in a solitary wilderness of magnificent but neglected things I stumbled on what seemed to be a piece of red brick. I carried it to my den, analyzed and found it to be phosphatic lime, highly ferruginous, and as hard as a fire brick. Carupano is a bed of many kinds of phosphates, in some places twenty feet deep. I no longer wondered at the marvels of the vegetable kingdom, but did wonder whether or not agricultural chemists knew all about the phosphate of lime when it is much mixed with the oxide of iron. Carupano would be an earthly paradise if the right sort of mortal mixture of earth's mould could be found and entrusted with its keeping. But no where, in no colony, golden or silvern, have I seen a people happy, healthy, or wholesome who were blessed with much of nature's abundance.

What a perfect wonder of beauty and plenty is Caracas; how glorious is its climate, and its situation. Who can tell its flowers, or call by their names its many other excellent things? And there how poor a thing is man. How poor and foolish has man been ever since Caracas was settled three hundred years ago.

If Caracas be a place begetting wonder, the road to it from La Guayra is worthy of it. I arrived very early at this oven, indeed long before La Guayra was out of bed. But even at that early hour the heat was overpowering. Within three hours after my arrival at the Hotel Nettuno I had changed my garments, bathed, breakfasted, and was fairly on the way to a new world.

On this way there are between forty and fifty turnings, some as rapid and abrupt as out of the Strand into Wych

Street, out of Cornhill into Bishopsgate, or out of the frying-pan into the fire. At every new turn there is a new region of colour and form. Not only does the colour of the sea change from green to blue, to sapphire and opal, emerald and pearl, but the earth in like manner puts on a different dress, all the dresses being beautiful and strange, begetting wonder. The heavens are in tune with all, and for once in my life I heard in the tropics a concert of such divine enchanting ravishment as made me forget the toil of the way, its dangers, and all of the troubles of life which beset a pilgrim on his road from the pigstye of La Guayra to the glories of Beulah.

Why are the men you meet with now like apes and now like men? How is it that the first impression you receive of human beings whom you meet in Caracas is an impression difficult to explain even to yourself, but which on mature reflection resolves itself into this: Here human nature is visibly seen to be made up of flesh and spirit, and can and does change its face as really as the varying light which falls on earth and sea on the Caracas way changes these in tone and tint? Here is patent to all, and at once, " God's image and the mould of clay," a being who is at once the heir of heaven and the heir of earth—an immortal, and a brute, the divine legend reversed, the beast of a dragon trampling on the fallen St. George!

I had not been a week in Caracas before I discovered that its principal men and women are all gamblers in mines, gold and silver mines—gold mines in Guiana and silver mines "close by" in the Cerro. I stayed at the Hotel St. Amand, the charges at which were higher than at the Grand Hotel in Paris, but neither the dinners nor the rooms could in anything be compared. It speedily became known in the town that I knew something of the metallurgy of gold and silver. Men whom I knew nothing of came to me with the most magnificent "gold ores" I had ever seen, seeking my advice, and asking questions on the best methods of treating such hard rocks, which contained so much of the beautiful yellow metal. Before these rocks were reduced to powder by stamping, all the auriferous wealth would be beaten into gold leaf so fine that the wind would blow it away. Could I, oh! would I, tell them how this beautiful fine gold could be got out of these very hard rocks?

If you want to see the immortal and the brute combined, or to see in actual operation the brute overcoming the immortal, go to Caracas. If you would see the seventh chapter of St. Paul's Epistle to the Romans changed into a living epistle that may be known and read of all men, make the acquaintance of men who hold shares in the gold mines of British Guiana. It will not prove a pleasing experience, but a very instructive one. You shall see one of these men, his face of a radiant brightness, charming to behold, giving off a happy smile that is so contagious that it influences the whole market-place; and six days afterwards you shall see this being again, and not know him. He has been changed, not from glory to glory, but from glory to shame, from a man to the "hairy eclipse of a manhood divine," from a Ferdinand to a Caliban, from the sweetest human companion to a black-visaged devil.

The change was wrought not by philtres or powders to be bought at the most respectable wholesale druggist's, but by the man's own will, his power of faith. While he bore a fair impression of the image of his Maker he believed that he was master of untold unrustable gold; when he bore the image of beast, or devil, he knew that all that he possessed in this changing scene of life was nothing but a heap of iron pyrites!

One of these men, whose *figura* had afforded me this study, offered me a fee of one thousand guineas to go to the Esequibo river and report on a certain gold mine whose name is now well known in Capel Court. I refused. Two mornings later he came to my hotel, inviting himself to breakfast, in an insolence of happiness; and as we were smoking our morning cigars he renewed his application and doubled the fee. I told him that I could not go. I was already retained.

Thereupon his feelings underwent a change, his manners changed, and he began asking several direct questions which I meekly refused to answer. He had taken up the notion that someone in Caracas had anticipated him. This he proceeded to ascertain. Not being able to come to any satisfactory conclusion, he began spreading abroad the most absurd stories about myself, all the recompense I obtained for not a little annoyance being the opportunity which this brute gave me of seeing what a devil a man can make out of no other materials save the elements of which his own nature is composed.

The public gardens in Caracas are very fine, being filled with trees and plants peculiar to Venezuela, a great and gorgeous collection. This garden was planted by that singular tyrant Guzman Blanco, who was then President of the Republic, a man whom all Venezuelans flatter hate and fear. It is only in a country where the men are all hens that such a magnificent dunghill cock as this could crow over them so lustily.

There was one exception, which I trust my reader may

be glad to hear of. It was in Caracas that I made the acquaintance of the most sweet-tempered man I ever knew. He was a Minister of State, a General in the army, and a negro—in the language of discourtesy " an unmitigated nigger," but in manners equal to the best of men. He was much beloved by the poor. He took me in a hired carriage to see the principal sights. It was a great treat to me to see this fine negro in active intercourse with all classes of people. He was, without exaggeration, adored by the women of all ranks; but to all he was as modest as he was, I believe, true and clean of heart. On returning to Amand's the driver refused to take any payment for the use of his carriage; he had, he said, been more than paid by having the honour of driving us about!

I left Caracas with regret and walked half of the way to La Guayra, that is from the half-way house, a distance of some twelve miles; it was the only way to enjoy the scenery, surely the most wonderful of any in the world. A sunrise in the Straits of Magellan, lighting up with ruby-fire the rippling snowy heights of Tierra del Fuego is a sight never to be forgotten by those who have seen it; but to see the sun go to his ocean bath from the heights above La Guayra is to have received a privilege that must for ever possess the mind and soul of those who have enjoyed it.

The railway to Caracas is one of several famous mountain railways which have been built in our generation. How long it will last, He who orders the earthquake and harnesses the lightning alone can tell. It is a work of great skill, carried through with courage and perseverance, and many Americans English and natives have played an honourable part in it; it has thrown many honest, hard-working people out of work, but it will save much suffering to innumerable horses, asses, and mules.

Still, to dwell for a moment longer on negroes. The negro General who helped to make my visit to Caracas so pleasant was a native of the province of Cumaná. I also know of my own knowledge that when an Australian black fellow is early taken on board ship, he becomes an expert sailor—handy, skilful, obedient, and supremely happy. The black people of Bouka, in the Solomon Islands—who, however, are not negroes—are a fine race of men. The "King," or head man at Bouka, with whom I came in contact very much—every day for a week—was a man of refined mind, of exquisite tact, and high breeding. He ruled his people with gentleness; he also worked as hard as any of them. There are in shallow water at Bouka beds of coral to be seen growing like flower beds, of infinite variety and beauty in form and colour. Noticing my delight at the sight, he asked me by intelligent signs if I would like to have some of these precious corals. I answered him in a manner that left no doubt in his mind that to carry away some of those wonders of the deep would give me great joy.

The next morning ten big fellows brought me two coral trees, each as big as a small gooseberry bush, nor would they or their "King" accept any gift in return from me for these things. They refused tobacco, and, to my utter astonishment, they refused a present of some of the much-coveted small beads. I made it up to them in other ways. The "King" I dressed in as much apropriate finery as I could muster, to his delight and that of his people. We also let off some guns and dynamite; a heavy lighted fuse being thrown into the sea raised a magnificent column of water and stunned a lot of fishes, which were easily taken.

To my horror, the skipper told me soon after we had left Bouka that he had given several charges of dynamite to the King, "he begged so hard for some." What happened it is not difficult to imagine. Perhaps some hideous tragedy which will never be forgotten or forgiven.

When Professor Moseley, of the *Challenger* expedition, had his soda-water stolen from him by the natives in Moresby Bay, there was much fun to be got out of supposing what happened in the bosom of those thieves' families when the bottles were uncorked. But dynamite!

I have seen the negro in many parts of the world, and know, as well as I know anything, that whatever was his social, moral, or intellectual state in those parts it was entirely owing to the treatment which he had received from his superiors. The negro in Colon and Panama, who had been debased in early life, in Jamaica is, perhaps, the most loathsome human being on the face of the earth. The negro in Barbadoes, a pampered sybarite, who has been allowed to grow up as a spoiled child, is a fine-looking animal, with homicidal tendencies. In Trinidad the negro is lazy as well as insolent. In Jamaica he and she are, as human beings, failures in every sense of that word, to an extent that is impossible to describe. English-speaking negroes, everywhere that I have seen them, are worse than French or Spanish negroes. Even in Peru, where this race has been living for more than three centuries, the negro is far more of a human being than he of the English-speaking breed.

Religious negroes—by which I mean those who have received a technical education in English religion—are much more hideous caricatures of human beings than the heathen negroes who have been left to themselves on the

Rio Negro, in the glorious wilderness which lies at the base of the Quindio mountains, and in other out-of-the-way spots of the earth, to which it would seem this most misused child of humanity has fled to hide him from the wicked white who made this earth for the black man a monotonous hell.

What an island is that of Trinidad. Who is sufficient to paint its wonders? If this were the only island of its kind in the world, the great powers of the world would contend among themselves for its possession. I stayed a month, meeting with much hospitality and many kinds of men, from whom I learnt many things. I visited several sugar plantations, and plantations of cacao, from which is made what the Mexicans called chocolalt, the Spaniards chocolaté, and we chocolate. The thing which struck me most in connection with Trinidad was to find that I was still alive on the morning after I left it. The feasting was so stupendous, the wine-bibbing so vast; but then the wine was so good.

Not the eating nor drinking—sugar, cacao, rum—or even the comet which at that time hung in the sky and made it so impressive, nor the Savannah, nor the pitch lake, nor delicious lap, nor the Blue Basin Falls made Trinidad so full of interest for me but coolies: I refer to the Indian coolie, not any individual he or she coolie, but the institution which is to disestablish the negro in the West Indies and the kanaka in Queensland, and give to the planters of both those countries the slave after their own hearts—apprentice, labourer, or by whatsoever other name the being is to be called whose days in this mortal life are to be passed in the sugar-field or the cacao-plantation, not so much for the purpose of making greater harvest of sugar and more chocolate, but for the primary purpose of providing more purple, fine linen, and sumptuous banqueting for los Señores Dives y Compania.

Of individual coolies I had some special experiences. One morning I was returning from an early ride some miles out of Port of Spain when it came on to rain suddenly, and as copiously as it only can rain in Trinidad. A hundred yards in front of me, coming along in the middle of the road was a shining woman—fair, with beautifully rounded limbs—walking in the soft warm rain. She had taken off her clothes, rolled them into a bundle, which she carried on her head, and over head and bundle, held by her left hand, she carried a long, broad, green plantain leaf, which gracefully hung down her back. She looked—to borrow a phrase from the English poet who sang of the orange—like a " gold lamp hung in a green night."

Another and very different sight was a coolie of the baser sex. He had cut open a fellow coolie's face with a knife, and two policemen were trying to haul him to gaol. He writhed, leaped, grinned, and glared like a tiger. He escaped from the grip of the constables several times, but being in the street he was always recaptured. Spare as the man was, his nervous energy was amazing. It occurred to me that a couple of hundred of such beings would give great anxiety to the town if each were in a similar state of excitement.

Every day there was some row, and a terrible outbreak occurred on one of the plantations, which caused great alarm. Some slaughter took place, and one or two valuable lives were lost.

There can be little doubt about the coolie being an admirable servant in a sugar-field. Coolies are both hard-working and thrifty. Deposits to the amount of £60,000 were then in the Colonial Bank of Trinidad all belonging to coolies. The sugar and cacao harvests were glorious. The coolie had in fact brought back the old prosperity, the good old days when the negro was a slave, not in Trinidad only, but in Guiana also. The coolie is the saviour not of West Indian society, but of its sugar.

I had procured statistics to show what a commercial success the coolie has been. I have advocated the coolie being engaged in North Queensland, believing that it would be good for all—the coolie, colonist, and capitalist.

But after going over the whole question again, calling to mind all that has happened during the past three hundred years on the West Coast and East Coast of South America, in the Gran Chaco, in the West Indies, and in North America, and what is happening in English colonies now, I think he would be a man of unique temerity who would try to repeat in Queensland the history of Peru, Jamaica, or New Orleans.

"'But,' you will say to me, 'this people, this Republic, this State, cannot be supported without Indians. Who is to bring us a pitcher of water, or a bundle of wood? Who is to plant our mandive? Must our wives do it? Must our children do it?'

"In the first place, as you shall presently see, these are not the straits in which I would place you. But if necessity and conscience require it, then I reply Yes! and I repeat it, Yes! You and your wives and your children ought to do it! We ought to support ourselves with our own hands; far better is it to be supported by the sweat of our own brow than by another's blood.

"Oh, ye rich of Maranham! What if your mantles and cloaks were to be wrung?

"They would drop blood."*

There are other considerations. Shall Presbyterians and others whose power of faith has been diverted from spiritual things and set upon carnal, who care little for the treasure in heaven, and much for the treasure which both moth and rust corrupt and thieves steal, shall these have it in their power to make of England another Spain, and turn her gold and silver into dirt by making of our colonies what Spain made of hers? Shall these rich, religious colonists make it the cry of England as it is the everlasting, tormenting cry of Spain, "The good that I would I do not, but the evil which I would not that I do?"

* The first sermon of the Rev. Padre de Vieyra, preached at St. Luiz, quoted in "The Conquerors of the New World and their Bondsmen," Vol. i., 241.

CHAPTER XII.

MORE GOLD AND SILVER COMPARISONS.

As in the silver, so in the gold colonies; as the rich Spanish colonists smothered better sources of wealth in their eager rush after silver mines, so have the colonists in the gold colonies. The Spaniards depopulated many a peaceful valley in order to get recruits for the mines of Potosi, Guancavalica, Carangas, and other places. There is a curious little book,* written by an English eye-witness, which is worth quoting:—

"The King's—that is the King of Spain—interest is to make provision that there be a sufficient number of slaves for all the mines that are opened. For this end he obliges all Couracas, or chiefs of the savages, to furnish everyone a certain number; which they must always keep compleat, or else are forc'd to give twice as much Mony as would have been paid in Wages to those that are wanting, if they had been present.

"Those that are destined for the Mines of *Potosi* don't amount (now) to above 2,500. These are brought and put

---

* "A Relation of Mr. R. M.'s Voyage to Buenos-Ayres, and from thence by Land to Potosi." London: John Darby in *Bartholomew Close*, 1716.

into a great Enclosure, which is at the foot of the Mountain where the Corregidor makes a Distribution of 'em to the Conductors of the Mines, according to the Number they want; and after six days' constant work, the Conductor brings them back the Saturday following to the same place, where the Corregidor causes a Review to be made of 'em, the Wages that are appointed 'em, and to see how many of 'em are dead, that the Couracas may be oblig'd to supply the number that is wanting; for there's no week passes but some of 'em die, either by divers Accidents that occur, as the tumbling down of great quantities of earth and falling of Stones, or by Sickness, and other casualties. They are sometimes very much incommoded by Winds, that are shut up in the Mines, the Coldness of which, joined to that of some parts of the Earth, chills 'em so excessively that unless they chew'd Coca, which heats and fuddles 'em, it would be intolerable to 'em."

I have quoted from this authority because it is the only English authority that I am acquainted with of what went on at that time. Spanish authorities supply a few more details and give the number of Indians employed at 5,000.

Not only were thousands of homes broken up, but Potosi itself and the country for miles around is a howling desert. All the highways have in like manner been broken up; no new roads have been made. The same with the bridges. There is not a single obstacle in the way of making a good carriage road all the way to Cobija, but this would have taken many Indians from the mines. The work has never been done, because no one thinks or dreams of anything but silver and silver mines. I may say here in passing that I have little doubt a railway will at no distant date be built from Potosi to the coast.

What has taken place in and around Potosi has taken place in and around every place in Peru, where were many precious permanent things to smother and kill, and some temporary silver to take away.

Take away? It fled, seemingly of its own accord. One of the permanent sources of the best riches in Peru was the storage and distribution of water. Nearly every one of these *azequias*, or artificial watercourses, like the many thousand homes the highways and bridges have also been broken up. The captive waters have broken loose, and now run about as a mob of East End roughs will overrun and spoil and carry off some of the precious things in the West if the police stand still sufficiently long or go away in the opposite direction.

The Incas built all the reservoirs, or nearly all, and all, or nearly all, the distributing watercourses. But like the Incas, these are no more, and the water like them is spilt on the ground, and cannot be gathered up again. The silver has been turned to dirt, or a peculiar kind of moth has turned it into corruption.

Before making any allusion to our gold colonies, or comparison with those of silver, let me for a moment divert the attention of the reader to another subject. Wishing to go the shortest way, I must go somewhat about, as Bacon observed. The Roman Catholic Church in China, as we know, was founded on Jesuit's Bark. The Roman Catholic Church in Western Australia was founded on a concert.

A band of Roman Catholic missionaries left Gravesend in the ship *Elizabeth*, 15th of September, 1845, for King George's Sound, intending to make Perth their headquarters. This band consisted of Spanish, Italian, French, Irish, and English gentlemen, priests, monks, and catechists. Some of these penetrated a hundred and twenty miles into the West Australian Bush in their endeavours to shepherd some of the aboriginal sheep whom they would bring into their fold. They went through incredible sufferings and privations, as all unworldly impracticable people do in Australia, but especially up country. Still, they were rewarded with some success, which made them stick to their posts. They were half starved and naked, having nothing to cover them but the skins of kangaroos. The mission was bound to come to an end; and merely on account of the lack of funds the Roman Catholic Bishop of Perth ordered his faithful shepherds to return. But they could not leave the sheep, and kept on sustaining themselves with roots, and covering their nakedness with skins.

The Reverend Father Rosendo Salvado, an Italian, resolved that the mission should not perish without an effort. Salvado made known his resolution to Colonel Clarke, the English Protestant Governor of West Australia. Salvado, who was an excellent musician, proposed to give a concert if he could only get a piano and a large enough room, to get money in order to keep the mission to the black fellows in the Bush going.

The Protestant English Governor lent him a grand piano, the Protestant English Mayor lent the Town Hall, Mr. Sampson, a Jew merchant, brought together some English ladies to sing, the Rev. Mr. Witnoom (?), an Anglican Protestant, lent the chandeliers from his Church to light up with, and a large number of Protestant English laymen and laywomen assembled to cheer the singers, and the Padre, who performed in his cassock. Ample funds were raised, and the mission to the black fellows went on. It has greatly prospered. I have never seen it, and do not speak from personal observation, but I derive my information from a reliable source.

The Rev. Mathew B. Hale, subsequently Anglican Bishop of Brisbane, and now resident in England, had great success in his labours among the aboriginals of South Australia. All who have had dealings with the aboriginals speak of them with kindness and pity, but never with disgust or in despair.

But what kind of missionaries did the Imperial Government send, and how did it further the endeavours of godly men to save the aboriginals of Western Australia from going to the devil?

In five years the Imperial Government sent to Western Australia, at the expense of English taxpayers, 3,661 sinners of a blacker dye than the Australian black fellow. Technically they are called convicts, which is a kind of sinner that for modesty I will not describe. To these 3,661 were subsequently added 1,476 kinsfolk and acquaintance of these convicts. The crime and outrage which followed, and the revelations which were made at the trials of these wicked men in the colony after their arrival there, produced an impression on the life of the colony which will take half a century to eradicate. Bishop Hale tells us that "there are men scattered broadcast through the colony who would shrink from no atrocity to which their fiendish minds could tempt them."* These are the men sent out to these favoured lands by the Imperial Government. In New South Wales and in Tasmania the like happened.

It had been better a thousand times that all the lions, tigers, jaguars, leopards, lynxes, hyænas, bears, and other effectually cruel wild beasts had been sent from all the

* " The Transportation Question," by Mathew B. Hale.

Imperial Zoological Gardens to Australia than the 3,661 convicts named above.

But the murders and outrages done in Victoria, the gold colony, on black fellows have been far greater than those done in the convict colonies. I mean greater in number and quality. It is true that in Tasmania the aboriginals were killed off almost at one swoop. That was merciful. In the gold colonies—Victoria and Queensland—the Lands of the Golden Fleece, there are many thousands yet to torture and to kill, who are being tortured and killed daily.

Horrible and hateful as the treatment was of the aboriginals in the silver Spanish colonies by Spaniards, the treatment of the aboriginals in the English gold colonies by Englishmen has been still more horrible and hateful.

We know of a truth that the primary cause of the outrages in Peru on the aboriginals was the love of silver. We have no difficulty in seeing this, and we like to see a text of holy writ well proven, so as to be plain to the meanest capacity.

We know of a truth that the outrages and murders committed in Australia sprang from a love of gold. But this we do not like to hear, and many will hate being reminded of it.

In the Exhibition of 1862 there was a gold coloured pyramid some 45 feet high, and ten feet square at the base, setting forth the quantity of gold taken out of Victoria alone in ten years. The value of the precious metal was one hundred and four millions, three hundred and forty-nine thousand, seven hundred and twenty-eight pounds sterling.

Up to that time there had not been any methods adopted for the storage of water, except the Yan Yean reservoir, which supplies Melbourne. Had the storing of water been carefully observed in Victoria, the loss by drought in cattle, and in pasture lands and houses by bush fires would not have occurred, and the prosperity of the people would have been enormously and permanently increased. But gold finding is as brutalizing and blinding as the finding of silver, nor shall we see any improvement of any sweet or healthful kind that will remain until the search for gold has dropped out of the Australian's mind, and that will only be when there is no more gold to find.

An improvement might begin now if the Colonial Governments were to issue a proclamation that no more prospecting for gold would be allowed—that all future discoveries should belong to the Crown—and that no one would be allowed to labour in this kind of diggings but convicts for life.

The land would then be made sweet to live in, all kinds of useful handicrafts would increase, and the pursuit of the fine and useful arts would provide a permanent means for securing a steady growth in good taste.

It would be easy to enumerate these handicrafts, but fruitless. So long as the storing of water is not done, it matters little what else is done. So long as the magnificent life of a fisherman and the craft of the sailor are neglected in any country, but especially in the Australias, it is useless to preach about elevating the national life.

If the gods would be as merciful to some Australians as the Indians of Castilla de Oro were to some Spaniards when they made their gold liquid with fire, and poured it down the hidalgos' throats, some good things might be hastened.

CHAPTER XIII.

AUSTRALIA.

I WAS not a little moved to laughter when I saw by the papers the other day that some of the London clergy had been applying to the Imperial Colonial Office for information on the colonies. They wanted to know something authentic on wages and labour, and getting on to the land, so that these clergy could advise their people—these shepherds find the best pasture for their sheep—at the Antipodes.

The colonies themselves can give no trustworthy information on these topics, and, therefore, the Imperial authorities cannot give any.

As a rule, the one statement that can be relied upon in connection with sheep—bi- or quadrupedal—is that they are chiefly wanted in the colonies for their fleece.

It is set forth in advertisements that domestic servants earn from £20 to £50 a year with board and lodging in Queensland. This is true. But the domestic servant, who in England, Ireland, or Scotland has been accustomed to the sweet influences of domestic life under a roof where master and mistress mean guide, example, and friend, speedily finds when she reaches the colony that she has made an irreparable mistake. It is not worth while even on £50 a year and "all found" to live in a solitude that is positively appalling except to a strong, trained, or contemplative mind. In like manner, the English workman finds that he has to compete with Germans and Chinese; the hours of labour are excessive, wages poor, treatment degrading, house rents high, neighbours shy and far between.

The real labourer—pick and shovel men—earn seven shillings and sixpence to eight shillings a day.

But under what conditions?

A fierce sun, which no pen can describe, and a very heavy job entails the need of a sustenance, the cost of which reduces the seven and eight shillings a day very nearly to the level of wages at home.

The Government, the squatter, sugar planter, and all employers of labour, screw the labourer down to the lowest farthing. Everything is done to keep the labourer in a menial condition. It is next to impossible for him to "get on to the land."

It must not be forgotten also that for the past generation labourers—working men of all kinds and domestic servants—have been born and bred in the colonies, and these, of course, successfully compete with new comers for the best places. Life in every condition, indeed, is very hard.

I am, of course, speaking of the majority. The Presbyterians and other respectable pharisees, grocers, Government clerks, and all who are attached to stables, public-houses and banks, the butchers, bakers, and gardeners, are well off, get drunk very often, and like it; all the more that there is nothing and no one to interfere with them. Colonial life, in short, requires an apprenticeship to succeed in it, but a great number of apprentices of both sexes never become master workmen, and remain apprentices all their days with no master to care for them.

There is much religion in the Australian colonies, but less morality. The hope which sustains the immigrant during his outward voyage crumbles to dust when he puts his foot on the shore where he is to end his days, unless, as many have done, the disappointed man resolves to work if only to obtain sufficient money with which to return home as quickly as may be. This resolve has saved many disappointed men from despair and suicide. A few have kept this resolution and returned. In the same ship in which I came this last time were more than one hundred respectable people of the working class who were leaving the colonies and returning to England because of the hard life and poor wage they found in Australia. In coming through the Suez Canal we met three English immigrant ships on their way to Australia. The third-class passengers crowded the bows of each ship to look at us as we passed them. They were greeted by our third-class passengers with the words, "*Go back home.*"

Others who went to work for the purpose of only getting the means with which to return to England remained did well, and will get on. But it requires great self-control, much common sense, a brave and cheerful heart to face colonial work. The number of immigrants who turn cowards on entering the battle field of labour in Australia is a melancholy sight to see. If we would ascertain the stuff of which our unskilled labourers are made we must see them on their passage out, observe their idleness and greed, their manners and spirits, and go with them to their first job on landing in the colony. See how they shape, hear the questions they ask, and observe the sullen, hateful cloud of cowardice and meanness settle on their brows; their look of disappointed lust, their currish slouch, and hear their hideous words as they turn tail at sight of the task that is set them.

Who is responsible for this state of things? It is a question that can be easily answered. But who cares for the answer?

As I publicly stated in Queensland, so I now repeat, that I have on two different occasions made two different journeys from England to Australia in ships carrying on each several hundred immigrants, such as serving maids from Ireland, Scotland, Wales, and England; tradesmen, deluded clerks, agricultural labourers, drapers' assistants, grocers, lawyers, and other useless and mischievous people with their wives and daughters; and I have now just returned from a voyage of 133 days in a vessel of 176 tons, carrying eighty-nine naked men and women; and I beg to say that in sobriety and cleanliness, in ability to amuse themselves, in industry and cheerful content, and in sweet human dignity, the unchristened children of the Coral Sea, to use a phrase, licked the baptized Britishers hollow.

That is a humiliating statement. But what is still more humiliating is that so few of us care to know whether it be true. We do not care to look into our debased national life, ascertain the sources of our debasement, and acknowledge, even with the courage of my poor india-rubber collector in Baranquilla, that we have done evil against our brother.

There is one picture that I have seen in our gold colonies which I would leave out of my collection of pictures if I could. It is the picture of the English immigrant woman.

I can quietly look on a poor drunken, half-witted hedge-carpenter, a cowardly pick and shovel man, a disgraceful, drunken bricklayer, a scandalous tailor, printer, rule maker, and a broken-down newspaper man, seeking in the colonies a refuge for the destitute, because I know what awaits them there, and how they will like it, but I cannot look on a friendless governess, nor even the slatternly, gin-loving cook, the gaudy, useless maid-of-all-work, the vain and foolish parlourmaid, the discredited barmaid, and others who are technically called maids, without a nameless horror seizing my faculties.

In the new Russian colony, where the new gold fields were lately discovered in the valley of the Djolgute River, some very simple laws were passed, which are worthy of the notice of the Australian authorities. Among these simple but severe laws, the penalty of death is inflicted for cheating at play, for adulterating gold dust, and for theft. For drunkenness during the hours of labour, or for bringing women into the colony, flogging, and flogging means death. They flogged a Jew for spreading false tidings, and he died.

Had these measures been taken on the Australian gold fields either the male population would be much less than it is, or those gold fields would have been worthy places for worthy men to live in, instead of places where everybody's wealth became everybody's hell.

But the women who have been brought to Australia. What about them?

I confess that I shrink from the question. I prefer to read a novel. Here is a quotation from a novel which comes in pat to the occasion. A great romancer,* who was fond of mixing facts with his fancies, writing of the silver colonies of Peru, calls them at the very beginning of

* Cervantes, El Zeloso Estremeño. Madrid, 1614.

his story *refugio y amparo de los desesperados de España, yglesia de los alçados salvoconducto de los homicidas, pala y cubierto de los jugadores (a quien llaman ciertos los peritos en al arte) añagaza general de mugeres libres, engaño comun de muchos, y remedio particular de pocos,* which, in plain English, is as follows:—These colonies are the refuge and shield of the hopeless ones of Spain, sanctuary of the fraudulent, passport of the murderer, gainful hell of the gambler (as certain experts in the art are called), general lure of free women, common trick for the many, and the special remedy for few.

Melbourne, Sydney, Brisbane, Townsville, Hobart Town, and other Australian towns, are general lures for free women. The treatment which these receive from the desperate, the gambler, the fraudulent and others is a treatment so shameful and horrible that it cannot be specified. Its effect on the community is obvious; its effect on the future life of the colony no one with any thought or compassion or patriotism can consider without dread.

The manner in which the immigrant woman has been treated in Australia is worthy of a people whose pasture lands have been manured with the blood of their aboriginal owners, and whose sugar-fields have been made the graveyards of many hundreds of slaves.

The best thing which some Colonial Governments could do for many of the domestic servants sent to them from home was to put them in gaol. The place for their reception on arrival in Brisbane, might have been designed to drive them on the streets. Some improvement has recently been made, and a new house of reception was, when I left it, a short while ago, in course of construction in Brisbane, the colony most guilty of all in its treatment of newly-arrived women.

Nothing in this world of common humdrum life—where little is of value that cannot be bought—would give me so much delight as to be able to bring up from the Antipodes the Brisbane Police-court, while it is occupied in "trying" the women who had been locked up during the previous night; and place this court, its occupants and proceedings, say, in Trafalgar Square, for all the world to see it; the front seats to be reserved for the Agents General and the Secretary of State for the Colonies, with the usual accommodation for the press.

We should then see the moral and physical pestilence which walketh about at noon-day in colonial towns—a pestilence from which all who suffer never thoroughly recover, which aggravates all other sufferings, and enervates, when it does not destroy, all the faculties by which a man may connect himself with that which pertains to immortal good.

In the middle of this court thus brought up should be placed a pyramid richly gilt, representing the bulk of gold which has been washed out of Australian dirt or crushed from its white rocks during the past thirty years, inscribed with the following golden words:—

> "O thou sweet king-killer, and dear divorce
> 'Twixt natural son and sire! thou bright defiler
> Of Hymen's purest bed! thou valiant Mars!
> Thou ever young, fresh, lov'd, and delicate wooer,
> Whose blush doth thaw the consecrated snow
> That lies on Dian's lap! thou visible god
> That solder'st close impossibilities,
> And mak'st them kiss! that speak'st with every tongue,
> To every purpose! O thou touch of hearts!
> Think, thy slave man rebels; and by thy virtue
> Set them into confounding odds, that beasts
> May have the world in empire!"

Round the plinth of this pyramid I would have in Old English the following:—

AUSTRALIA.

> "Take any brid, and put it in a cage,
> And do all thin entente, and thy corage
> To foster it tenderly with mete and drinke
> Of all deintees that thou canst bethinke
> And kepe it so clenely as thou may;
> Although the cage of gold be never so gay,
> Yet had this brid, by twenty thousand fold,
> Leven in a forest that is wild and cold,
> Gon eten wormes, and swiche wretchednesse.
> For ever this brid will don his besinesse
> To escape out of his cage when he may;
> His libertee the brid desireth ay."*

In order to turn the exhibition to the best account I would ask Mr. Walter Besant, President and Founder of the Earthly Tract Society, to write a two-paged tract on Domestic Servants, and I should give a commission to Mr. George Du Murier, to draw a picture that would illustrate in black and white the following passage from *La Vida Es Sueño*, by Pedro Calderon de la Barca :—

> "Cuentan de un sabio, que un dia
> Tan pobre y misero estaba
> Que solo se sustentaba
> De unas yerbas que cogia;
> Habra otro (entre si decia)
> Mas pobre y triste que yo?
> Y cuando el rostro volvio
> Hallo, la respuesta, viendo
> Que iba otro sabio cogiendo
> Las hojas que el arrojo."

Which I should translate, to suit my own purposes, as follows:—

> They tell of a maid who one day,
> Miserable and poor, went on her way,
> Plucking up roots her hunger to stay.
> "Is there another more miserable than I?"
> She would say. She turned and saw close by
> Was another maid to hunger a prey,
> Eating the leaves which she threw away.

This last would be the one who stood in the dock of the Australian Police-court.

* "The Manciple's Tale."

CHAPTER XIV.

CHILE.

THE rapid rise of Peru to opulence and power by means of its silver wealth was equalled in nothing for wonder and surprise except by its rapid fall. There is probably as much silver still in Peru as has been taken out of it, as it is certain there is quite as much gold in Australia as has been sent to the mint. Yet what a miserable Peru it is; over head and ears in debt, beaten in battle, hopeless, ashamed without being repentant, disgraced in its own eyes; yet too idle to work, and because it always despised wholesome industry has become too ignorant to learn the simplest lesson by which it might even pick up a decent living. There is something appalling to see a man once well dressed, indifferently honest, very religious, well off, with a houseful of servants, fine stables, garden and coach-house, lying in a pigstye, too feeble even to die. But to see a republic in this melancholy condition is a thing which compels wonder and demands inquiries, which cannot be shirked even if we try to shirk them.

Very few people, if any, in our gold colonies care to trouble themselves about the ruin which has come on the silver colonies of the Andes. Probably a few deluded bondholders in London, who at this particular period would be glad if they had in hand the money which they had lent to Peru ten years ago, have still a little interest in her real condition. But the number of Englishmen who see in the ruin of Peru a lesson which affects themselves and their own country I trust may be many, although I am afraid that, like the chosen, they also are few.

Never having visited the republic of Chile until recently, I accepted with alacrity a retainer from some merchants in London to go and inquire into the particular mining industry which had secured to Chile the high character which makes her to differ from every other republic in Spanish America.

I sailed from Liverpool to Valparaiso, touching at Madeira, calling at Montevideo, visiting the Cape de Verdes, and steaming over the fathomless waters of the Straits of Magellan, whose banks are hung with ever-green woods. A very remarkable voyage, which was accomplished in forty-four days, with gorgeous summer weather all the way. We carried a few Scotch Presbyterians among the first-class passengers, who sufficed, amid the glories through which we passed, to remind us that we were still in a world of woe. They were grocers and drapers and general dry goods men with their wives, who had been "successful" in Valparaiso; had been home to see the old people, and were returning from a land where they were nobodies to a country where they were somebodies. Why it is that grocers and other necessary traders should make a louder and more ostentatious profession of religion than even parsons, grave-diggers, or churchwardens I could never make out.

On approaching the mouth of La Plata we ran into a *pampero*. This was nothing more substantial than one of

> "Heaven's cherubin horsed
> Upon the sightless couriers of the air,"

a wind blowing off the *pampa*, the mighty plain of Uruguay. I have been in many kinds of winds at sea, and was never vexed; but this *pampero* was as different to any wind I had ever experienced as the bagpipes played in a room are different to every other kind of noise. It not only penetrates every part of your body, but smites every part with a resistless palsy; and the chill it brings is bewildering. The effect on the sea is also remarkable, the waves being fretted into little things in shape like unto shark's teeth, very peculiar; and it was trying to the Presbyterian ladies and their husbands.

Montevideo was agreeable, as all places are to landsmen who have been long at sea. Its climate reminded me of the climate of Bogotá—cold in the early morning, hot in the middle of the day, and very suddenly cold at night, especially if there was a wind. The food was good, so was the market-place, with its great heaps of oranges and other fruits. It is the only place in the world where you can fully appreciate *yerba maté,* the *cha* or *té* of Paraguay. There was a great dearth of people in Montevideo; there were even no beggars. Many beautiful women there were, and a large orphanage, or rather foundling hospital, with the inscription in Latin: "When my father and mother forsake me the Lord taketh me up." The hospital was served by nuns. There were some handsome shops, and I was invited in the most simple Quaker-like way in one of them by an astute young person to buy some French photographs of living creatures. Very much annoyed and astonished did she seem at the terms in which I expressed my refusal. I had seen similar works of mechanical labour exhibited publicly in the shop windows in Dunedin.

We reached Sandy Point, *Puntas arenas*, the entrance to the Straits of Magellan, early on Sunday afternoon, too late to admit of our finding anchorage at night if we went on; and, therefore, we tied up, hoping to get an early start next morning, so that we could reach the Pacific before the sun went down. We rose, however, to meet with a dense fog, and we had to remain tied up another day. This gave us time to go on shore, and also to receive visits on board from some of the natives of Patagonia, who had come in the day before to sell skins and buy provisions, also from some dealers in those skins. A villainous-looking wretch, who turned out to be an evil son of the United States, offered me some curiosities and "a fine guanaco robe" if I would get him a bottle of brandy from the purser.

Puntas arenas was once a penal settlement, and an evil spirit still seems to cling to it.* Among our visitors from Patagonia was a very handsome chief of considerable stature, well proportioned, and equally well mannered. No doubt their way of wearing the "guanaco robe" gives the tall men a seeming height which does not really belong to them. Had I not measured our tall example, I should unhesitatingly have set him down at seven feet. He measured six foot four without his shoes.

We got away very early next morning, and to my great delight Captain Hammell came to my cabin and called me on deck. Tierra del Fuego may derive its name from

* See "Cambiaso: Relacion de los acontecientos i de los Crimenes de Magallanes," par B. Vicuña Mackenna." Santiago, 1867. A most interesting study in human wickedness.

belching volcanoes, but whether that be so or not we were certainly in the region of Cielos del Fuego—a heaven of fire, but fire without smoke, ruby fire, so red, yet soft, so dazzling bright, yet beautiful, that I could well-nigh have shed tears for the speed which was carrying us away from the sight of heaven revealing its delight to the earth. Below the gold light were "motionless cataracts" of silver snow, below the silver snow were emerald islands flung in the air, and there was a staircase of sapphire built up on the slopes of two mountains called in guide books glaciers, and if that name conveys to the reader an idea of the triumph of heavenly beauty in an earthly paradise of colour let it be so called.

The sun went down at evening earlier than we expected, and we could now only see our way by the wild, white waves that came tumbling in upon us through the Strait from the Pacific, threatening to swallow us up. It was ten o'clock, and we were still in the jaws of the Straits, the ship pitching like a cameleopard mounted on a rocking-horse. Most of the Presbyterians had said their prayers and were gone to bed, some of them were still praying. All the plated wares belonging to the ship, the spoons, forks, dish covers and cruet stands, were put away at the stern end of the saloon on a gallery over the rudder. In one of her pitches, the ship going down as if bent on standing on her nose, she tossed all those Birmingham goods into the middle of the saloon with a noise that cannot be described, which drowned even the roar of the wild waters and made the Presbyterians believe that

"Hell is empty
And all the devils are here."

The women were very pious, and glad even of such cheer

as I could give them. Them I comforted with hot beef-tea and other carnal delights, and when we at length got into smooth water they went to sleep and I went to bed to rise in the morning to another world of wonders impossible to describe, although I can never forget it. The mountains of Chile seemed glad to see us.

Valparaiso is unlike any other place that I have seen. It is the European quarter of the new world. The Italians muster in thousands, the Germans muster in thousands, the French muster in thousands, the English muster in thousands, and the Spaniards muster in thousands. There are more than thirty thousand Europeans in Chile, and they most do congregate in Valparaiso.

Chile began life in a very humble way, and gained a living by selling tallow to Lima to light up its streets and houses, also *charqui* for its negroes, and other small commodities. To these it presently added ropes and yarns of all kinds—its hemp is still famous—and it boasts of a thread which even the new world cannot surpass. To these it subsequently added mules, and the traffic in these beasts of burden was very great, especially with Potosi. It then began to cultivate wheat, and grind flour, which it sent to all parts of the Pacific Sea, and then it began to smelt copper. Chile has had three ages since the year 1640— the age of tallow, tackling, and *charqui*, the age of mules and corn, and the age of copper. In shorter form, the foundation of the prosperity of Chile was agriculture, and when this was well laid it took to mining and manufactures. Chile has always been industrious and thrifty, proud, pious, and pure of blood. Chile was settled by Spaniards from the North of Spain, who were too proud to wive with negroes or Indians, too proud to live without labour, and scorned idleness as much as they abhorred impiety or running into debt. Like all strong races, the Chilians were cruel, and showed their cruelty most in their religion. They boast of the victims which they supplied to the maw of the Holy Inquisition, and of the two thousand, mostly women, who were burnt to death in La Iglesia de la Compania, less than three-and-twenty years ago from now, while they were at their devotions before the shrine of Maria, and they rightly boast of their recent conquest of Peru. They are fond of their own land, and pride themselves on their commercial integrity. They like to be called the English of the Pacific.

The Chilians have been much indebted to the English for capital which has been invested in mines and for money lent to the executive Government. The relations of the two peoples have been a benefit to both. Englishmen have married Chilian women, and Chilian men have married English women. The family institution, the home, without which no nation has ever been formed, and only where it is found in its purity is there any certainty for the continuity of the community in all that is good, and sweet, and gracious, flourishes in Chile.

The easily available gold was taken away from Chile by the Spaniards; its silver has never been great, but its copper has in times now gone been in quantity the greatest in the world. There is still gold in Chile, but it does not turn the people into oromaniacs.

It takes more skill, time, and patience, to produce metallic copper than silver or gold. Had copper been as easily produced in Chile as silver was in Peru under the crown of Spain, or as guano was under the filthy tyranny of the Republic, Chile would have been as poor and blind and naked as Peru now is, her agriculture would have been neglected, and her morals would have followed in the fall of her agricultural industry. Even when copper had reached the height of its glory its agriculture was still in the ascendant. The greatest amount of copper which Chile ever exported in one year was in 1876, when the value reached to somewhat more than eighteen and a half million of dollars. Since then there has been a disastrous fall in the price of the metal, and competitors have increased in all parts of the world, so that if Chile had devoted all her attention to copper her beautiful country would have been as desolate as the shores of Lake Superior, and her people as destitute and miserable as those of Peru.

Before the war with Peru in 1879 Chile occupied and worked all the principal mines of copper and silver that were in Bolivia and Peru. But for Chile energy and Chile capital the silver mines of Caricoles, in the desert of Atacama, would not have been opened up. She still supplies Lima with flour and vegetables, as well as all the towns along the coast, as she has done from the earliest time; and now, by means of her navy, she dominates the entire coast from the Straits of Magellanes to Panama. The nitrate of soda deposits of Tarapaca now belong to Chile. It is impossible to doubt that the ship canal through the Isthmus of Panama will give an enormous impetus to whatever is doing in Chile.

There is a great deal of weather in Chile.* All the rain that has been denied to Peru and the desert of Atacama has been added to the natural downpour of the southern republic. This gave rise to much prayer for many years,

* See a valuable little book, "Ensayo Historico sobre el clima de Chile desde los tiempos prehistoricos hasta el gran temporal de Julio de 1877." Valparaiso, 1877.

but it became obvious to the Chilians that this was not the proper means to use in order to escape from being drowned at one season or dried up at another. They gave themselves to hard work, and built canals and reservoirs instead of wasting their substance and losing all their people in building an ark. Indeed, what with early wars with the Araucanos, earthquakes, floods, the low price of copper, and having to fight Peruvians on sea and shore, and other serious calls on their time and attention, the Chilians have had a great deal of very hard work to do.

But they have done it.

That is the secret of the difference between Chile and Peru, Chile and Ecuador, Chile and Bolivia, Chile and Colombia, and all the other beggarly republics of South America that were born with gold and silver spoons in their mouths.

There are few countries in the world, and none with which we English have been so intimately connected, that have so interesting a social, commercial, and moral history as Chile. It is full of lessons to ourselves and examples to our colonies, especially those colonies that belong to the family of the Kielmanseggs.

Although Chile has done so much hard manual work, none of the gold or silver colonies have been so productive in works of scientific and literary merit as she.

I trust it will be taken in good part if I end this chapter by translating some of the laws and customs of that people whom the Spaniards "conquered." Here is one from Chapter IV. of the Fifth Book of the Royal Commentaries of the Incas written by one of themselves :—

"In the lands where there was little water for irrigation they gave it by order and measure (as they did all other things that were distributed), for among Indians there were no heartburnings about the administration; and this they did in the years when there was little rain, when the need was great. They measured the water, and experience told them how much was needed to water five hundred square fathoms of land, and according to this rule they gave amply to each Indian so many hours of water according to his span of land. Each received the water in his turn one after the other; neither the rich, nor the most noble, nor the friend or kinsman of the chief, nor the chief himself, nor the minister or governor were preferred. He who was careless to water his land within the appointed time they publicly and ignominiously chastised, giving him three or four blows on the shoulders with a stone; or they scourged his arms and legs with osier rods as an idler, and a slothful fellow—a people that were much despised among them, whom they called Mizquitulyu, which means easy-bones, composed of Mizui, sweet or soft, and Tulyu, which is a bone."

A horror creeps over me every time I am reminded that the wonderful land of Peru was deprived of the services of a people who could give and administer such a law as this.

I like to increase this feeling of horror, and would much like to give the same feeling to every thoughtful man in the gold colonies, or the lands of the Golden Fleece. Therefore, here are a few more characteristics.

"Idleness was punished as a crime. There were no beggars in the land. As gold and silver and precious stones were not necessaries of life, but fine things for adorning and giving pleasure, these were gathered when there was nothing of importance to be done, and presented to the Inca for the adorning of his palaces, or the temple of the sun. They only used their spare time in searching for gold!"

These were the people whom the gold and silver grabbing Spaniards murdered!

"Copper was of more value to them than gold, for out of it they could make mirrors, warlike arms, knives, tools, pins, spades, and hammers." "No Indian was called upon to pay ought out of his own property. His payment for the service of the State was personal, given in the form of labour, time, or skill. All were equal in this, the rich with the poor, for they were all an educated people."

These were the people whom the gold and silver grabbing Spaniards murdered!

"They called a man rich when he had children. He who had no children, although rich in things, was called poor! A man with a large family was regarded as a very rich man! The poor who had no children were helped by the children of the rich."

These were the people whom the gold and silver grabbing Spaniards murdered!

Among the annals of the people we come on such things as the following:—

"Among the works that the Inca Viracqocha constructed was a channel of water more than twelve feet deep, and as many feet wide, which flowed for more than five hundred miles. Its rise was in the mountains between Parcu and Picuy, at some beautiful springs which are there. The channel flowed thence to the Rucanas, watering the pastures in those desolate wilds, which are sixty miles wide, and in length stretch almost over the whole of Peru."

"There were many such channels throughout the empire, and were equal to the greatest works in the world."

These channels were allowed to get out of repair by the gold and silver grabbing Spaniards. The waters got the upper hand, and swept away the walls as the Spaniards swept away the people who built them.

Many sayings of the Incas are preserved. Here is one by the great Viracqocha worthy to be held in remembrance.

"Fathers are often the cause of their sons being lost, or what is the same thing, corrupted by evil habits acquired in childhood. For some train up their sons in over indulgence, leaving them to do as they please, without caring for the future when they shall become men. Others treat their children with too much severity and harshness, which ruins them. Too much indulgence weakens body and mind, and too much severity enfeebles the spirit, making the child to hate instruction, and to make learning hopeless. Those who are made to fear everything cannot have the courage to do deeds worthy of men. The proper way is so to train children that they may be brave in war and wise in peace."

This voice the Spaniards choked with blood.

Here are a few more sayings of these wise people.

"Envy is a worm that gnaws the vitals."

"Drunkenness, anger, and madness are all one, except that the first two are voluntary, and the last inevitable."

"He who kills another without authority condemns himself to death."

"Thieves and adulterers who destroy the happiness of others must be put to death."

"The noble and generous are known by their patience in adversity."

"Impatience is a sign of a base mind, ill taught and worse mannered."

"Judges who receive gifts are thieves, and to be punished with death."

"He who tries to count the stars where he can't count the *quipos** is worthy of scorn."

This voice the Spaniards choked with blood.

"They planted colonies in those regions where the climate was fine, in order to multiply such fine things as would best grow there, and obtain greater perfection. These colonies were planted first of all for the good of the people, then for the good of the Inca, and lastly for the good of the kingdom."

Now the fine climate of Peru is so much waste in the earth. The precious things which grow there fall into rottenness, the land is clothed with the "muddy vesture of decay," because the gold and silver grabbing Spaniards murdered the gardeners, and all their wives and children.

One remarkable custom which the Presbyterians of our gold colonies may imitate, if they please, was that the Incas insisted on all tradesmen marking the cost price on every article of food or clothing offered for sale—not in cipher or marks privately known to the vendor, but in figures that could be "understanded of the common people." The sale of fuel as well as the distribution of water was under control of the State.

---

* Quipos, plural of quipo, an arrangement of coloured threads and knots. A description of this method of keeping the public records was made by an English sailor, but never having heard his name I cannot find his book, which I am told is in the British Museum.

CHAPTER XV.

COLONIAL RELIGION AND MORALS.

I HAVE remarked already that there is more religion than morality in the colonies, as there is, let us say, in Ireland or in the ranks of the Salvation Army; and I have often thought that it would be worth while to throw a little light, if it were possible, on the ease with which we can propagate religion, and the difficulty there has hitherto been in cultivating good morals, and thereby acquiring good manners. In the course of my travels I have met with many clergymen, by which I mean men in Holy Orders, or clerks; ministers of the Gospel, by which I mean men who are not in orders, but whose profession it is to preach; and priests, by which I mean men who offer, or pretend to offer sacrifices, and if I ever speak of clergymen or ministers of the Gospel as priests it is for shortness and to express dislike of the priestly character. I have also travelled much with sailors and soldiers, lawyers, doctors, actors, botanists, and other men of science, fishermen and farmers, carpenters, engineers and blacksmiths, painters and poets; and when my ship comes in, by which I mean when, in the words of Antonio,

"My merchandise makes me not sad,"

I shall charter the finest steamer of the Cunard fleet, give a picnic that will last a year to all my friends—if the ship is big enough to hold them—and re-visit all those ports of the world where I have left and received marks of affection. But there would not be a single priest among the lot. Of sailors there would be many, for they are the best of mankind in all nations. Of soldiers a few, and only those who have been in battle; lawyers one. Of carpenters, engineers, and blacksmiths, there would be a host, which would include many other handicraftsmen, as well as fishers. There would be several doctors, who would be also botanists, chemists, and historians. The only historian I ever knew was the best doctor I ever knew. There would be also a few women who can sew and wash linen, besides the wives (some of them) of the sailors and soldiers, the fishers, carpenters, and blacksmiths. Also if we had on board any poets or novelists (and there would be some of these) all the wives of these, with the painters. Of actors the number would be great.

For it was entirely owing to some actors that I owe what I hold as most dear, and that is the recollection of the days of my childhood. But for them I could not go back into the playground, or the gardens where the big gooseberries grow, or the rivers where the fishes are mighty prey, or the meadows where the birds sing, or the sky where the stars always shine, or the world where the villain is always caught, where marriage means love, and home joy.

It is always dangerous, at least it is not always safe, to take illustrations from Plato, especially such as he puts into the mouth of Socrates, but there is a passage in the "Ion" which I will venture to quote from Jowett's translation, which, as Sancho would say, fits like a glove to the hand, or a ring to the finger. There is a divinity which moves an actor, "like that in the stone which Euripides calls a magnet, but which is commonly known as the stone of Heraclea. For that stone not only attracts iron rings, but also imparts to them a similar power of attracting other rings; and sometimes you may see a number of pieces of iron and rings suspended from one another so as to form quite a long chain, and all of them derive their power of suspension from the original stone. Now, this is like the muse, who first gives to men inspiration herself, and from these inspired persons a chain of other persons is suspended, who take the inspiration from them. For all good poets—epic as well as lyric—compose their beautiful poems not as works of art, but because they are inspired."* The magnet which first picked me out of a heap of rubbish was hung in a lowly theatre in a provincial town in the Midlands, and though I have not kept my place I have never ceased my connection with the magnet which first laid hold of me. At a remote distance I am still moved by Shakespeare, and those whom he has moved. The muse of fire that did ascend the brightest heaven of invention still keeps my little candle alight.

I could not have been more than twelve years old when I first saw "Mary Jane Woolgar," as she was called among her intimate friends, who became so great a favourite as Miss Woolgar, and subsequently as Mrs. Alfred Mellon, of the Adelphi. When I first knew her she belonged to a company of strolling players attached to Bennett's Theatre, which went the "Midland circuit." She was a charming actress, and the most beautiful girl that up till then I had seen. According to my childish ability I used to take her

* "Dialogues of Plato," Vol. i., 237.

flowers, and even bought pieces of music, which I carried to the theatre for her, and gave for delivery to an actor of the name of Fenton, who kept my secret. She was my first love, although I never made her personal acquaintance.

I allude to my early recollections of the play in order to help me to say what I would about the propagation of religion and the cultivation of morals in large towns, and the religious and moral condition of our colonies, and I would remark in passing that if we would see a nation in its naked reality, appreciate its energy, its tendencies, its meanness and nobleness, its cruelty and pride, in short, if we would see the bent of a nation's genius, we must see its colonial life. If the professional historian wishes to instruct us on the downfall of Spain, and point the awful moral of its disgrace, a story that certainly remains to be told by some man whose love of truth is invincible, he must not go to Simancas, or the Escorial, or the Colombina, or the picture galleries of Madrid or Seville, but to Peru; he must visit Cuzco, Santiago de Chile, Santa Fé de Bogotá, Caracas, Old Panama, Potosi, and Chihuahua. Precisely as if we would see the value of a father's example and the influence of a mother's love on a son who has never been from home, we must see the young man, let us say in Paris, alone and by himself, and, especially if he has been brought up in the Presbyterian faith, we must observe how he spends his Sunday evenings in what used to be called the gay metropolis of France. The "principles" of the young man are nearly always found to be as easily put off as they were put on, to be resumed, like his clothes, when he returns to the bosom of his family.

How often have I been amused in watching the agony of some men in what is called "society" in London when at a garden party they have unexpectedly met some of their kinsfolk from the Antipodes dressed not in peacock's feathers, but in the real plumage of the barn-door fowl, which for ease and pleasure they prefer, because it is natural to them; in brief, who never were of gentle blood, but only good commercial people in the egg line. And I think if the strait religious denominations, who sometimes hold high festival in the Strand in the merry month of May, could see the result of their teachings in some of the big towns in Victoria and New South Wales, Queensland, and Tasmania, they would become very anxious, and even ask me for a little advice. This I should be glad to give, because I think after a long experience they are prepared to relinquish many things that are worn out now and worthless. The first thing I should venture to say to my own friends in the colonies, who belong to the Lion and Unicorn party, who stick to black bombazine and lawn, would be —

"You perceive that religion is an acquired taste; and as you cannot get real Stilton cheese, nor real Chambertin, nor real fine old port, nor even the meanest "fiz," in any of the colonies you would not dream of investing for your own use in any base imitations of these, so you would not, if you are wise, dream of getting an imitation religion. Nor is there any need for it; all that you have to do is to cultivate the native article, instead of importing imitation trash. Pure religion is infinitely more precious than pure wine, but you can only get either one or the other by natural causes and the use of appropriate means. The first means to be used is to get hold of real men, who are religious and learned. If you have to wait a thousand years for men whom you want to teach you religion, let me advise you to wait for them rather than put up with religious men who are ignorant and mere formalists; who are not real men at all, but only imitation men. The preaching and praying men you want are the men who can do something, if it be only fishing or tent-making; who have already done something, not men who are soldiers only in uniform, but men who have been in action; not men who know how to spoil a good thing, but who would rather die than not do the best. Even if you began by discarding the imitation man, that would be a fine beginning, and the best beginning towards getting the real man."

Now, I make bold to say that the clergyman who does not cherish the play, the drama, the theatre, in a colony; who does not think more of it than of any other means of recreation; who does not strive night and day, wrestling all the time to get good actors for playing the best plays, is an imitation man, a stick, a dumb dog, a sentinel who sleeps at his post, a watchman who tells lies about the weather, and is in league with the thief.

The hard work that is the daily portion of every colonist is always followed in all our colonies by a long night. A man to work well under an Australian sky must have the best of rest, and that is a rest which is looked forward to with joy and delight, not the rest of guzzling the bad liquor which is sold as Scotch whiskey or French brandy in a hateful atmosphere, but the rest which comes from looking into that mirror which shows virtue her own feature. The best rest for an Englishman is that which makes his soul to sing and dance with joy, which excites his wrath, and rouses his admiration. The only rest for a hard-worked wife, capable of restoring her vigour and enabling her to keep by the side of her husband in the hard journey of life through colonial mud, mosquitoes, and heat, is to laugh and be glad, with such laughter and gladness as are only to be got at a good play. The best recreation for the domestic servant is to be found in the pit or gallery of a theatre, where she can have something to cheer her into a wider sympathy than that which she finds in the frequent inhuman drudgery to which she is often condemned.

When the history of the English theatre is written, it will be seen that by its being divorced from English everyday life, English life became a very dull thing, youth was robbed of its best teacher, manhood of its charm, the community of its best moral stimulant, and religion of its purity. The priests who shut up the theatre opened the new gin palace, and enlarged the gaols; the statesmen who made education compulsory but neglected the encouragement of the national theatre, made the best provision for sapping the intellectual vigour of the people. If we would see the proof of this statement we must go to the Australian colonies, where we shall not fail to find much refined cruelty, and a life so vulgar and selfish that men who see it for the first time think of nothing but the shortest and quickest route back to Warwickshire, or Devon, or Yorkshire, or anywhere, where there is a church porch, if only for shelter, or a peal of bells, if only for a little music that will remind us of happier days, or that will link us to someone or to something that is better than ourselves. The profession of technical Christianity is not always associated with kindness and charity even at home; what are called the religious newspapers are quite sufficient evidence of this, and this profession is not infrequently associated with narrow-mindedness and even bitterness, which are destructive of good fellowship and provocative of ill blood. But in the colonies, where good nature and sweetness of disposition, frankness, openness, honesty, courage, charity, and kindness should be specially cultivated, the hotter the religious enthusiasm is the more sickly are the other growths; indeed, I think it is true that sectarian religion at the Antipodes may be likened unto a bush fire which consumes the grass. Fierce religion burns up all natural feeling, and every lowly and sweet instinct that belongs to cultivated human nature, and leaves behind grotesque results which are the incarnation of monotonous ugliness and lingering sullen death.

There is by no means a lack of sport in Australia; on the contrary, there is a great deal of sport. But women are not expected to play cricket, or football, hunt kangaroos, join in boat races, or join the volunteers. They want something more suitable to their taste and ministry; besides, it is not a woman's place to contend at all in anything; she ought to see and enjoy beautiful sights, hear good music, and never want to play on the piano, unless she can play well. But to return to my meagre thesis for a brief space, there is more religion in the colonies than morality. I think this worthy of consideration. The great majority of good people who look to the colonies as a stand-by for the mother country, philanthropists who look to emigration as a means to improve our national poverty and ragged-legged condition, little think what emigration means—and they do not know. It is impossible for them to conceive what an "assisted emigrant" has to go through on arrival at Melbourne or Sydney, Adelaide or Hobart, Brisbane or Perth. We may be quite sure that the emigrant who comes as an outcast to Australia is a very ordinary being, with no other knowledge than was doled out to him in the Sunday School, and with a religion that only excites his fear, or appeals to his imagination—and as a rule the power of this imagination is very strong; he has no mental training of any kind; he has received no discipline which has produced one wholesome habit, or confirmed him in one good custom; from the moment he puts his foot on board the ship which is to carry him fifteen thousand miles to the time he leaps on to the new soil which is to receive him, he lives the life of a hog. The effect of a storm at sea, when every heave of the ship threatens to drown him, is to bring back the memory of the little child when God was like his earthly father, whose anger and sudden ill temper made his life miserable. The British emigrant is not a coward, but he is always superstitious, and never knows his own mind. Everything around him when he gets on shore is as indefinite as the sea which surrounded him for three months—no familiarity with which ever bred contempt for it—and he is not only superstitious, but he is also very religious, and his religion he keeps to himself. I don't care by what name his priest or his parson calls this religion, be it Roman Catholic or Protestant, Presbyterian or Methodist, the British emigrant has always got a religion of his own. I never in my life met a man of the emigrant class who had the remotest notion of a systematic religion, not a Roman Catholic who could tell me his church's meaning of a sacrament, a Church of England man who knew the meaning of the word repentance, a Methodist who could explain Wesley's doctrine of the witness of the Spirit, or understand it when it was explained to him, or a Presbyterian with a settled conviction about the duration of hell—how its fires were supplied, or in what was to consist the happiness of the elect. Indeed, each was

> "A pupil in the many-chambered school,
> Where Superstition weaves her airy dreams,"

and all seemed to be

> "Lost in a gloom of uninspired research."

I took much pains to inform myself of the quality of the religious services which are celebrated every Sunday in colonial churches and chapels. In all my experience of calling at the various ports to which we carried emigrants, I only met one clergyman who came to see the new-comers on their arrival to offer his sympathy and advice.

The Roman Catholic priest is very earnest in beating up recruits among the emigrants after they are settled. As a preacher he is singularly lacking in human sweetness, and I never heard him preach without his larding his discourse with indefinite but powerful language on the future torments of the wicked. The altar of his church is always decorated with artificial flowers, lighted candles, and gilt ornaments. The gaudy clothing which he occasionally wears, mingled with the white surplices of the choir, the tinkling of bells, the swinging of censers, the fumes of incense, perfumed sometimes with the penetrating scent of the tonquin bean, together with some approach to refined music, cannot fail to produce a sensuous delight that may soothe and bless, even if it does not elevate and strengthen the mind.

The Church of England services are well attended by respectable, substantial, well-clothed people, and the women are as fashionably dressed as when they go to the play. There is more preaching than in the Roman Catholic

Churches, but it is far from good. With one or two exceptions it was very bad. I was puzzled to ascertain what motive a man could have in delivering in a monotone voice a string of words which sounded all right, but which did nothing but buzz about your ears without ever getting inside either to stimulate to action, or to hope, or to wholesome sorrow. Nor was I less puzzled to find out what kind of composition the sermon belonged to, how it was put together, and what sort of a mind the preacher had that could make words of such a sort that the moment they left his lips began to float in the air, sometimes like slow snow, sometimes like fine dust, and sometimes like feathers. I gave it up, never expecting to make anything of it. But to my delight and surprise, one Sunday I solved this mystery, and it has since been of much use to me. A young and good-looking parson, noted for being "a good fellow," a promoter of cricket, football, boating, tennis, and picnics, a favourite at Government House, and much liked by the rich young women of the town, preached from a text which made me prick up my ears. The words were, *"Ye cannot do the things that ye would,"* Gal. v. 17. In the course of his sermon the preacher said, all on one note, "Let me impress upon you, dear brethren, the importance, the value, the weightiness of the great truth that mortal man, poor, sinful mortal man is nearly always made to consist of high and ennobling thoughts, which sometimes, it may be in church, it may be in the market-place, or in the social circle carry him away from this world into a better, a higher, and a truer world where God is, and low, grovelling, sordid, sometimes wicked desires, which degrade him, and which, if he gratifies, must bring him into trouble, perhaps, alas, into a long life of suffering and disease; and he has grand ideas and the weakest, feeblest, yea, it too often happens, I am afraid, very worthless results. He has bright, it may now and then be ecstatic, visions of some important or noble work that he means to do, but which through his infirmity and the sin which so easily besets him he never does. He has bright and fond hopes for himself that never come to any fulfilment, at least, not in this vale of tears. He has the very best intentions of being something better, greater, perhaps holier, but these intentions, alas, my beloved brethren, are overcome by the influence of the world, or the influence of the flesh, or the influence of that fell being by whom, or through whom, sin came into the world, and all our woe."

Some time after he had preached the sermon of which the above is only a short extract I made his acquaintance, indeed, we became friends. Among his books he had a volume of sermons called "Spirit and Form,"* and in one of these which is called *The Meaning of Limitations,* is the following passage, p. 151 :—

"Man is made up of high thoughts and low desires; of great aims and small means; of grand ideas and poor results. He has visions of work that he will do which he never does; hopes for himself that are never fulfilled; intentions of being what he never is."

The whole sermon, which is one of uncommon vigour and helpful sympathy, is designed to set forth the true mortality of man, and is of the greatest practical value. But my priestly young parson had simply spoilt it. Every word of the second extract is contained in the first, but is so smothered with platitude that it sends to sleep the reader

---

* "Spirit and Form," Sermons preached by Edwards Comerford Hawkins, M.A., Vicar of St. Bride's, Fleet Street, London.

or the listener. He had not availed himself of this volume of sermons to shirk his own work, or to strut in borrowed plumes, but *to improve on the sermons.*

"There is no religion in these sermons," he said to me in all seriousness when we were talking about them. "*I fill in the religion, and then find they go first-rate!*"

It is this filling in of religion that takes out all the bone and marrow from colonial morality, and by thus separating religion from daily life, it becomes a very dangerous thing, because they who look upon religion as an antidote soon come to regard it as an anodyne. In the colonies religion is taken as an opiate, and not infrequently swallowed as a dram.

I found the same "vain repetitions" in all the services of the Presbyterians, while their sermons, made up of weary doctrinal argumentation, never could have produced one manful resolve, or one rational conviction. Using the key which had been supplied by my young Church of England man, I was always able to follow the long-winded extemporary prayers which make the Presbyterian services so very terrible. Here is one to which I call especial attention, which I took down with great care.

"O thou dread Being, who art *our* Almighty all-loving *Father*, though Abraham be ignorant of us *which art* to come, and who dwellest *in* that *heaven* the light of which sinful man cannot approach unto; holy and *hallowed be Thy* great and wondrous *name:* and, O, in mercy and in grace let *Thy* righteous *kingdom come* into our fallen world, and on our bended knees before Thy awful throne we beseech Thee let *Thy* perfect and good and holy *will be done* amongst us *on* this polluted *earth*, and in our sin-stained hearts, from the Queen on her throne to the humblest of her subjects, O Lord, even *as it is* done by angels and archangels who delight to do Thy will *in* the *heaven* of heavens. And do Thou of Thine infinite mercy and tender compassion, who feedest the ravens and dost mark the sparrow's fall, *give* to *us* Thy servants even on *this day our* manna from heaven, such *daily* and hourly *bread* as may be good for our souls and our bodies, *and* in the tenderness of Thy compassion, and remembering that we are but dust, *forgive us* the sinful thoughts of *our* hearts, the *debts* of gratitude which we owe to Thee, our sins of omission and commission even *as we* trust, O our Lord, that we are desirous to pardon and *forgive* all the debts of *our* earthly *debtors*. *And*, most mighty, do Thou of Thine infinite compassion and tender mercy blot out all our transgressions and forgive us all our sins, and *lead us* by the still waters of Thy grace where the pleasant pastures are, and *not into* the mire and marsh of deadly *temptation ; but* do Thou make bare Thine arm, O Lord, and come down, *deliver us* in the time of trouble *from* all *evil,* of whatsoever kind, and from the evil one who goeth about seeking whom he may devour. *For Thine*, O omnipotent, *is the* everlasting and glorious *kingdom,* which shall become the kingdom of our Lord and of His Christ, *and* Thine *the* almighty *power* which shall bruise Satan under our feet, *and* shortly, shortly, O Lord, as well as *the* refulgent *glory* that shall last *for ever and* for *ever*, world without end. *Amen."*

If the reader will take the trouble to read only the words in italics he will perceive that they form the Lord's prayer as given in Matthew vi. 9-13. All the rest is the "much speaking" and the "vain repetition" of the heathen, and it is this which makes preachers vain and wooden, and congregations stupid, vulgar, and, I am afraid, immoral. It is far from pleasant to say these things, but they belong to our colonial life and are of greater moment than they may seem at first sight. I once heard a colonist in Queensland, a man of much cultivation, and who occupied a place of great public trust say, and he said it to me —

"I only wish to God my father had been a convict!"

He was referring to a cruel controversy that was then occupying every family and every newspaper in the colony on the appointment of Mr. Groom to the Speakership in the Queensland House of Assembly. In early life this Groom had been a convict, and some of the vulgar wits went the length of saying that the only place he was fit for was that of groom of the stole. But the man had thoroughly purged himself of his wickedness, and had become an able journalist, a clever speaker, a thorough man of business, well acquainted with parliamentary life, Mayor of Ipswich, and rich. He had to exert himself—and, of course, without friends—and this compulsion, coupled with a poignant compunction, made him, as it had made many a hopeless convict who had been shipped from England to Botany Bay, an independent and a powerful man.

What my friend Mr. Ballard meant by that apparently wrong-headed saying was that he wished his father had come out from England, and been compelled to begin life anew at a time when men were valued, not for what they had been, but for what they could do; men who would not have been troubled about pleasing this or that kind of man, or currying favour with the commonplace people of the community, but who would push ahead, wisely improving the present, and going forth with a manly heart to meet the future careless of favours and frowns. There are thousands of respectable men in Queensland, but they are superstitious, and allow their hopes of heaven to interfere with their growth in robust moral health, who are very much shocked at the elevation of Mr. Groom, and all because when they say the Lord's Prayer they smother it with so many words of their own, and with so much " religion " that they cannot see its beauties or feel its power.

Therefore I say with all humility that there is too much religion in the colonies and too little humanity, too many churches and chapels, and far too few theatres, too much work and too little play, and that what there is of this overmuch religion is not of the best kind, but of the lowest kind, that it leads to vanity and self-conceit, and widens the space between rich and poor, between lowly saint and lordly sinner, by which each loses much that would be of the greatest service to both. And finally, and I say it with reverence, knowing what I say, that for the colonies the Son of Man has yet to come, and up to the present very little has been done to hasten His coming.

CHAPTER XVI.

THE UNITED STATES.

IF we care to look at modern colonial life and compare it with the past and comprehend its spirit, we must live in the United States for more than six weeks at a time. Indeed, they are worth living in for many reasons for a much longer time than even six months. I should be content to live in this nation for ever but for one thing, and that one thing is that it persists in calling itself a great nation, and yet every day of its life it does one of the meanest things that can make man little or a nation little, and this daily exercise of this mean thing has become a part of its daily life, and greatly belittles the national life of this nation, which persists in calling itself great, but is not.

It is great certainly in one thing—it is the greatest pirate in recorded history. So great are its piratical acts that no one sees any immorality in them. Napoleon was not a murderer, he was a soldier, and the horrors with which he overspread the earth, or some of the fairest parts of it, are only not called murders because they are murders on a large scale.

If a man picked your pocket of a story which cost you twelve months to write you would not presently think it any the less a crime if the thief got it printed, sold it in thousands, made much profit by the transaction, and then excused himself for his theft by pointing to the fame which he had procured for you.

This is what the Americans do every day. You can't pick up a newspaper, no matter how respectable it is, but the best part of it consists of something stolen from the best men in England. All the bright things in the current *Temple Bar,* or the *Cornhill,* are at once appropriated; if there happens to be anything good in the *Saturday Review* it is at once transferred to the leading newspapers, and the small up-country weekly papers copy from the leading daily papers. This is common enough to a limited extent in England, but I only know of one paper here that lives entirely by its scissors, whereas in the United Sates, as in all the colonies, there are "editors" who never handle any other tool in making up their columns but a pair of scissors. If Mr. Louis Stevenson gives us a new story, not only is it at once put into a cheap form and sold for a "nickel," but it is copied into many newspapers. The same holds good with the short stories of Mr. Walter Besant, Mr. James Payn, Mr. Haggard, and others. And all the time that this piracy is going on the sneers and the abuse go on. If any garbage about the Queen or her family appears in a London paper it is at once laid hold of and put into large type with edifying remarks in a language that is only heard among riverfaring men. And if any trial is going on in the Law Courts in which some unhappy lords and ladies are implicated the proceedings are sent to New York as fast as lightning can carry them, and are printed in special editions. How many publishers and proprietors of newspapers in the United States have become rich by robbing English authors will never be known. It is easy enough to understand why their Government should impose taxes on pig iron, copper, and other articles of that sort, even though the Government has more idle money in its purse than it knows what to do with; but that this same Government, which is richer in hoarded coin than any Government in the world, should go on screwing money out of English authors is, to say the least of it, very remarkable.

There has been no piracy carried out on so vast a scale since the days of Sir Francis Drake.

Therefore I repeat that the people of the United States may call theirs a great nation, but it is essentially a little nation, because a great nation would not condescend to do acts of systematic piracy.

Drake turned pirate to please Queen Elizabeth;* but three centuries ago kings and queens were different beings to what they are now, and it is quite certain that if Lord Brassey, or any other yachtsman, was to go out on his own account and intercept some commercial steamer and take all its treasure and offer it to the Queen, the Queen, through one of her policemen, would certainly hand him over to a stipendiary magistrate.

We know that the "throneless homicide" of Waterloo

---

* "The quantite of bullion brought into ye Tower by Fr. Drake was of silver, it weighed 22,899 lbs., the coarse silver 512 lbs., and the gold 101 lbs.," in round numbers. This is not a vast sum, and the risk was great. There also was some glory in "singeing the King of Spain's beard." If there were any glory to be got by singeing English authors, or even any risk, I would be the last to make any reference to the matter.

was a murderer, because we know that he was a measureless liar, an All Evil Spirit whose

> " Evil deeds are writ in gore,"

and that weighed in the balance the hero dust

> " Is vile as vulgar clay."

And we know that the United States cannot be a great nation so long as it continues piratical practices, which are all the more despicable because its victims are too poor to put to sea in armed ships.

The truth is, that the United States have not yet grown out of their colonial smallness, their colonial vulgarity, their colonial religion, which dwarfs their morality; and they will continue to be colonials so long as they continue dependent on English art and English literature for their culture and pastime, obtained not by fair playing, but by thieving.

Let the United States show their greatness by becoming honest.* For my part I am morally sure that the high-spirited people of the United States never think of this wrong, any more than the English people ever thought of how they got their sugar at one time, or the godly people in Manchester—for there are a few such people in Manchester—ever thought of how they once got their cotton.

---

* It is retorted that we English steal more American books than the Americans steal of English books, and that if Mrs. Harriet Beecher Stowe had her rights she would be $200,000 richer to-day than she is. That is to say, we English people owe that lady for "Uncle Tom's Cabin" £20,000. Let us pay it. If I thought my banker would honour the draft I would draw on him for that amount, and send it to this lady, whom Americans say we have robbed. Let everybody in England who has read "Uncle Tom's Cabin" subscribe towards paying off this debt which Americans say we owe. I very well remember the first English edition of "Uncle Tom," which appeared thirty-five years ago. It was poorly printed and sold for a shilling. But how it was

I have great love and admiration for American people; especially those of its beautiful women, who do not know that they are beautiful any more than Eve knew she was naked before she took a certain apple. But that is the greater reason why I should talk plainly of their continuous thieving; for it must stop before it is too late for repentance, or the greatness of the United States will be indefinitely put off.

But I make bold to say that in a peculiar sense the Americans are not dependent on English art and English literature for their culture and pastime. It only seems that the Americans are thus dependent; the American people do not think about English literature, or English art, nor do they "feel after it." But when an English newspaper publishes a highly-flattering notice of an English writer's work, and this is copied into another and another paper, and the voice of the English press is as unanimous as a chorus of brass trumpets about an English novel, history, dictionary, poem, or other work, then the American publishers run for that work. No American publisher ever reads an English book before venturing on its publication in the United States; he simply reads the reviews of it, and the newspaper paragraphs which puff it up; in short,

devoured! It was read by everybody. I well remember saying in a public meeting after reading it "that the tears which that book had made to flow in England would fall on the fetters of the slave and dissolve them." Nor am I now ashamed of the words or of remembering them. Among the people whom I know to have derived great inspiration from that book who are now living are the Duke of Argyll, several Sutherlands, R. W. Dale, and Florence Nightingale. These alone are capable of stirring up the people to pay Mrs. Stowe. It is true that only a set of publishers ought to be made to pay up, and not the people; but as the people shared in the publishers' stealing they must be made to pay for it. What fun it would be. But then, as certain lewd Frenchmen say, "Englishmen have no sense of fun." So I suppose the thing will not be done.

he watches the market, and listens to the racket which is made in the market-place. It does not in the least matter if it be a clean or an unclean book, a great or a little book, if the thing is a much talked of book then there is no hesitation in publishing it. Literature in the United States, therefore, is simply a matter of trade, and reading English books is only a fashion. Americans deal in books as they deal in pigs, or pig iron, or oil, solely for the purpose of making money. This is the true colonial spirit; the spirit which subordinates everything connected with the fine as well as the industrial arts to the principle of getting on, the undivine science of trying to make the best of both worlds,* the old world and the new.

* The American people need not be dependent upon England for new books. One of these days there will be a list of American works produced by American authors in one year with a list of English works which have been stolen. It will then be seen how native American talent is rewarded, or rather how it is snubbed, belittled, put in a corner, and made to wait. If an American man of genius takes a really great work to Messrs. Harpy Pickpoke, Dam-the-Old-Ten and Co., these great publishers say to the American man of genius: "Thank you, so long as we can steal all we want we need buy nothing from you. But say, look here, why in thunder don't you go to England and publish there; they'll pay you well, better nor we, and then we can come to terms. You just try it." The baseness of this traffic in English books is only possible to a people who defended slavery for so long, who parted with it by accident, who made their coloured brethren citizens, and then set up a turnpike gate on the Republican highway through which all negroes must pass and pay toll to get to heaven, or even into the Post Office, while all white men and publishers go over free.

The following appeared in a London paper August 7, 1889 :—
"SPOILING MR. RIDER HAGGARD.
"Mr. Haggard's 'Cleopatra' is believed in by the publishers at any rate (says the American *Journalist*). The Messrs. Harper are the authorized representatives in America of the writer, but the return which they will be able to make to him will be of the smallest. The Munros followed the Harper edition within three days, and Rand, McNally and Co. followed with another. Perhaps the most amusing thing in connection with this legalized thieving is the statement of the proprietor of *Once a Week*. In his announcement of the publication of the book in his paper he says: 'In consequence of the unexpected receipt of the last chaper of "Cleopatra," we publish,' etc. The truth is that the enterprising owner of this sheet had clipped the columns of 'Cleopatra' as

Nor will the United States cease to retain its colonial complexion, even if they renounce all literary piracy and lead an honest life in that particular, unless they also do something more of far greater importance than recognizing the rights of authors, their instructors in wisdom and good taste. They must recognize the rights of man before they can become a great nation. They must carry out their own declaration of independence * before they have the right to call themselves the great Republic. For the past century this declaration of independence has only been so much bounce and bluster. The American people declare in a voice as loud as Niagara that all men are equal; but the voice has been as false as it has been loud, and is more false to-day than it was when it first uttered that declaration.

they came out in the *Sun*, and this 'unexpected receipt' was the cause of the sudden publication of the book by the Messrs. Harper. How much there is in the way a thing is put. 'In consequence of the unexpected receipt' sounds so much better than 'in consequence of an unexpected opportunity to steal the last chapter, we publish,' etc."

* "Our declaration of independence was held sacred by all, and thought to include all; but now to aid in making the bondage of the negro universal and eternal it is assailed and sneered at, and construed, and hawked at, and torn till if its framers could rise from their graves they could not at all recognize it. All the powers of earth seem rapidly combining against the negro. Mammon is after him, ambition follows, philosophy follows, and the theology of the day is fast joining the cry. They have him in his prison house; they have searched his person, and left no prying instrument with him. One after another they have closed the heavy iron doors upon him, *and now they have him as it were bolted in with a lock of a hundred keys, which can never be unlocked without the concurrence of every key; the keys in the hands of a hundred different men, and they scattered to a hundred different and distant places;* and they stand musing as to what invention in all the dominions of mind and matter can be produced to make the impossibility of his escape more complete than it is."— Abraham Lincoln's speech at Springfield, quoted in the *Century Magazine*, June, 1887.

These striking words of the martyred President are more emphatically true now than they were when spoken thirty years ago, while the words I have put in italics express with awful precision the political and social bondage of the negro in the United States at this present hour.

Therefore, the Americans are not a great nation, but only a provincial or at the best a colonial people, and they only pretend to be, or say they are a great nation, for they know well enough that in spirit they are mere colonials.

It is eighteen years since I first made the personal acquaintance of America, during which time I have visited many of the States several times at long and short intervals. My recollections are all pleasant. I have never had any trouble—except once, when I challenged a man to fight with equal pistols for a vulgar threat he launched at me and on account of the disparity in our size. I was the little one, but it ended in a whiskey sour. I have met with more noble men without titles in America than in my own country, including the titled ones; and, as I have before said, I love the American women, some better than others of course, but all better than I can express. Yet they are more colonial than the men. The American woman is only a subordinate when she is unconscious, and she is never conscious that she belongs to a great nation. No wealthy creole lady in Cuzco or Lima, Tucuman or Potosi, or in the West Indies, ever showed a more willing disposition to become the wife of an Hidalgo from Seville or Madrid, however poor he may be, than some of the rich creole * ladies of New York or Boston, Chicago or the States of New Jersey, or New England, to become the wives of Englishmen or English peers, no matter whether they were good men or bad. In fairness it should be said that this never happens without indignant comments from all, or nearly all who have married plain undecorated men.

* A creole is commonly supposed to be a person of colour. This is always the case in the States. It is a vulgar error. The word, as is well known outside the colonies, is made up of two Spanish words, the verb *criar*, to breed, or to bring up, and the adverb *alla*, there, in that place. A creole in common parlance is one born or raised out yonder, and has no connection with colour.

The changes which I have noticed, and are to be seen by all who are acquainted with the States, are great and worthy. I defy any Englishman, even though he has been to Jerusalem and Spain, India and Egypt, or wheresoever Cook and other couriers have conducted him, to visit the United States and not be wonder-stricken by the wonders which he shall see in that great country.

It was, perhaps, natural for me to be struck with what I am about to relate, because, go where I may, I am more interested in human beings than in bridges and railroads, or mines, steamboats, or even mountains, icebergs, or trees four hundred feet high. The lakes are glorious. Niagara is the most beautiful thing I have ever seen, but none of these things move me so much as the people. Any man with eyes can see that if it is possible for man to make a great nation, greater than any that has ever been, the men of the United States will do it. That is my firm conviction. But it will take more than five hundred years from now to accomplish. Such speculations as these, however, are not reminiscences, and I resume my tale of things which I have seen.

Last year I made the acquaintance in New York of a scholarly man, who on account of his being a native-born American and possessing an uncommon vision attracted my notice, and our acquaintance ripened into friendship. During the early period of our intimacy we were a good deal together, and together we visited some of the popular institutions of New York. One of the most ephemeral of these is the Young Men's Christian Association. My friend and I strolled into the building to see what was going on. We were no sooner inside and began to take an interest in the proceedings, than one of the Christian young men, with a Bible in his hand, came to us and said in a sweet, low voice —

"We do not admit negroes."

My scholarly friend is a negro, and his manners are as good as mine, or yours, or anybody's. There is nothing the matter with him except that he is black.

I was thunderstruck. I turned to my friend, who said to me in a tone of voice which I shall never forget —

"We must go. Come."

We did go, but not before I spoke to that Christian young man, and said in a sweet, low voice—but it was pure imitation —

"You Christian young men *may* go to heaven, but take my word for it, you are just now on the track which goes in the very opposite direction."

And he went on with his Bible studies, and I went out with my negro.*

To say that I was suffocated, mad, and shrivelled up, is to say a small thing. It was in this way that the

* Here is an extract from a newspaper of the day on which the above was written:—"St. Louis, Missouri, May 24.—In the general assembly of the southern Presbyterian Church on Monday morning, the special committee on organic or co-operative union, consisting of thirteen ministers and thirteen elders, made a majority and minority report. The majority report had sixteen signatures and favoured union, on conditions that the church, as a religious organization, consents to totally eschew politics in every shape and form, and that the negro membership in the church must worship separately and distinct from their white brethren and meet in separate sessions for church legislation. It is considered extremely doubtful that the northern branch of the church, now in session at Omaha, will accept these terms. The minority report, signed by the members of the committee, vehemently opposes unification in any form. Action on the reports was deferred."

We are distinctly told in the Acts of the Apostles that Philip sat with an Ethiopian while he opened up to him the Scriptures and rode in the same carriage with him. Who are these Presbyterian Democrats that dare fly in the face of apostolical practice? (see Acts viii., 27, 38).

negro question first pressed itself on my attention, but since then I have made up for lost time. I continue to be amazed at my own ignorance, but every day I make a point of learning something new on this vital question. It is the one question that will keep the United States in a subordinate position until it is settled on the lines of their declaration of independence. They will not cease to be mere colonials until they act up to that declaration. It is quite impossible for the bulk of Englishmen to understand this matter. They do not understand the difference between Republican and Democrat, and there is not, probably, a single editor in London who a year ago knew the meaning of mugwump, and but very few—they may be counted on the left-hand fingers—who know the meaning at this moment. And it is impossible for anyone who takes an interest in human affairs to care for these distinctions unless he knows that they are of vital importance to the progress of the human race in all that is excellent and precious in all the wide world.

These political distinctions exist in the States because the declaration of independence is a mere literary document, and not an article of faith for the guidance of human conduct. It certainly never seemed possible that I, who am nothing but a pair of hands and feet used for fetching and carrying knowledge from the ends of the earth to the heads of departments, should ever find anything worthy of notice in a Mugwump, a Michigan Republican, or a Democrat from the Mississippi, and I now find that these distinctions carry more interest than the distinctions of Whig and Tory, Radical and Conservative, for they concern humanity more.

The future Presidents of the United States will be elected by the negro vote.*

This startling statement can only be fully appreciated by those who understand the difference between Mugwump, Republican, and Democrat.

And yet the negro is not admitted into the assemblies of the Young Men's Christian Association in New York!

This Christian young men's insolence is a mere straw in the street, but it tells which way the wind blows down on the river. The negro is not allowed to share in the Lord's Supper when it is spread in Holy Trinity Church. The negro was good enough to fight for during one particular crisis in the history of the States. The blood of some Americans was good enough to redeem the "niggers" from slavery, but the sacrifice of the Saviour was not meant for negroes!

This is a mistake, and arises solely from the colonial mind caring more for religion than for morality.

* This is a very serious thing. It appears that the white population of the United States, increasing at the rate of twenty per cent. per annum, doubles itself every thirty-five years. The black population, increasing at the rate of thirty-five per cent. in ten years, doubles itself in twenty years. Hence we find:

Whites in Southern States in 1880 (in round numbers)	12,000,000
Whites in Southern States in 1985...	96,000,000
Blacks in Southern States in 1880...	6,000,000
Blacks in Southern States in 1980...	192,000,000

In the year 1902, or thirteen years hence, each of the States lying between Maryland and Texas will have a coloured majority within its borders; and there will be eight minor republics of the Union, in which either the coloured race will rule or a majority will be disfranchised.

So that not only are the United States a subordinate people, they stand confronted with the possibility of becoming subordinated to the people whose race they once enslaved. Will the United States, by persistent blindness to their own national dignity, hasten the time when the declaration of independence shall be interpreted as excluding the white race?—See an "Appeal to Cæsar," by A. W. Tourgée. New York: Fords, Howard, and Hulbert.

I do not say, of course, that the object and purpose of the civil war between the North and the South was to liberate the negro from bondage. Far be it from me to say so. It is, however, the commonly received opinion, and it is not altogether wrong; that is, it is sufficient. The object of the war was the preservation of the Union. The Union remains intact, but slavery has gone to the devil, and will never be restored, hence the common opinion that the war was undertaken for the abolition of slavery. To prevent the possibility of the South ever again enslaving the negro the Republican party made the negro a citizen—a full citizen of that great and free country. That is to say, the negro was made free in order that he might defend the freedom which is set forth in the declaration of independence. And there is no question that this was a wise thing to do and worthy. A negro now can only become a slave in the same way that a white can become a slave. This equality of rights is fully recognized by Mugwump and Republican although not so fully by the Democrat. But a negro is not allowed to partake of the Lord's Supper when it is spread in Holy Trinity Church. This is unwise and unworthy. But it is essentially a colonial view. When the United States cease to be colonial all the citizens of the States will have equal rights in no limited sense, whether they are black or whether they be white. So long as there are citizens in the United States who can slam the door in the face of other citizens, and can keep them out, and can refuse to allow them to partake of supper with them, when the supper has been prepared for both by the Lord, so long must the United States hold a subordinate position. They are not a great nation.

I will give the latest instance that has occurred up to

now of the colonial spirit which rules in the United States. An Act has lately received the signature of the President called the Inter-State Commerce Act, one section of which reads as follows :—

" It shall be unlawful for any common carrier, subject to the provisions of this Act, to make or give any undue or unreasonable preference or advantage to any particular person, company, firm, corporation, or locality, or any particular description of traffic in any respect whatsoever, or to subject any particular person, company, firm, corporation or locality, or any particular description of traffic to any undue or unreasonable prejudice or disadvantage in any respect whatsoever."

The negroes naturally saw in this provision a protection for themselves against the injustice and insolent tyranny to which they are as much exposed on railroads as at the Lord's Supper, and they prepared a document which had better be given at length, as it will explain much. It is as follows :—

" *To the Honourable Inter-State Railroad Commissioners.*

" As constituents of railroads whose operations are governed by the Inter-State Commerce Law, we respectfully ask you to place a construction on the third section of the said Act. In our opinion the evident spirit and letter of the law is to obviate discriminations of all kinds, whether of person or property.

" The discriminations of which we complain are against persons of African descent; throughout all the Southern States, with the possible exception of one or two, persons of African descent travel at great inconvenience and disadvantage by reason of the inferior accommodation accorded them by railroads. A few among the many disadvantages and inconveniences which we suffer are as follows :—

"First, We complain because in travelling *we pay the same amount for fare from place to place that any other class of passengers does* but do not receive the same equal and indiscriminate comforts, privileges, and advantages from the road selling the ticket. For instance, we pay five dollars and twenty-five cents for a ticket labelled 'first-class' from Atlanta to Montgomery. On entering the train we are assigned, peaceably if possible *by force if necessary,* by the officers in charge of the train who claim to be acting under orders from superiors, to some particular car known in the common parlance of this section of the country as the 'Jim Crow' car, 'Smoker,' or 'Negro Annex,' *which is always inferior in every respect to cars occupied by white passengers paying the same fare, and travelling between the same points,* which car is also *the retreat for drunkards and all low and unprincipled characters of the travelling public of other races,* thereby subjecting *our wives and children, mothers and sisters, to horrible outrages and indignities and forcing them to listen to language which is heard in the brothel and seraglio.*

"Secondly, We complain because the cleanliness, ventilation, and sanitation of the cars to which we are assigned are not such as will conduce to the best health of passengers.

"Thirdly, We complain because of the injustice involved in this sort of treatment, and because of the injurious effect it has upon the morals of any people who are subjected to such indignities; that is to say, that filthy and squalid surroundings have an effect detrimental to the highest intellectual and moral development of any people who come in contact with them. We are aware that the railroads claim to give equal but separate accommodations. A casual investigation will prove that the accommodations, while separate, are not equal; and if they were equal yet separate, would this condition satisfy the demands of the law?

"In our opinion the grievances herein enumerated can

and should be remedied by that section of the Inter-State Commerce Act now in existence, known as section third.

"Each and every allegation contained in this petition can be proved if a question arises in the mind of the commission as to its truthfulness.

"In view of these facts, we whose names are hereunto subscribed in behalf of our race whose rights and privileges are being trampled upon, and whose patience, long-suffering and forbearance is being tried, respectfully ask your interpretation of the third section of the Inter-State Commerce Act.—Very respectfully, J. S. FLIPPER, H. A. RUCKER, J. N. BLACKSHEAR, J. W. YOUNG."

This document speaks for itself. It is written by negroes, and signed by negroes, who are citizens of the United States. Again, it is scarcely possible to open a newspaper without encountering some shocking tidings of the lynching of negro citizens by white citizens of the United States. There are sinful negroes as well as sinful whites who break the laws. Both have equal rights to be tried in the courts, but this right is frequently denied to the negro, and negroes are taken by force out of gaol by white citizens, and without trial—simply on rumour or very flimsy testimony—are hanged in the fields. Such citizens do not belong to a great nation, because a great nation does not allow such things to happen, for various and serious reasons.

I am quite aware of what has taken place in Ireland, and still stand to my statement that a great nation does not allow one set of citizens to hang another set of citizens on their own responsibility, and without taking some sufficient notice of it.

A negro cannot marry a white nor a white marry with a negro in the United States. The utmost license will be allowed in the mingling of these races, but it is against the law to marry; and the United States cannot be allowed to call themselves a great nation without exciting much derision so long as they abide by that law.

If Othello were to come to the United States, bringing Desdemona with him, they would not be allowed to stay at the Brevoort House, nor Palmer House, nor Sherman House, nor Cleveland House, nor Hoar House, nor Hoffman House, nor any of the fashionable houses; nor travel in a Pulman Car, nor take the sacrament in Holy Trinity Church, if they had a mind to do so. They would not be received in society. Their marriage would have been illegal.

* Now I understand for the first time why it was that Forest played Othello in a copper-coloured skin, and not in blacklead.

The Republican party made the negro a citizen of the United States. The Democratic party have never recognized the full legality of that act. The negroes naturally voted for and with the Republican party, and by that means the Republican party held a long lease of power, during which time the Republican party would go to the Lord's Supper with the Democrats, and Democrats and Republicans agreed together to slam the door in the face of the citizen whose face had been burnished by the sun, and keep him from partaking of the same table. The Republicans at one time had it in their power to make a full citizen of the negro, after they had made him one by statute, but they joined the Democrats in not doing it.

"We cannot make citizens by Act of Parliament," say the people of the United States. Therefore, by their own confession, the United States are only a subordinate people. They are not a great nation.

The mugwump is a dissatisfied Republican who will vote

for measures, not for men, merely because they belong to the Republican party ; for good measures and a good President, even if they have to seek for them in Democratic Nazareth. Therefore, there is some hope that the United States will not for ever continue to be an agglomeration of colonies. They may become a great nation.

"We are engaged," observes the Reverend Dr. Strong,* "in what Lord Bacon called the 'heroic work of *making a nation*,' for which heroic sacrifices are demanded; and our plea is not America for America's sake, but America for the world's sake." The Doctor means well, but his eloquence not unfrequently makes him blind to the truth of some of his own sayings.

By living in the United States for a sufficient length of time we may see a mean colonial spirit actuating fifty or sixty millions of people. It is the same spirit which presided over the silver colonies of Peru and which presides over the gold colonies of Australia. They all worship one god at the behest of him who said "All these things will I give thee if thou wilt fall down and worship me;" and nothing makes people so much alike in looks and ways as worshipping at one and the same shrine.

It is only fair to hear what an American has to say on behalf of his country.

Bishop A. Cleveland Coxe, in an article upon "Government by Aliens," printed in the August number of the *Forum* of last year, says:—

"We are confronted by the terrible fact that we are undergoing changes similar to those which have been the ruin of ancient peoples in many examples. Successive invasions of Spain made for her a mongrel race, and have

---

* "Our Country: Its Possible Future and its Present Crisis," by the Rev. Joseph Strong, D.D. New York: Baker and Taylor, Bond Street.

fastened upon her a chronic state of decay and imbecility. The great world-changes of the sixth century were effected by the movements of Goths and Vandals pouring into the sunny south, as the Gulf Stream rushes into the cold waters of the north. The Salian Franks made a great kingdom, but they did so by wiping the Gauls out of their inheritance as one wipes a platter. In a more stealthy fashion, but with equal powers to obliterate, hordes of barbarians are now flooding our fair estate, and taking possession of our heritage. We do not recognize the immigration as an invasion, which it really is, simply because the invaders land without arms and ammunition. We forget that they come with weapons of fatal import to our civilization and to our race. Vice, ignorance, corruption, superstition, and hereditary enslavement to a foreign Court which makes war upon all free institutions are the destructive elements, worse than dynamite bombs, which they distribute through the land. What boots their lack of guns and bayonets? We give the invaders votes, and they are soon drilled and magnified into a 'balance of power' which makes them our masters. Look at the City of New York—invaded, seized, and held by aliens, who have presumed to make it the seat of war; turning its Government into the hands of a religious sect governed by priests; conquering and now sacking the metropolis, and even raising an alien flag over our *hôtel de ville,* not merely as a menace and a defiance to the older inhabitants, but as a step toward embroiling us in the political conflict that rages between England and Ireland. The alien flag is the symbol of organized warfare upon a great nation with which we are professedly at peace. Our invaders, who have sworn fidelity to our laws, and who claim to be Americans, are practically Irish, and nothing but Irish always. Everybody knows that they are engaged in supplying the sinews of war, if not destructive weapons, to the factions that stained Phœnix Park with the blood of a cowardly assassination, and that placed dynamite under London Bridge and in the lobbies of the

Parliament Palace at Westminster. Such facts are serious tokens of a political decay which works towards dissolution. We are rapidly becoming a conquered people.

"Is there national spirit left among us (the Bishop concludes) to assert that the time has come to govern America by honest American voters, and to demand that no such prefix as Irish or German or Mormon shall be suffered to qualify the American name? If not, free institutions and popular government must perish even here. Have we so speedily reached the terminus predicted, as by Cassandra herself, in the pregnant warnings of that pure and lofty genius, Fisher Ames? He said, long years ago:—'The sovereign power being nominally in the hands of all, will be effectually within the grasp of a few, who will combine, intrigue, lie, and fight to engross it to themselves. . . . The idle, the ambitious, and the needy will band together to break the hold that law has upon them, and then to get hold of law. . . . Our country is too big for union, too sordid for patriotism, too democratic for liberty.' But even this far-seeing statesman had nothing to forewarn him of the real character of the combinations which have actually come to pass; of alienism entering like a Trojan horse, drawn over broken walls by our own infatuated hands, and already threatening our inheritance with *Fuit Ilium* for our premature and ignoble epitaph."

CHAPTER XVII.

SPAIN.

WHEN I was preparing my translation of the "Don Quixote" for publication I went a second time to Spain, and passed several weeks in Albarracin, Teruel, Calatayud, Daroca, and Valencia, in the very heart of the Castiles, and lived in a house not far from Daroca, which, three centuries ago, was the home of renowned hidalgos and fine women not a few. This is a region in which it is possible to catch glimpses of the power and glory of Spain, when Spain was in the height of her glory, and to realize what a wonderful country it must have been. Here, if a company of a dozen men wanted a holiday, they might enjoy some of the ruins of departed splendour, the enduring glories of a landscape which man cannot spoil, and live on the fat of the land for tenpence a day. I am astonished that Spain is so little visited by men who can paint, women who can sketch, and others who would understand the present time by moving amongst some of the finest monuments of the past. But it is absolutely needful to be able to converse, to joke, and to sing songs in the native language. The most learned man in the world visiting Spain would be considered a nobody if he could not speak, and speak well, the Castilian tongue. The old house in which I stayed as a guest was in perfect preservation, but its contents were in a state of hopeless confusion. Pieces of quaint old furniture were thrown into one corner, covered up with old folios in vellum and gold. In another corner were old wood carvings, pictures, pieces of gilt leather embossed, ancient manuscripts which the rats had been investigating for their own selfish purposes—like some English historians at Simancas have done with the old records which are there—pieces of ancient armour, covered with rust, and tattered flags, to say nothing of the men servants and maid servants who waited on me, laughed at my questions, and made me laugh with them at their simple ways and speech.

The old gentleman who occupied this ancient house lived in one of its smallest rooms, where he slept and took his meals. A rich mine of manganese had some time before been discovered on his land, and there were deposits of fine hematite iron ore to be seen everywhere. Coal was also abundant, and also close by, and Don Felipé de Quiñones, as poor as a church mouse, was living in hope that some day these riches would be turned into ready money. He knew no more than a child what was to be done to get the iron and coal to market. When he found that I knew something of these things he began to thaw, and carried me from one place to another where the hematite ore cropped out in marvellous abundance. The hills were simply masses of fine rich iron ore, the like of which I have not seen either in Cumberland or Bilboa, or on the Agogebic range. One day he took me to see the works of *los antiguos*—the ancients, probably the Phœnicians—and lo! a vertical chimney had been bored through one of the highest hills, at the foot of which could still be seen the hearth where the ore was smelted into iron. This is probably one of the oldest blast furnaces in the world. The slag which is lying about is very rich in iron, and resembles what is known as kidney ore. So interested did I become that Don Felipé waked up under my influence. I plied him with schemes, and so effectually excited his avarice that I found it difficult to leave him. The dinners became much improved, the wine was better, and we sat up later at night. There was nothing he would not do for me. At length he found out a way to detain me, which I could not resist. Among his old books was a copy of the first edition of "Don Quixote," printed in Madrid, 1605. It was the veritable first edition which I call *the shirt-tail edition*, to distinguish it from the other first edition, which was really the second, published in the same year by Juan de la Cuesta, in which the knots made out of the shirt-tail to make the rosary of are changed into gall nuts. I believe there are not more than five or six copies of this shirt-tail edition in the world. Don Felipé there and then made me a present of this book, which perhaps Cervantes himself had not only seen, but handled. If I had found a fragment of the tables of stone on which the original Ten Commandments were written I could not have been more affected. There was no sleep for me that night, and although I had read the book a score of times already, I did nothing but sit in the sun all the next day reading it once more and laughing and crying over it more than ever. All the iron and the coal and the manganese of the world became as mere dirt to me. I cared no more about the blast furnace of the Phœnicians than I cared about last year's clouds. Don Felipé could not move me out of my corner and away from my glorious companion. I was with Cervantes in his own beloved Spain, beneath his own sky, hearing him talk, seeing him smile, and asking him questions, which were answered in a most sweet voice. I did not want any dinner or to go to bed. I only cared for some Rioja, of which there was plenty, a favourite wine of Cervantes. Don Felipé was too good; certainly too courteous to take me away from my book, but to my disgust he came and sat by me and began to talk.

"Why, think you Don Alejandro, did Cervantes write this book?" he asked, intending to draw me away from it, and to talk about iron ore.

But I wasn't to be drawn away; wild horses could not have drawn me away. I said in answer to this—

"You know, Don Felipé, that Cervantes had served under Don Juan of Austria and had greatly distinguished himself, and when he would return to Spain he carried on his person letters to Philip II. from Don John, which set forth all his bravery and the noble example he had set at the battle of Le Panto, and you know that when Cervantes was taken captive and carried to Algiers these letters were found on him, and you also know that it was these letters which made Dey Azan think so much of Cervantes that he took special care of him, loading him with chains and keeping him in the cellar of his own house, believing that not only Philip II. but all Spain, would part with all their gold, and even sell the shirts off their backs to ransom such a man as this. You know, also, how Cervantes behaved in his captivity—how he was always plotting to escape—and yet, when all his fellow captives expected that he would be impaled or hanged when his plots were discovered, the Dey did not even scourge him, partly because there was something divine about this noble Spaniard, but chiefly because he still believed that all Spain would even sell the shirts off their backs to pay his ransom. It must be also well known to you, Don Felipé, that Cervantes wrote often to Philip II., telling the King of the twenty thousand Spanish Christian captives held in bondage in Algiers, urging him in the name of his father Charles the Great, in the sacred name of Christ, and by all the obligations of a Knight of the Cross to come to the rescue of these captives. He showed how easily their redemption could be accomplished, and reminded him of the glory with which he would be covered if he sent a sufficient armada against this infernal tyrant, whose daily cruelties were turning many noble Spaniards into renegades, losing their souls in order to save their bodies from pain. But Philip II. was at that time too much occupied in the Netherlands to attend to the ravings of a mere captive dreaming in the baginos of Algiers, and the letters of Cervantes remained unheeded. In 1580 Cervantes returned to Spain. He had been absent nine years, five of which were spent in cruel captivity, two years in active service in war, one year in the domestic service of the Colonna, and the rest of the time in hospital or travelling through Italy."

Don Felipé had more than once shown a little restlessness, but he was now all attention, and turned his face full on mine, as I continued—

"Cervantes who you remember lost the use of his left arm in the service of his country, found it very difficult to get employment of any sort. He was willing to do anything, even to go to Peru as an exciseman, if only to earn his bread. But he was neglected, and probably he was proud and hated the idea of standing on some hidalgo's door-mat waiting for an answer to his application to serve the State. He did go to Portugal and served under the famous Santa Cruz. Then he found some time after some subordinate employment at Seville in the commissariat department, for which he was not fitted, but it involved much travelling about the country, buying up provisions for the galleys of Spain. His profession brought him in contact with the highest and lowest class of men and made him acquainted with village customs and general rustic life. There is a tradition that he was thrown into gaol in a village of La Mancha for libelling a lady of Toboso, that he was also confined in a gaol in the town of Argamasilla, where some believe, if he did not write his 'Don Quixote,' he designed it. It is certain that Cervantes suffered much from poverty through the treachery of false friends and the neglect of all who should have been proud to help this maimed and noble soldier."

"Ah, Don Alejandro," said Don Felipé, "the world never knows its great men."

"Es la verdad," I replied. "But see how lengthy an answer I am making to your short question. 'Why did Cervantes write the "Don Quixote?"' Bear with me a little longer; I will give you the best answer I can. When Cervantes began to write the 'Don Quixote' he was more than fifty years old; he was fifty-eight when he published it. He had seen much of the world, and probably more of Spain than any strolling player, or missionary priest, or muleteer. He was an avaricious reader, he sympathized with all men, and could find something good in the most stupid book ever printed. He associated with Jews, Gipsies, Moors, carriers, soldiers, wine growers, wits, and men of the highest distinction in every walk of life. He was a personal friend of Don Bernardo de Sandoval y Rojas, Cardinal Archbishop of Toledo, a learned and most humane man, and of many others who mourned over the corruption of manners, the degradation of letters, and the immoralities, irregularities, and puerilities of the stage. The best writers, orators, and the holiest of men tried in vain to put down the novels of the day, but the more these holy men preached against the loves of Amadis and Oriana, the indiscretions of the Imperial Princess with Belianis, the revels of el Caballero Don Cupido, and the very naughty things that were to be found in the Amadis of Greece, the more did everybody read these pernicious books; and to bring them more into fashion the Government put a tax on them, and the higher the tax and the more lewd the book, the more it was multiplied and read."

"All that I never knew, Don Alejandro," said Don Felipé.

"It is quite true," I continued; "indeed, before the 'Don Quixote' had been published a year the revenue of the Government fell off so seriously owing to this tributary stream having been dried up that political economists wrote on the subject and complained; for I have no doubt that you, Don Felipé, know well enough that not one more of these lascivious books was again printed in Spain after the appearance of the 'Don Quixote.'"

"I had heard it so said," he replied; "but never appreciated the statement until now."

"Very well then I go on. Wearied with neglect, weighted with poverty, bowed down with insult, Cervantes resolved that he would make his ungrateful country repent its conduct towards him. And now I must translate for you an English story as it is told by one of the greatest of English writers of prose.* But I warn you that the story will lapse into nothing at all unless you yourself are able to dilate it by expansive sympathy with its sentiment. "A young officer (in what army, no matter) had so far forgotten himself in a moment of irritation as to strike a private soldier, full of personal dignity (as sometimes happens in all ranks) and distinguished for his courage. The inexorable laws of military discipline forbade to the injured soldier any practical redress—he could look for no retaliation by acts. Words only were at his command; and in a tumult of indignation, as he turned away, the soldier said to his officer that he would 'make him repent it.' This wearing the shape of a menace naturally rekindled the officer's anger and intercepted any disposition which might be rising within him towards a sentiment of remorse; and thus the irritation between the two grew hotter than before. Some time after this a partial action took place with the enemy. Suppose yourself a spectator and looking down into a valley occupied by the two armies. They are facing each other, you see, in martial array. But it is no more than a skirmish which is going on; in the course of which however an occasion suddenly arises for a desperate service. A redoubt which has fallen into the enemy's hands must be recaptured at any price, and under circumstances of all but hopeless difficulty. A strong party has volunteered for the service; there is a cry for somebody to head them. You see a soldier step out from the ranks to assume this dangerous leadership. The party moves rapidly forward; in a few minutes it is swallowed up from your

---

* De Quincey, "Autobiographic Sketches." James Hogg, Edin., 1853, p. 127.

eyes in clouds of smoke; for one half-hour from behind these clouds you receive hieroglyphic reports of bloody strife, fierce repeating signals, flashes from the guns, rolling musketry, and exulting hurrahs advancing or receding, slackening or redoubling. At length all is over; the redoubt has been recovered; that which was lost is found again; the jewel which had been made captive is ransomed with blood. Crimsoned with glorious gore the wreck of the conquering party is relieved and at liberty to return. From the river you see it ascending. The plume-crested officer in command rushes forward, with his left hand raising his helmet in homage to the blackened fragments of what was once a flag, whilst with his right hand he seizes that of the leader, though no more than a private in the ranks. The soldier, stepping back, and carrying his open hand through the beautiful motions of the military salute to a superior, makes this immortal answer—that answer which shut up for ever the memory of the indignity offered to him, even whilst for the last time alluding to it—'Sir,' he said, '*I told you that I would make you repent it.*'" Has not all Spain repented of its insults to its soldier-hero, who was never anything but a private, although he heads the entire army? Even now not a soul knows where the bones of Cervantes rest, but the meanest Spaniard that lives knows that when he died there died the greatest of them all. The most highly decorated Spaniard could do nothing for Cervantes but insult him, and there is not a Spaniard now living that would not kiss his bones if he knew where to find them, and who is not consumed with ineffectual repentance for the treatment which hastened their one great man to his nameless grave."

"Hombre, vamos á comer!" said Don Felipé; and I,

looking at my watch, found that it was long past the hour to dine, so we went in to dinner.

Happily for me the next day was one of cold rain—although it was the middle of June; walking about to look at hematite iron ore was impossible, and I was left in peace to read my most precious and absorbing book, then made more dear to me than ever. A couple of hours before dinner I was so cold that I thought I would go for a run over the hills. Don Felipé thought I was mad. "You'll catch your death of cold; you will be laid up with rheumatism; pray do not go."

I begged of him to have filled for me the large wooden trough that was in my room with cold water, and I would return in an hour. He, thinking that I was about to make some experiment, promised to do so.

I came back dripping with perspiration, and found half-a-dozen lasses carrying water up the great staircase in long jars on their heads, and looking like so many living caryatides stepping out of a frieze. The tub was nearly full, I dismissed the caryatides, and began to undress, when, to my astonishment, I found these curious maids anxiously looking on through an open window at the other end of the large room. I sent them away with some very harsh words. They ran to tell Don Felipé, who, in great terror, rushed into the room to see what I was up to. He found me splashing about in the tub. He began to call on a great number of saints in pious ejaculations, and I was out of the tub rubbing myself down before he had finished.

He hurried out to look after the dinner, I believe; and when I joined him, instead of finding me pale and trembling with cold, he saw me red, warm, and happy, he was agreeably surprised, and inquired if that was an English custom. When I told him that all English gentlemen in sound health tumbled into a tub of cold water every morning all the year round, in winter and summer, he exclaimed, good-naturedly —

"Que barbaros son estos Inglesas"—what barbarians these Englishmen are.

I was very glad to find that Don Felipé was quite ready to resume our talks on Don Quixote. He was only the second or third Spaniard whom I met in Spain who did not get away from the subject as quickly as possible. Of course I do not include my friends Don Pascual de Gayangos or Don José Maria de Asensio. I have sat up for hours together with these learned Cervantistas talking of nothing else but the neology of the famous man who was as great a coiner of words as Shakespeare was, and more remarkable as an inventor of names.

I had brought with me from Seville a copy of the recently-discovered letter of Cervantes, which was found in the Biblioteca Colombina by el Señor Don Aureliano Fernandez-Guerra y Orbé, and as this magnificent "find" was quite unknown to my host, I thought I would try his patience and my own skill in making known its literary value.

The next morning, therefore, as we were sipping our early chocolate, I asked him if chocolate was a Spanish word, hoping to wean him away from his beloved hematite, and his manganese, and my magnificent schemes.

"Of course it is a Spanish word," he said.

After a good deal of gentle manœuvring on my part he acknowledged that he was wrong, that he was grateful for my learned company, and would never forget that the original word was chocolalt, and that it came from Mexico.

"Now," I said, "Don Felipé, as I have told you this great secret, and added, although little, yet something to your knowledge, do me the favour to tell me in return for this service why it was that Don Quixote, after many promises to visit Zaragosa, not only did not go there, but after getting almost in sight of the city, where he intended to take part in the great tournament that had been announced so long before, he turned his back on it in disgust and went to Barcelona instead?"

"You, my dear Don Alejandro," he said, "can better make answer to that long question than I can, and therefore I beseech you to answer it for me, and I shall listen with joyous gratitude."

"I tell you, Don Felipé, that it will make you happy for the next six weeks, and when I am gone —"

"I pray you not to mention your going."

"When I am gone you will be delighted that I ever came, and I shall always think of you as often as I think of Don Quixote, and I do not expect ever to give up thinking about him, either on this side the grave or the other."

He smiled, rolled up another cigarette, and ordered me to go on.

"You have read the false 'Don Quixote,' by Avellaneda?" I began.

"How could I read a false 'Don Quixote'?" he exclaimed. "Is there in the world such a book as a false 'Don Quixote'?"

"Oh! oh!" I said, with some excitement. "This will be as great a glory as a three days' bull fight."

On which he exploded a volume of inarticulate satirical

incredulity. For a bull fight to a full-grown Spaniard to last three days would be like all the hydrants in London running free gin for the same period to its male and female roughs, and why an exhibition of so much cruelty and cowardice should so delight a mob of ten thousand Spaniards is as inexplicable to me as the ever-recurring description of this brutal sight by English travellers in Spain.

"Yes," I answered, "Avellaneda published a second part of 'Don Quixote' in which, knowing as he did that Cervantes intended to take his hero to Zaragosa, he devotes three chapters to the Virgin de Pilar, the patron, you know, of that famous city. This book came into the hands of Cervantes at the time that he was just writing the advent of Don Quixote to Zaragosa, and when Cervantes read it he broke out into a rage so terrible that as you read you can perceive it must have been a rage that was increased by intense pain. For Cervantes had intended to be very humorous, and playfully satirical, in dealing with the worship of the Virgin de Pilar."

"Como?" exclaimed Don Felipé, opening his eyes with energy.

"Oh, yes, my dear Don Felipé," I answered, "you must bear with me and with Cervantes in this matter. Remember that he had been nine years away from Spain, travelling through Europe, and living, or rather dying, in slavery in Africa. He had mingled with all kinds of men; he had noted their morals and been moved by their immoralities; he had seen the awful divorce of religion from morality; he had pondered on the inhumanity of man to man, and all this while human life was a dread reality to him, while shams of all kinds claimed his most serious thoughts, for he pitied man, and laughed at the delusions which man imposes upon himself. I must also tell you that Cervantes made the acquaintance of some of the early reformers of Spain, who were hunted from pillar to post, ' from Meca to Zeca,' who had to hide in hovels and stables, and in mountain caves, from the wrath of Philip and the myrmidons of the Inquisition, and if he did not believe their doctrines he sympathized with them in their toils. You must keep all this in mind as you think of Cervantes turning the stream of his sunny satire on to the worship of the Virgin de Pilar. 'I know that it is difficult for you to remember this, or to make any allowance for a man whose experience of life is so much wider and deeper than your own. You, my dear Don Felipé, have never been out of Spain. You have, as you tell me, lived all your days in Castile. You know nothing of the hardness of man, nothing of the corruption and the arrogance and tyranny of priests who have frightened men and women out of their souls, nothing of the moral slavery in which millions of Italians, Frenchmen, and Englishmen were then held. The cries of the victims of Saint Bartholomew were still ringing in the ears of Cervantes, mingled with the laughter of Philip when the news of that massacre reached him. Cervantes knew that the Netherlanders were fighting for liberty against Philip's troops, against a persecution which makes us tremble for the name of man when you read the history. And Cervantes knew better than any man then living that Spain and all her people were as fond of vice in all its varied forms as Philip himself was. He knew that the people were profoundly ignorant—in morals deeply degraded—for the books they read were as demoralizing as the plays they saw on the stage, and that the Church which watched over the good of the community was in its officers as unholy, cruel, and tyrannical as he who was the head of the State."

"Por Dios Señor Don Alejandro Vuestra merced es algo exaltado," said Don Felipé, breaking in.

"I will be as calm as I can," I replied. "I say that it was inevitable for Cervantes not to see, to feel, and to know that there was no inherent quality in Spain that could justify her in lording it over other people. Much less was there any morality in her to qualify her for dictating what other people should believe, and that it was the people's own fault if they lived in slavery or in terror, and their own pusillanimity which made them sweat to win money in order that Philip might walk up to his knees in human blood as he went to say mass or to worship the Virgin de Pilar. *Basta!* Now when Cervantes found that Avellaneda had handled the subject of this worship in a gross and carnal way in his false 'Don Quixote,' Cervantes shrank from it as you, Don Felipé, would shrink from pollution, and so instead of the joust at Zaragosa we have the visit to Barcelona, and a series of isolated and unexpected accidents for which no preparation had been made, and which are not linked with anything that has gone before, all sprung upon the reader as if to bewilder him or make him forget the way he has come, in order, apparently, to show that the road leads to nowhere. This, querido Don Felipé, is one of the greatest disappointments you shall meet with in the whole range of secular fiction. It can only be likened to the 'Merchant of Venice'—which I am glad to see you have translated into Spanish, with the trial scene omitted—in which the revenge of the bloody-minded Jew is backed up. His plot of vengeance is supported by a technical and masterful reading of law, and the cup of Christian blood is carried to the thirsting lips of revenge when it is dashed to the ground by the wit of a woman. Without that scene Shylock would be to us nothing more than a common-place 'bull' or 'bear' on the Rialto of Venice. This is the fatal loss we have in our 'Don Quixote.' Zaragosa and the Virgin of the Pillar are left out. The great promise remains unfulfilled. Dulcinea remains a garlic-eating wench—

> "'She glided like a spirit, and her light
> Did all fantastic seem. And yet her form
> Was human, I touched, yea—felt its substance,
> She, too, had mortal fears, and woman-like
> Shrank back with crimson modesty!
> Then like illusion faded—
> And unsubstantial melted quite away.
> If now to nice conjecture I give place
> By heaven I neither know nor guess
> What most I doubt—nor what I most believe.'

This is the painful attitude into which we are all brought at the very moment when we expect our hero to crown his life with one achievement which shall eclipse all other achievements which preceded it. Instead of this we have the rebellion of Sancho against his master; the trees on the highway turned into so many gallowses—a horrible picture of domestic lawlessness in the most beautiful province of central Spain—Roque Guinart—the incarnation of provincial license; the beautiful Claudia, another victim, like Dorothea, of the pernicious reading of the time; the first view of the sea; the insult to Rozinante by the rabble of Barcelona, showing the estimate in which the 'Don Quixote' is held by the lowest and most brutal; the enchanted head illustrating the intellect of the Spanish middle-class mind; the visit to the printing office; a view of the pirates of the African coast; the expulsion of the Moors, the only life-like picture which has come down to us of that insane act of an ignorant people and a priest-ridden king; the return to the duke's castle, which Don Quixote thought he had quitted for ever, but to return to go through the burlesque of the Holy Inquisition; the descent into hell! the scourging of Sancho—a profound mockery—and a new use of the rosary; the return home; the recovery of his reason; his peaceful death in bed, and taking the Sacrament—thirty or more striking incidents, all new, all gems of genius, hurried together in a short space, and to no purpose! This is not Cervantes' way. His 'Don Quixote,' as it was the first great novel, and the father of all modern novels,* so it was a novel with a purpose—and the main purpose is lacking—because a lewd priest had touched his subject and profaned it. Just as some stage carpenter, to catch the gallery of the Globe, made Shakespeare's La Pucelle invoke the help of fiends and to offer hell

"'Her soul, her body, soul and all
Before that England give the French the foil.'

After which the whole Globe, including pit and royal box, was ready to believe anything that was said of 'the holy maid' of France. Allow me Don Felipé, to repeat that the great tournament that was to take place in Zaragosa had been long promised. There had been many such in Spain, at which Charles V., Philip II., and Philip III. assisted. Valladolid, Salamanca, Seville, Madrid, and Naples had held their jousts which were nothing but masquerades, the revels of an idle time—a dying world—whether for pastime or in

---

* Including the Waverley Novels, which would be an incredible statement if Sir Walter had not said so himself. See Lockhart's " Life."

profound pretence, mimicking the glorious enthusiasm, when the sword welded to the cross swept the accursed crescent from the earth and planted the standard of the Church on the highest rock of the world—as it was thought; and now there should be another joust, and the scene the Celtiberian Salduba—Καισαραυγυστα—the glorious free city of a glorious king and the shrine of heaven's queen. But, as I have said, the promise was not kept for the reasons which I have given you."

Don Felipé laughed at my *elocuencia,* as he called it, and marvelled that so much could be said about "Don Quixote." He had read it for pure amusement and nothing else. Nor did he believe that Cervantes had any such intention as I had ascribed to him. Don Felipé firmly believed that the Phœnicians had once visited Spain and had made iron out of some of his own hematite ore. That blast furnace was sufficient evidence for him; but he could not see that the work of a man of genius was like the pie in the nursery song, in which the four-and-twenty blackbirds were baked, when the pie is opened the birds begin to sing." Hereupon three-fourths of the company run away in a fright. After a time, feeling ashamed, they excuse themselves by declaring the pie stank so they could not sit near it. Those who remained behind—the men of taste, the epicures—say to one another, "We came here to eat. What business have birds, after they have been baked, to be alive and singing? This will never do. Here is an invasion, for who will send a pie to an oven if the birds come to life there? We must stand up for the rights of ovens. Let us have dead birds, dead birds for our money." Then each sticks his fork into a bird, mangles it awhile, and then holds it up and cries, "Who will dare assert that there is any music in this bird's song?"*

I was now in great dread that Don Felipé would not ask me if I had any proof of my assertions, in which case I should have had to conclude that he did not care a fig about this matter, and that I should lose the opportunity of making use of the new discovery in the Colombina. This oppressed me a good deal because I felt that I had already given him quite enough of 'Don Quixote,' and it would be gross cruelty in me to press upon him more if he did not wish for it. But to my great joy he returned to the subject, and inquired how I became possessed of all this knowledge, and if it had ever been of use to me further, he hastened to add, "than entertaining your friends." "Have you ever made any money by it?" he inquired, as if he were an American, and it is true that we had become very familiar.

I told him that I had once delivered two lectures on this subject before the celebrated Philosophical Institute in Edinburgh, for which they paid me £10; but that, as I had had to pay my railway fare to London and back, which by going third class amounted to £3 6s. 8d., and my hotel bill at the Caledonian for six days, which came to £6 5s., I did not make much profit by my labours. But I had great pleasure in recollecting that by means of the same lectures I once raised £200 for building a house of refuge for young women in one of the English gold colonies.

On hearing this his interest increased. I did not care to tell him of my translating the 'Don Quixote' into English, and the great pecuniary profit and universal praise I gained by this work, because a man is not unseldom an object of

---

* Julius Hare, I think, in "Guesses at Truth." It is a long time since I read this passage. But I am sure that I have not spoilt it in quoting.

doubt when he tells the tale of his own successes. Don Felipé was glad to have me read to him the document discovered in the Colombina, because he was a real Spaniard and full of Spanish sympathies; but it would not interest the English reader.

It was necessary to draw my visit to Don Felipé to a close, and I had to resort to a stratagem in order to escape getting still deeper entangled in the toils of his hospitality.

I ordered José, the major-domo, to have my horse saddled early in the morning, as I intended to reach Murviedro the same night. This I knew he would not fail to communicate to his master, and, as I expected, Don Felipé was down to see me off. He had also ordered his horse to be in readiness. The moment I saw him I went to him with the copy of the precious first edition of "Don Quixote" which he had given to me, and I said—

"Don Felipé, you must keep this rare book in your own house. Do not part with it on any account to anyone; it is one of only some five or six copies that remain in the world. Let this be kept in Spain, and let me help in showing to the world that even in Spain Cervantes is no longer neglected."

He took the book in silence; he embraced me; we drank our chocolate, and mounted. He rode with me as far as Valverde; and a very windy ride we had, talking was impossible. Arrived there we breakfasted, and then I bade him farewell, and I have not seen or heard of him since.

CHAPTER XVIII.

CANADA.

SOME TIME ago when I was in the pay of the Government of the Dominion, Canada became more and more every day a land of much importance to me, for always have I found that the people who supply you with money are much more interesting and worthy than others, even though they may be superior in manners and talents who do nothing in your behalf. On one occasion I enjoyed the hospitality of a man who at one time was a great friend of some connections of mine, and by means of his commercial acquirements and relationships in the grocery and lumber trades, of which trades he was a pillar, I was able to see much of one particular part of Canada, and to make the acquaintances of many men, both good and bad.

One day as this grocery man was driving me in his dog-cart, I think he called it—and it certainly was his own—to see some salt wells which he thought of buying, he said pointing to a house half-a-mile in front of us: "Yonder is the house of the man I am going to see. He is one of our self-made men."

The house pointed out did not appear to me to belong to

the ordinary self-made man. It was surrounded by one of the best gardens I had seen in the district, which is rightly called the Garden of Canada. Not far from it was Natawasauga Bay, which stretches into and forms part of the waters of Georgian Bay.

Now, there is never any difficulty in making your way into a Canadian house, provided your entrance be marked with goodwill and courtesy; so my friend and I found easy access to the pleasant and substantial dwelling of the Canadian self-made man. I was not anxious to make his acquaintance—preferring to remain outside and look at things which, although not self-made, were beautiful and of infinite value. But my friend, who was great on all matters pertaining to common salt, and had, in fact, come to consult with the self-made one about some salt wells, of which he was the owner, insisted on my going into the house with him, and in I went. I expected to find the self-made a ponderous, square-shouldered man, of heavy jaw, high cheek bones, a long chin, small eyes, who had forgotten to get a forehead in the process of his creation, and who, if he had ever been endowed with any of the simpler graces which help to make up human character, had obliterated them all in making himself anew.

The moment I saw him I enjoyed an agreeable surprise. He was still young, well built, with a good English face, a rich voice, a clear eye, an uncringing gait, and fresh and open in look and gesture. He received us in a quiet, but frank and easy manner; he took us into his private room, which was well littered with books and papers; he went himself to the pantry, and brought out wine and other things, which he set before us with that sweet politeness which can only proceed from kindness of heart.

This natural behaviour of the self-made, whom I shall call Job Spring, showed itself in other ways than by supplying us with refreshments. He took us round his garden, introduced us to the pigs, the poultry, and the dogs, and explained those improvements which were of his own planning, together with certain projects for making his homestead famous.

After a while my grocer friend interposed, and said that as he had come to see the salt wells, he would like to be shown the way to them. On which Mr. Spring called to a serving man who was there, and said to him —

"Take this gentleman to the springs; show him everything; tell him all you know; and be back in an hour whether the gentleman returns with you or not." Then, turning to me, he said, "Do you wish to go with your friend, or will you remain here? I shall be glad of a talk about the old country."

There was a mixture of peremptoriness and kindness in his tone and manner that was pleasant to see and to hear, and I answered that I should prefer to remain and give him such home news as I could, if it would please him.

"I shall be more than pleased," he said; "I shall be grateful."

No sooner had the others left us, and gone in the direction of the salt property, and we were alone, than a strange feeling took possession of me. It was a troublesome, half-awakened consciousness that I had met this man before, and known him under some conditions that were not of the pleasantest kind. This feeling did not last more than a second, nor did it again return, until, after awhile, it came back attended with a few veritable facts which made me speculate, as I had often done before, and still oftener since, on the mysterious manner in which the lives of some men seem to be linked together.

From the garden we strolled back into the little room where we had been received, and, after shutting the door, but before taking a seat, I was asked in a quiet, untroubled voice —

"Do you know London, and the country round about— I mean in the direction of Surrey?

Now it was to Surrey, while Job and I were together in the garden, that my thoughts had suddenly flown.

Quick as lightning the truth flashed across my mind, and I knew the man's early history, although, as I have said, I had never before seen him, or heard his name, nor had he said more words than I have here set down concerning himself which could have given me the least hint of who he was, where he had come from, or what had been the course of his life. It was not until my friend had left us for the salt pits that this secret communion between my own spirit and that of the unknown man before me had begun; and it continued to increase after the first moment of uncertainty had passed away. I discovered that he did not care about mere newspaper tidings from England; his wants were deeper, and we fell into a vein of homely talk chiefly about ourselves. I even got the length of calling him by his Christian name.

I had risen from my seat, and was walking about the room talking to Job all the time, and now and then looking at the goodly row of books on the shelves. The first book I picked out contained a name, the sight of which sent through me a thrill of pleasure. The name belonged to a relative of mine.* Job saw me take out this book, and saw

* The Reverend Charles Walters, M.A., late Chaplain of the Redhill Reformatory, Surrey.

me restore it to its place again. Then, turning my back to him and going to look through the window in order to hide what he must have discovered in my face had he caught sight of it, I said to him in a cheerful voice —

"Job, they call you a self-made man; how do you like it?"

"Like it?" he replied; "it is one of the worst names a man can go by. I have often tried to stop it, but it is of no use; the people here are so accustomed to it."

"What arrogance and pride there is about it. Talk of self-conceit, this is the conceit of the devil," I said. "Do you not think this vile phrase to be a real Yankee product of Yankee independence and bluster, and springs from their money-making republicanism?"

"I think," answered Job, with much seriousness, and as if he were pained by my alluding to Americans in terms which he considered to be intended for an insult or a sneer, "I think that the phrase 'self-made man' was at first a mere idle word—and it is so still in many cases—and seldom or never intended to bear the meaning you would put upon it."

"Then why should it offend you," I inquired, "when it is applied to yourself?"

"Well, you see, it depends upon how people are brought up. In this country," he continued, "a man is taught very early to rely upon himself; the children are much smarter than our children are at home. I have seen young lads do things which, for intelligence, would put a whole English village to the blush, including both the parson and the squire."

"What do you mean by being brought up differently?"

"Well," said Job, "I mean chiefly the way that sacred

things are taught to them. From their earliest days, English children—at least the children at home of the class to which I belong—are made to feel that they are nothing else but prisoners: the earth their prison, the great Father their gaoler, and His Son the one who comes and persuades the Father to be kind to them, and let the little gaol birds go free. These terrible symbols stick in the child's mind; they haunt it, and fill it with images of terror. Such imaginings make the child timid, and very pliable to the first powerful influence which comes upon it."

Job's sentences were very nearly missing fire, so he pulled up in this rhetorical fashion —

"Whereas," he went on, "in the children's schools here, while they are taught much that is like this, it is not all like it; there is something else besides. They learn much of natural objects; they get ideas; they get abundance of fresh air —"

"They get, in short," I struck in, "a variety of moral and mental food. But do you mean to say that the English child is taught the fear of God in some way that it hurts its moral nature; and that this is not the case with the American child?"

"Yes," he said, "I do mean to say that; and I say more, that this over-much talk about the Almighty, dressing Him in black like an undertaker, surrounding Him—not with the charm of mystery, but with its jargon—stifles in the child all power to reach after Him, except as a Being who can do anything and everything He likes; and, although they soon discover that He never does interfere with them in the way they have been led to expect, yet they get the notion that He is as changeable and as full of interference as their own parents."

"Job, you are an atheist," I said, with as much grim humour as I could throw into my voice, putting a bold, unaltered face upon the whole matter, hoping to divert his thoughts from what I knew to be at that time directing and colouring them.

Job, however, went on unmoved, and proceeded as follows:—

"I think I can safely say that no man has tried more than I have to help poor fellows who left the old country and came out to Canada 'to better their condition,' as they were told they would, but which they never did and never will, because they never had anything to better. They are not men at all—except in shape, and not much of men in that; they have the brains of birds or rabbits, who build their nests and make their holes, as they did at the creation; and if you insist on their being men, and learning different ways, and obeying a different master to what they have been accustomed, they simply jib, or go and get drunk, and enter the hard and active service of Satan, because, indeed, they are not strong enough, and were never taught to fight in the active service of God."

To which I replied—

"Job, all this is very dreadful; and I am beginning to suspect you to be a Republican, or, as I said just now, an atheist, and let me tell you I ought to know what that is, for I think I have known more men of the clerical profession than any man who has lived for sixty and odd years in various parts of the Christian world."

But Job apparently did not hear my remarks, or what is more likely, did not care for them; he was like a hound on the scent, and not to be diverted from the pursuit by the babbling of a shallow brook.

"I mean, of course," he proceeded, "the untaught, ill-fed poor; the beings who cannot think, nor even see anything but the food they eat; or smell anything but what they give off in sweat; or feel anything but what they wear to hide them from the cold, and who are as much good in a country like this as a wheelbarrow is for helping a man over ten miles of soft snow three feet thick."

And all this ignorance, imbecility, and stereotyped or wooden notions which belong to the poor emigrant classes who leave England for Canada, he traced to the defective training, or no training, which they had received, as well as to a certain religious cramming which, he said, stifled them in childhood.

The impression which Job Spring's conversation produced on me was that Canada was a splendid man-growing country. It had certainly produced Job Spring, and I think that if some of the Englishmen whom I know in various parts of South America, in India, in Africa, and the Spanish Main, even in Australia, had selected Canada as the field of their future lives, instead of going to the bad as many of them have gone, they would have strengthened the good that was in them, and reaped the very opposite kind of harvest to that which they have garnered, and might now be living on corn instead of having to feed for the rest of their lives on husks, in the company of swine.

If Job had been left to himself when a boy in England, he would have added to the number of its permanent criminal population; but being taken in hand at the right time—supplied with the physic appropriate to his malady—in other words, made to labour with his hands, taught to plough, and sow, and reap, he became, as he now is, one of the most perfect men I have ever met. To Job every new day seemed to be an addition to his personal pleasures, and he convinced me that he went to bed for the express purpose, and with the fixed faith, of rising to a better day than he had as yet seen.

"Job," I said to him, as the above passed through my mind, "what splendid health you have."

"Well, you see," he answered, with an easy smile, which I verily believe had in it the slightest curve of a sneer, "I have no debts, except one that I can never pay. I have no fears, no anxieties, except such as now and then come to make me ashamed of the manner in which I have wasted much time. But," he added, with a curious dash of suspicion in his eyes as he looked at me, "do you think good health comes from being well off?"

I replied that I had a sort of belief that good health was much mixed up with good conduct, and perhaps right thinking.

"It has, I think, more to do with right doing," said Job; "and as for opportunities of doing right being so few, I can't agree with those who so complain. It is not my experience. I know that the more right things a man does the more he can do, and the easier he can do them; and one of the most mischievous errors ever taught in book or pulpit is, that it is easier for a man to do wrong than right."

"What a spectacle of shame it is," I remarked, "to see so many beggars and thieving tramps not only in Canada, but through all the Eastern States of America. How does it come about?"

"There are faults on both sides," said Job, with great promptness and moderation; "it is a long story, and an awkward business to discuss. There is no use in going back, or quarrelling; if there were, a few Cabinet Ministers would have to be dug up and hanged, as well as innumerable jobbers in land, and not a few local jobbers in colonial politics, but," continued Job in his dogmatic fashion, "I am myself a living example of THE RIGHT THING TO BE DONE. The exactly right and appropriate thing to be done with me was done; had I been sent from the old country to Canada without first being taught to do the things I had to do, or had I come here without guide or friend to receive me, I should even now be a beggar, or a thief, or at best a mere splinter in the bucket, instead of one of the staves which compose it."

"Or one of the hoops which bind it together," I said.

"A steady stream of emigration has set in from England to Canada," Job continued, "which nobody can stop, and which nobody ought to try to stop, but it might and should be regulated; it might and should be a blessing to both countries. There are a good many people in England who are worth a matter of £5,000 sterling, and all that they can make this sum to yield will be £250 a-year, or £300 a-year at the most, and with this the man has several children to educate and provide for, besides other things. These men would flourish in Canada, and Canada would flourish the more their number increased; and what is more, they would be of greater use to England in Canada than they are at present by remaining at home."

"How do you make that out?" I inquired.

"Easy enough," was the answer. "These people, so long as they stop at home, merely live from hand to mouth. Every year they buy fewer things, for their purchasing powers are diminished every year by such expensive luxuries as fantastically educated children; but once out here their ability to buy would only be limited by their ability to consume, which I assure you grows amazingly. That is one class of men who ought to be encouraged to emigrate to Canada; the others are those who should be compelled to do so, and by a hearty co-operation this would be easy enough."

" How compelled ? " I inquired, with much amazement.

" Just as some folk from being cold are compelled to work to get themselves warm ; or as the epicure is now and then compelled to take a blue pill to aid his digestive organs ; or like the people of the highways and hedges who were compelled to come in to a wedding feast."

" Do you mean that you would have the Colonial Secretary of State go tramping up and down the kingdom, beating up recruits for the Colonies ? "

" There are plenty of officers of the kingdom already to do that, if they would only do their work," said Job. " The British Colonies ought to have been held out to the British workman as prizes to win and rewards to earn, and as places of distinction for which all were to contend; and this idea is fast making its way among the people, who know that by thrift, uprightness, and the practice of other virtues, there is a career open to them in the Colonies equal to that which made many obscure men famous in England 300 years ago. Unluckily for us, the first use that we made of one of the most splendid of our new domains was to transport there our desperate criminals, instead of honest, industrious men. These latter, when British capital became devoted to manufactures, and machinery displaced operatives, and operatives became herded in great shops, and labour became more and more divided, we then proceeded to do the enormous wrong of building for them great houses of state, called workhouses, keeping them and encouraging them in idleness by outdoor relief, and even indoor protection, clothing them, and teaching their children at the expense of those who still had work to do, and could get paid for it. Again, the word 'emigrant,' which should suggest ideas of health, hope, and prosperity, has been degraded into low meanings by its association with the very scum of the people; and so, what with transportation, and able-bodied paupers, to say nothing of filthy emigrant ships, and wrecks of emigrant ships, pilfering, over-paid, Colonial Government emigration officers, land sharks, and money sharpers, thousands of good, sound-hearted English work-folk have been deterred from even thinking of emigration; and they have gone through many years of a cheerless life, its only charm to them being that it was unstained by crime, and that they had never troubled the parish."

Here my friend, who had been looking after the salt property, returned, and having taken a seat with us in the same room, Job, with the decision which distinguished him, plunged swiftly into the matter, and settled it in his own way, and after his own original fashion. It was his method of dealing with the man of salt that increased my curiosity and interest in his knowledge of emigration. He began as follows, addressing my companion —

"Do you like the property?"

"I do," replied the other, who did not much relish saying so point blank, Scotchman as he was, but could not help himself.

"Are you quite satisfied that you can do with it all that you can reasonably expect?"

"Well, Mr. Spring, I want to know how much money you want for this property; how you wish the money to be paid, and so forth; and then you may leave me to form my own opinion as to what I can make by the bargain."

"Not so," answered Job. "I have no need to sell, but I am in need of a good neighbour; and if I could make up my mind that I should have a good one in you that would go a great way with me in coming to terms. From this letter you have brought me I find that you have been a lumberman."

"Lumbering is still my business, but I have taken a fancy to salt," said the other, who was beginning to feel a little more at ease.

"Very well. I don't ask you for any money, but you shall have the salt springs for $5,000 worth of lumber, to be delivered here next fall at current rates, and you shall pay me 6 per cent. on all profits you make above $5,000 a year for the next five years. Those are my terms. We need not discuss them if I have made myself clear; it would be waste of time for you to try and alter them."

"The terms are clear enough; but I should like to think them over," replied the man of lumber.

"Take a turn in the garden," said Job, rising and giving the man his hat, who could do nothing else but go out into the garden, whether to think over the said terms or not. Then, addressing himself to me, he said, "You did not tell me your name, I think? Or have I forgotten it?"

"ADALID," I answered, unblushingly.

"He repeated it, and said that it sounded more like a woman's name than a man's.

"I did not say Adelaide," quoth I, "but ADALID," giving to it its full Arabic sound.

"Then it is not an English name?" he said, interrogatively, which I answered in the affirmative.

"It came from Spain," I added, "and let me tell you there are many useful lessons to be learned in Spain. For example, the last time I travelled through Castile I came to a little farm-house by the wayside in the middle of a hot day in August, and my companions and I turned in there, and we were kindly entreated by the people to whom the house and farm belonged. We six, in the space of two hours, consumed three gallons of wine, a dozen small loaves of fine bread, and several pounds of delicious raisins, such as you never taste out of Spain, and how much, think you, did that elegant wayside repast cost?"

"Perhaps ten dollars," was the reply.

"It cost exactly ten *pence*," I continued, "which uncommercial transaction took place near to the village of Calamocha, in the valley of the Jilloca, once one of the most fertile tracts of country in the Peninsula; but, alas! there are now in that region more ruins than habitable dwellings, and more houses than men."

"How came that about?" inquired Job, who, like a hungry fish, rose at every strange fly that was cast above him.

"It came about," I said, nothing loth to tell, "through a religious difference. That romantic valley, like many another in Spain, now so desolate and dreary to look at, was once alive with thousands of men, women, and children, by whose constant free labour and skill the hills and dales gave fragrance to heaven, and health to the earth. But one fine morning all these busy people were turned out bag and baggage, because they could not be made to believe in the Pope, or make believe that Mary, the Jewish Maiden, was the mother of God; and ever since that sublime act of sweeping the Roman Catholic House of Spain clean of heretics it has become occupied with the worst of evil spirits, for which there is now abundance of room. The country, to speak in plain English, has been ever since going from bad to worse; people starve in the midst of plenty; poorer than poverty-stricken Job, they are as proud as Lucifer, and are more piteously ignorant than the romantic person who ripped up the goose which laid the golden eggs."

" Oh ! " said Job, " you are speaking of the Moors. I have often read about them, but never till now since you began to speak of them have I ever realized the force or meaning of what I read. What a wonderful thing sympathy is. I shall go back to my lessons to read and learn again the chapter of the expulsion of the Moors from Spain."

" And you may add the Jews "—but wishing to get back to the subject of emigration, I added, " If you go offering such a premium as that of making English labourers and artizans landed proprietors in Canada, there will be no need of a profligate Duke of Lerma, or an eloquent bachelor of divinity, or crusading bishops, and an imbecile, easily-terrified king to make Devon and Dorset as desolate as the Valley of Daroca."

" There's no such fear, nor are the two cases the same," said Job ; " for the more the colonies have prospered, the more has England prospered ; and if it had not been for her colonies there is no telling where England might be now. Empty back into England at any moment the Canadas, the Australias, and the real English-feeling people now settled in the United States, and you would have a revolution—as great as any of the past, and very different from all of them."

" While I admit what you say," I replied, " that there is

no parallel between the expulsion of the Moors from Spain and the emigration of skilled and unskilled workmen from the Mother Country to the plantations, yet the same result might follow to England as followed to Spain. If, for example, all the colonies, after receiving the English army of workers which England has trained and taught and led to victories, in which the whole world has shared, should take it into their heads to impose prohibitive duties on British merchandise, as some of them have done already."

"I have no fear," Job answered, "about what you say of prohibitive duties ever coming to anything serious. Here and there you may find a few political philosophers who are to the rest of British colonists what the Irvingites are to the great bulk of British Christians, but they are too fantastical to do any permanent harm."

"Do you think that any widespread tendency still exists in Canada to give up the Union Jack for the 'Stars and Stripes?'" I inquired, intending to keep up the discussion under a new guise.

"Such a tendency exists, but it is not widespread," said Job. "It is confined to men whose existence depends upon competition, who live to keep up the contagion of competition, and who believe competition and nothing else to be the one spirit that rules the universal race, and guides, prompts, and sanctifies its progress. But those men are becoming fewer in number every day, and every day their number will grow less the faster the colonies of Great Britain determine the peculiar character each is going to play in the future."

We talked on many subjects, and Job was ever on the alert for knowledge. Knowing that I had been staying for a year or so on Lake Superior he begged me to tell him what I saw up there, and how the people lived and what they were like.

" There is not very much to see," I replied, and begged him to be more specific in his demand.

" What is the extent of this copper region, and what is the general appearance of the landscape? How many towns and villages are there, and how do they look?"

" If you include iron mining, together with the copper, the mining district on the American side of Lake Superior is in one continuous line, 400 miles long and 80 miles wide in some parts, in others it is less. From Marquette to Ontonorgan, the last village to the north-west, before reaching Duluth, the distance is 250 miles, and all the land between those two points is highly metalliferous. There are more than a dozen towns and villages scattered over that space, and all, with the exception of Marquette, are the most abject-looking and misery-stricken towns I have ever seen. The landscape looks like a murdered thing. You see nothing for miles and miles as you travel along in summer-time but signs of violence; the blackened stumps of great trees which have been burnt down, look like charred corpses. There are also great mounds of waste sand, and mountains of broken stones; forsaken mines surmounted by fragments of machinery, which hang silent in the air. All is like this until you come to Calumet, where you find the largest native copper mine that is known in the world. All the little streams which once ran through the Huron Hills, and carried copper in them, would appear to have emptied themselves into what now seems to be an inexhaustible pit of copper, called the

Hecla and Calumet mine. Here the town is substantial looking, even healthy; and carries itself as if it were not to be frightened out of its wits in the night-time."

"Did you know any of the working-people—the miners, for example, in any of those towns?" inquired Job Spring.

"I made it my business to know as many as I could in every one of them," I said. "I lived among them, ate and drank with them, and I know more about them than I like to tell."

"Give me," said Job, "a general idea of the people; who they were, where they came from, how they looked, and how they lived."

"The great majority," I said, "were from Cornwall; there was a good sprinkling of Germans, a few French, not a few but a good many Irish, and an odd lot of Bohemians, Poles, Hungarians, Swedes, and Finlanders. They were, for the most part, hard-working, kind-hearted men, and full of sterling character. A good number had saved a little money. The Germans and French were given to spending their Sundays in shooting little birds or going after deer. The Cornish were, in their general ways, less intelligent, having no religious excitement to keep them up to their old standard, and these relapsed into sulkiness and general dulness. A few of their number had, however, become rich, and were very good, kind-hearted, wise men, according to their light and opportunities; but the native-born American was always superior to them all. The women fared the worse, and the poor Cornish women worse than any. Many went mad. One poor fellow, whose children were growing apace, who had built himself a very decent home, and earned good wages, was married to one of these unhappy creatures. She had taken to drink. The stillness of the lake-shore, with its stretch of unruffled water, the cloudless sky, the flowerless earth, the murdered trees, the absence of church bells, and of every other familiar thing which belongs to English life, the value of whose ministry is never known till it is lost, bewildered her, and then she lost her senses. She made her man's home a hell; she starved his children; she broke his furniture, and smashed his crockery. At last he left her, then she followed after and found him, but he refused to take her back; until one day, as she stood moaning in the street, she deliberately stripped herself stark naked and stood before his door until he, for very shame, was compelled to take her in."

"That will do," said Job. "I do not want to hear any more. I had an idea that some such life must be the outcome of passing Acts of Congress by the arts of the gambler. I knew that the worst forms of human misery are to be found where competition is the order of the day. I thought I knew the full meaning of the cant phrase, 'protection to native industries' in our Colonies. I perceive that I had something to learn; and I thank you for the knowledge you have given me."

Here the man who wanted to buy the salt-pits again interrupted us by putting his head in at the door and inquiring —

"Is the six per cent. on the five thousand a-year to be paid in cash or lumber?"

Job replied that if that was all he stuck at he might take his choice. When the bargain was struck, and all necessary documents signed, Job asked us to take dinner and remain with him for the night, which we did.

The dinner to which Job invited us was of an early

English type; I mean that it was not what we now understand by a dinner-party. We began at once on roast beef, without any prefatory soup, fish, or anything else. But the beef was a marvel of succulent tenderness; so were the vegetables. The fruit pies were delightful, so was the bread, which, somehow, made you believe that it was made by the hand of a woman; so light was it that it retained the perfume of the wheat from which it was made. Job drank home-brewed ale, but provided wine for those of weaker stomachs. We were waited on by a maid.

The man whose soul was in the salt-pits went early to bed; and Job and I remained alone till very late before we said good-night, and we talked chiefly about the eternal question of emigration.

The earnestness with which my host spoke of the ignorance, ineptitude, and stolid idleness of the poor emigrants who were sent out of England to Canada, in the vain hope of bettering their condition, approached to fierceness.

"Is it not all their own fault," he continued, in a milder tone, "as you may see after five minutes' talk with them; at the same time it is easy to find out that they have simply been got rid of for the good of those who remained behind—at least they come to think so themselves. For they speedily discover that everything they have been told about Canada they have been told wrong; their stupid hopes have been raised by pretty pictures, and no pains taken to help them towards realizing them."

"But, Job," I struck in, "this matter of the emigration of the poor is still going on; what would you do to improve things? You appear to have thought about it, and to have some experience in it. Give us some practical advice."

"Do?" he exclaimed; "I would begin by undoing."

"Oh! you would send us back all the moral cripples—the drunkards, thieves, and thriftless ones. I remember the Australians once threatened to transfer back to England all the convicts which she had sent to Van Diemen's Land."

"Did they?" replied Job, with much astonishment. "Well, I do not mean that; nor should we gain much by it. But let me say that before I was allowed to emigrate they first put me on to a farm for three years, where I had to work, and to work much harder than I had to do when I first came here. I was then fifteen years old. When I arrived here there was a friend to receive me. And then I had to begin to learn things which, if I had not before been taught the way of learning, I should soon have got sick of, thrown them up, and run away perhaps."*

To me it was very delightful to hear Job thus refer to his early life, and I remarked —

"That is the way they began with you; but how do you propose to begin with those who have been begun with at the wrong end?"

"Oh!" he sighed, "it shames me to think of the laziness, the misery and waste of human life always to be found in England which need not be."

"Come to the point, Job," I cried out, "and do not go fretting and fuming in that painful manner. What would you do, I ask again?"

"There are so many sides to the question that it is not quite so easy as choosing a knife to choose which side of the emigration question to provide for first; but, no doubt,

---

* My dear relative when chaplain at Redhill paid more attention to the industrial training of the boys than to their reading, writing and arithmetic. He was besides a High Churchman, and the services in the delightful little chapel were as much a part of the drill as digging on the farm.

if we can get hold of the master principle all the rest will follow like a flock of sheep."

Here there was a silence, and, to my disgust, it was broken by Job asking —

"How many parsons are there in England, do you think?"

I was getting somewhat wearied with what seemed to be a mania of his. I believe that Job Spring had not an idea in his head that was not connected with a parson, so I answered with some indifference —

"Oh, as many as jackdaws, I should think—perhaps fifty thousand of all kinds."

"A vast population, devoted, for the most part, to the propagation of talk," remarked Job, in a tone that carried no malice, but some evident regret. "Hundreds of thousands of starving men and careworn women consoled by hearing of paradise, who never get the slightest chance of learning how to behave in paradise should they ever get there."

"Pray go on," I interposed; "don't mind me, I am accustomed to free speech and free thinking."

"In this our Canada," continued Job, as quietly as if he were winding a ball of worsted, "there are hundreds of thousands of acres of land waiting to be made into a garden, and yonder in England are hundreds of thousands of labourers standing idle, not earning a penny—many preferring to steal it; and the preachers of paradise seldom or never open their lips to these idlers to tell them of a vineyard to which they might go, and in which they can work, much less to command or hire them to go to work in it."

"What rant is this?" I demanded. "Where have you

been?—what company do you keep? Do you perchance correspond with the author of 'Modern Painters'?"

"I never heard of the gentleman," Job continued. "You asked me for my ideas, and I am trying to give them to you. If you do not interrupt me, I shall the sooner get through. Now if those shepherds of the sheep were to offer a real paradise to these poor, as they might, not as a boon, but as a joy—an inheritance to improve and beautify —what men, sheep, and shepherds they might become, and what a change would happen in the world! There might be held here in Canada fifty farms of forty acres each, and two of these farms should be six times the size of the others, for larger and more varied work, and where model farming would be carried on. There should be also farms where the untaught labourer would be received on his arrival from England, drilled on it, and kept at his work and prepared for better and higher things. One of the better things would be his own land, on to which he would pass when he had laboured for a period of two years. He would be enrolled in the Dominion Militia at once, and if he stuck to his duty he would receive farm implements, seed, and oxen on easy terms from the General in command, after a certain time, which, as I have said, need not exceed two years, and —"

"Hold!" I cried. "Do me the favour to tell me, where are the poor parsons to get the hundred thousand pounds or so with which to start this delightful militant-agricultural man-helping Utopia?"

"Get it! Where do they get their stained glass from? and their brass filigree and twisted candlesticks, to say nothing of the gilt cocks stuck on spires, which cost hundreds of pounds a-piece? Let them build churches of

T

living stones; they will cost less money, and endure much longer than any that are built of blue stone or Portland. Say we start with a capital of a hundred thousand pounds, we should have no difficulty in getting it. We could draw up a prospectus that would make men's guineas start out of their pockets like fleas start when the blinds are drawn and you begin to move. We should not have the least trouble in getting labourers, in getting the farms, in raising corn and beef, potatoes and barley; and we could become the greatest cheesemongers that the sun ever shone upon.

"Oh!" he exclaimed, in fervent language, "how many hundreds of thousands of pounds have been thrown into such quicksands as the Eliza mine, oil wells, and schemes of impossible railways, and not a groat into the only profitable one of all investments, namely, that of human industry guided by knowledge!"

"That is an idea which I should think would be able to fight its own way in the world, if it got a chance," I said.

"It is a great idea," said Job, "and like many another of its kind, no one knows who first gave it out. Is it not a strange thing that we should have among us so many men of really great intellect, and so few with what may be called great ideas? If money-making could only for once be connected with a great idea, even money-making might become a means of grace. I could name three men who by themselves could make a sensible impression on the food supplies of England—a marked sensible impression on that hideous spectacle called able-bodied pauperism—and gain ten times more profit than they gain at present by dealing in other people's money, taking care of it, or doing the easy work of mere pawnbrokers. But they cannot commit themselves to this, because these men are as innocent of great ideas as a guinea-pig is of a purse. They are, likewise, mighty timid, and also somewhat ashamed of looking singular, and so they remain the commonplace beings they have always been, and always will be — "

" Job," I exclaimed, " you have been reading the history of William Paterson * and his bubbles."

" Yes," he answered, " and there has been no great colonization scheme since the disaster of Darien. It failed because it deserved to fail, but so far from that history, even with all its horrors and its immortal disgrace, deterring us from attempting great things it ought to encourage us. Paterson was ignorant of everything pertaining to Darien; he misrepresented its climate, its capacity, its productions, and his title. There was a truly great idea in the plan, but the enthusiast had not paid the least attention to one of the details which it was essential to observe. If another William Paterson could come and organize flour grinding on the St. Lawrence or at the Sault de St. Marie we should see a result worthy of the times in which we live. The valley of the St. Lawrence would become a garden; the Pacific Railroad would run through a thousand miles of corn fields; and a million men, women, and children would in less than five years be living in their own homes, who up to then had had no home and no hope of getting one!"

As I lay in bed that night, before falling asleep, I thought it a good sign of the times that a man like Job Spring should be found who thought on these things.

The joyous sun of an autumnal morning in Canada does its best to rouse anyone out of bed who has the least taste for enjoying the charms of a new-born day. At an early hour I was awakened by the sun coming into my room like

* See Macaulay's " History of England," Vol. iv., pp. 91-498.

a turbulent friend in search of a companion, whose advances admit of no denial. I got up at once, opened the window, and received a breath of air as delicious to breathe as it is to eat ripe fruit freshly gathered. I then proceeded to make use of a tub of water and an enormous sponge which had been placed in my room by the thoughtful master of the house. While I was in the midst of my ablutions a thundering attack was made upon my room door, which hastened my movements.

"Come in," I was at last in a proper condition to sing out; but as no one came in, and the noise being repeated, I half opened the door to see who my visitor might be, when, to my great surprise, and altogether against my will, the door was pushed open, and in bounced a Newfoundland dog rather less in size than one of the lions in Trafalgar Square. "Holloa!" I cried, in as cheery and confident a voice as was possible to me, and the great beast bounded over the tub of water, and at once turned round and faced me, lying down on his stomach; he then stretched out his two forepaws, opened his mouth, rolled out his bright-red tongue, and began beating the floor with his tail as if he were threshing wheat and expected to be paid for it. I was as polite to that dog as if he were a man of superior intelligence, who had come to confer on me some favour. Each garment I took up and put on suggested some remark, which I addressed to that dog in the most musical tones I could throw into my voice. I called him in a familiar way all the endearing names I could think of. If I could have turned all the money I had in my pocket into bread I should have done so at once, and in the most playful manner thrown it into the jaws which yawned before me.

At last I was dressed, which Newfoundland seemed to know quite as well as I did.

"Come on," I cried to the great fascinating beast, making a dash at the door, and as if we had known each other all our lives. To my intense relief the enormous brute bounded out of the room, downstairs, and through the front door, which stood wide open, on to the grass plot, and once there he gave a bark which shook the dew-drops from the trees. Of course I followed him, and I was no sooner outside the house than he scampered off to a remote part of the garden, I meekly going after him, evidently much to Hector's pleasure—Hector was his name. As I turned the corner of the house, Hector watching my approach, prostrated himself on the gravel walk in front of a bower, some distance off, opened his great jaws, put out his great tongue, and began beating the ground with his great tail as he had beaten the carpet in my room. Up I went to this summer-house, as Hector, of course, expected, and there I found Job Spring, dressed for the day, seated inside, smoking a pipe, and reading.

"Good-morning; how did you sleep? You like dogs, I see," was the greeting I received.

And I had to confess that I did like dogs, but was not quite sure if I liked being taken into custody by one of Hector's size.

As I was quite sure that Hector was listening to all I said, and understanding it, I was very guarded in my remarks.

I learnt that Job had sent the dog to call me, and instructed the creature to bring me to the summer-house, and very faithfully had the dog done his master's will.

Here there came into our shady retreat a dairymaid carrying a large white jug of milk. The appearance of this girl, the way she came in, and the curtsey she made when she went out, made as much impression on my mind as anything else I had seen in that house. It was the only curtsey I had seen a woman give to a man in the New World, and I could not help reflecting how much the New World had lost by allowing that act of grace and worship to fall into desuetude. Probably, if the Job Springs were more numerous, there would be more women to make curtseys.

" Did you notice the servant who brought us the milk? " inquired Job, in cheerful seriousness.

I told him that it was a habit of mine always to notice a man's servants, and sometimes I preferred the servants to the man.

"You," my host continued, "wish to have a plan or idea for conducting emigration. There is no plan to be had for individual cases. Every individual case requires a plan of its own. This servant, whose name is Rose Marigold, was dairymaid at home to a man whose name or calling I will not mention. All I will say of him is that, without being a scoundrel, he wrought the social ruin of that girl; had she remained in the old country she would have certainly added to its evil and shame, but her master put an advertisement in a London paper, which quite by accident caught my eye, and it moved my heart. I answered it. Rose has now been my servant three years. She is a jewel. That little fellow, whom you see toddling across the lawn yonder, is her boy, and he will become a Canadian farmer. He might have died in a ditch, and his mother on the gallows; but God is merciful to all who hope and trust in Him."

I was greatly affected, and will not trust myself to write what I heard of Rose Marigold, or the passionate feelings which flooded my heart on hearing all that Job Spring told me of her.

The attachment of my generous host to Canada as a place to live in was as plain to be seen as the blue sky which stretched above us. It coloured his conversation; it never left him; and in some form or other it was constantly coming up.

We were sorry to part. Job pressed me with great earnestness and affection to remain with him for a week, but the cares of this world forced me away from further communion with one of the stoutest-hearted men it has been my lot in life to know and to love.

As my grocer friend and I drove away from the house, I said to him —

"You told me that Mr. Spring was one of your self-made men."

"So he is," replied my companion.

To which I answered that Mr. Spring was as much a self-made man as yonder oak was a self-made tree. But the man, although a friend of mine, did not seem to understand the remark.

Job Spring is one of the treasures of the ancient English kingdom, which are dispersed through one of England's many mansions that we call Canada. And there are others like him, with plenty of room in which to grow, and who hold within them a sufficiency of power to hand down for centuries to come the English name, and who know that there is no need that a single Englishman should perish, either for lack of bread, or the lack of a noble human love.

CHAPTER XIX.

STILL IN CANADA.

I WILL tell of one or two more of these chance acquaintances, because they will help us to understand some of the ways of life peculiar to Canada, and appreciate the novel conditions under which a man lives in that ever-improving part of the New World. I made the acquaintance of which I am now to tell on board a great pleasure steamer, while running down the St. Lawrence on a trip to the Thousand Islands, which in the autumn put on a painted pomp worth journeying several thousand miles to see. An imaginative person might be excused on first beholding the coloured trees of these islands for believing that the gold and purple clouds of the summer had fallen there from the skies, and were held by some unseen hand among the leaves and branches. The native Indians must have taken their fashions of tailoring from these gay and gaudy princes of earth and sky; and certainly an Indian chief, in all his magnificence of red and white plumes, his porcupine quills and coloured leathers, is not unlike a maple tree whose leaves have undergone much kissing of the Canadian sun.

I had occupied a few monotonous hours in reading a book called " Man and Wife ; or, How to Become a Brute in Six Lessons," or something like that, and a book more false it had never been my lot to buy—at least, I thought so at that time—and, in revenge for my folly in buying it, I flung it into the river, where at the moment I would also have flung its author had my power been equal to my will. This ostentatious act happened to be observed by a fellow passenger, who, like myself, had nothing else to do but stand bolt upright among several hundred people, and look over the side of the steamer at the rapid river, over whose rippled waves we were going at the rate of sixteen miles an hour. Presently he and I began discussing the demerits of the book I had consigned to a watery grave. This led us on to other things, and ended in our dining together at the same hotel in Montreal, where we stayed that one night—occupying the same double-bedded room—and returning to Toronto together in the same steamer on the day following. He turned out to be a young doctor who had taken up his abode in the region which lies on the Canadian side of Lake Ontario, between Toronto and Lake Simcoe—a good wide region, sufficiently indefinite for anyone curious to discover the dwelling-place of one whom I may now call my friend.

It seems to me, from the little experience I have had in the matter, that what the doctor of souls once was, such is the doctor of physic of to-day in the estimation of certain well-to-do people. No professional man inspires such thorough-going devotion in the female breast as your handsome doctor, provided that to ability in his art he adds great firmness of character, coupled with sweetness of manners. This is not to be wondered at; the confessions which some women are ready to pour into the professional ear are of a kind to beget confidence. It is no doubt this passion for confession in women which makes such thorough-paced charlatans of certain doctors; and it is remarkable how like a fawning priest goes your thorough-bred money-making fashionable doctor. His dress, including the white necktie, his sleek ways, his complexion, the whites of his eyes, his measured walk, his serene and equable conversation, his universal knowledge, his smiling despotism, his steady and unshaken faith in things long ago exploded, the awful sanctity of his behaviour when in the company of the superior clergy, all show a curious parallel with the professional priest. It would seem that when to a man—be his vocation the saving of souls or the healing of bodies—the vocation becomes a profession in which the money he is to make, or the social distinction he is to win, become the paramount objects of life, in that same moment do the two quacks become transformed into the same likeness, especially if the sphere in which they both move be noted for its love of ease, its insincerities, and its fondness for what is only common to the superior brutes who are ever dumb. Then are you sure to see your sleek family physician, and the family priest, or the fashionable parson, of one and the same colour in cloth and in skin, both equally and scrupulously clean outside, both as empty and sometimes as undesirable within, as a stranded boat on a bank of mud.

It was the somewhat free handling of some such subjects as this that established a common feeling between my young doctor and myself—so strong that we became friends, as we remain to this day. I stayed with him several days at his own house.

It was the snuggest place a man could desire, and only wanted a wife to make it the happiest—provided she was a wife and not a Dushenka, a milliner or money-monger, or any of the other equally objectionable things which pass under the name of wife. There was a garden of about half-an-acre, which contained for the most part pot herbs of every sort, vegetables innumerable, and fruit trees; attached to the garden was a field in which, besides a cow, there were pigs, geese, and innumerable egg-producers, all hemmed in on two sides with brick walls, and the other two sides fenced with shingles. The house was built of wood, but was commodious and weather-proof, the rooms large and lofty, and the stories were two. At the back was a large yard paved with brick, with dog kennels, in which were housed spaniels, pointers, hounds, and a bull-dog with a very observing eye and a curled tail; there were stables and two horses, a four-wheeled buggy and a sleigh. The inside of the house was plainly furnished, the bedrooms were like the soldier's quarters, who is above all luxury in that department except of a clean bed, a tub of water, and rough towels. A man servant as well as a maid waited at table. The dinner was better, both in the quality and variety of food, in cooking and serving, than will be ordinarily found in the houses of wealthy people in London. The wine was good, the beer excellent, the whisky Old Bourbon, which Prince Napoleon once said was the only good thing of the name he had ever known.

During the hours of day the doctor rode out to see his patients, or he drove out, and then he took me with him. He introduced me to many admirable people whom it was a pleasure to meet, who had cut their way through many troubles, while weighted with heavy sorrows, to safety and repose. Many of these not only had carried on their backs their poor relations, but their sinful relations likewise, and made long journeys through life with such impedimenta, coming to rest at last, thankful that they had done such service.

One evening the doctor was visited by some officers of the British army, who were quartered not very far off. They had come to borrow the dogs, and to invite the doctor and me to a day's sport on the morrow. They remained the whole of a night, which will live in my memory as one of the merriest a man may spend. We had all of us travelled far and wide—in India and Africa, in Australia, New Zealand, and Peru; and from the Pacific to the Amazon, and from the western shores of the Atlantic to the Meta and the Cauca, and heaven only knows where besides, and we were all born on British soil, and not a renegade among us.

Not with an income of less than five thousand pounds per annum could a man command the social distinction, or find such society and comforts of life, not to mention a long string of health-yielding duties, as my friend found in Ontario, and which cost him certainly not so much as three thousand dollars a-year.

But behind these three thousand dollars was a free, open-hearted, brave, handsome fellow, as full of health as he was of knowledge, as modest as he was true of heart, and with only one failing—which was, perhaps, the secret why he had not married, or which kept him from dipping his hand into what he called the bag of snakes called marriage, on the chance of securing the one being that could not poison his life or sting him—and that failing was, that he would always have his own way, and think his own thoughts, and carry them out in a perfectly original and masterful fashion.

"How came such a magnificent fellow as you to leave Old England?" I ventured to ask once, when we were alone. We were smoking our pipes after dinner, in front of the great fire of logs which blazed on the wide hearth of my friend's dining-room, when I put to him that stereotyped question of mine.

After a pause, and looking at me over his pipe, out of the corner of his right eye, he said —

"It seems to me that you have asked that question before. There is a dryness about it, and about your way of putting it, that smacks of the diary-keeping man, who is callous to human frailties or tastes and feelings, and only looks upon human beings as so much raw material for using up in ink. Come, confess."

"It is true," I said, "that I have asked that question often, of many and different people, but never from lightness of heart, nor because I am going to write a book—though if ever I do write, it shall be a book as unlike any other as I am unlike my neighbours. There must be some sort of pleasure in writing books, or so many women would not engage in the occupation; and one of these days I may try and find out in what that pleasure consists. But I am not thinking about it at present."

"Gentle and harmless creature," he replied, in assumed sarcasm. "Might I ask what first prompted you to put that question, to whom you first put it, and what answer you received?"

"Well," I said at once—for I thought I perceived a slight suspicion of my having trespassed—"the first person I ever put that question to was myself. The occasion of it was my being lost in the Desert of Atacama, when I was near becoming food for condors, and the answer I received was so amusing, that I have come to believe there is more fun and humour in us who wander over the face of the earth than may be found in the good mortals who stay at home, and that both the fun and humour are of different stuff. We get into the habit of bullying ourselves, which is even more amusing than playing with dogs or parrots. When I went wandering in the dark on that, to me, eventful night, beneath the tropic of Capricorn, I could not help laughing, amidst all my woe at the question which seemed to come from my household soul to the wandering soul then mounted on the top of a mule, 'What the devil was it that brought you here?' and the answer which the fireside soul obtained made me laugh, and almost hold opinion with Pythagoras that the souls of animals infuse themselves into the trunks of men, not in Gratiano's sense as he conveyed it to the immortal Shylock—for I suppose your worship believes as much in hell as in heaven—but rather as Malvolio would have it. I need not tell you the answer I gave to myself. I am only accounting to you for having acquired the habit of asking some of the men whom I meet abroad what it was that first set them thinking of leaving home."

"Very well," returned my friend, "I need not answer your question either. But what kind of answer have you received from other folk?"

"Oh," I replied, "one man said that his reason for emigrating was that he was fond of a garden; and another that he was hungry."

"A very good answer too, although for that matter I have known men emigrate because they had no appetite; but go on."

"Another said that he came out to America because they insisted that he must doff his bonnet when he went for his wage. He refused, and came out to a land where he could be free. A third said that it was for love."

"Ah! that must have been a woman. Love and pride are potent causes of motion, as well as heat."

"While another declared that his sole reason for leaving England for the New World was the decline of the drama."

"All this," my friend said, "is surprising and delightful. Here is a new object in life for my idle hours, and one that will supply me with a fund of delight; but then I haven't got that fascinating eye of yours, or that remarkable impudence, which seems to belong to you as its perfume belongs, shall I say, to the dandelion? How, in all wonder, did you get at that woman's answer who said that she came out from the Old Home for love?"

"Oh, I flattered the baby," I replied, "who was caressing its mother and kissing her in the most delighted manner, which excited my envy, and I made some remark about man being an unthankful, restless, ambitious animal, seldom happy, and always wanting to be in somebody else's shoes.

"'And whose shoes do *you* want to be in just now?' she inquired, with a pleasant intelligence.

"And I said 'The baby's,' on which of course we both laughed, and then she told me her story."

"That method is quite beyond me," said the doctor, "and I suspect you to be a Jesuit, for it is a conviction of mine, on which I invariably act, that any fellow who is cleverer than myself is bound to belong to the Society of Jesus; but I repeat, all this is interesting. Here do we find all the elements of national greatness, the passion for pastoral pursuits, love, pride, the drama, and the lower appetites, to satisfy which men consent to till our soil, black our boots, dig coal and iron, sweep chimneys, and do all the other hard and necessary things which certainly neither you nor I could or would do, but which must be got over if we would live as superior creatures ought to live. Well, I had intended to give a rallying answer to your impertinent question, but I relent and forgive you, for there is some admirable use to be made of this method of pumping people. I shall adopt it and cut you out, for is not competition the glorious attribute which distinguishes the man from the ass? Know then, oh wandering sage," he continued, "that the reason why I left Old England was fatty degeneration—peristaltic action—aconite, together with a dogmatic condemnation of Dr. Sangrado's treatment; all these at one time or another got me into such hot water with my governor, who was physician to Bishop Sweetapple, as well as to the Dowager Duchess of Patchouli, that I was glad to pack up my traps when the governor suggested it, and give up lies and imposture for the sake of living as it becomes a man to live who cares more for fresh air than lavender powder, and prefers freedom to the sleepy monotony that is afraid to laugh lest it should land you on the shores of silence to live in the cold. And now, take my answer, and add the same to your *repertoire,* and to be as epigrammatic as possible, write down for your answer 'Science *versus* Humbug,' and give that as the reason why I, among the many of your acquaintances, left Old England, and why I am now here in this new land. The dear old bishop, who was very fat, fell sick of a fever, and at a certain stage of the disorder my old quack father proposed the Sangrado method of letting blood from the Episcopal arm. I not only remonstrated, but was guilty of the indecorum of swearing at the practice of my venerable parent, and all the venerable humbugs associated with him in their treatment of the case of Bishop Sweetapple. I went further, and said to the friends of the right reverend prelate that if he were then bled he would die. Humbug shivered in its shoes, but as my fate would have it, I had to compound with Humbug; and to save my dear old father from humiliation in his own eyes, as well as to wash my hands of a set of murderers who commit homicide through ignorance, I came out here, and I may tell you that I am right glad I did so."

We continued on the best of terms, and I never visited his part of Canada without going to see him, or without receiving a warm reception, and I had to promise always to make his house my home when I passed that way.

Not all the men of whom I asked the reason why they left the old country answered with equal alacrity. Some put on an expression of countenance that was far from pleasant, as if they had been reminded of something painful, while others were glad to have the time recalled to mind when they began life anew, in a new land, under a new sky, surrounded by new faces, and inspired with the strength of new hope. These I found were generally men who had started with a definite idea, bent on realizing it, and finding each day's happiness to consist in advancing towards it if it were only the advance of an inch—the saving of a sixpence, or the removal from an acre of ground of a handful of stones.

It was a habit of mine to stroll outside the towns where I happened to be staying, with the object of discovering traces of English tastes, customs, or ways that could be recognized at a glance, as an old mode or fashion kept up for its own sake in new circumstances and under new conditions. I have made agreeable acquaintances by recognizing certain old words in the talk of people who had come from certain English localities. But this was easy compared with such tricks as trundling a mop—the way of cleansing a bucket—adorning a window with flowers, or painting a door, and dressing out its step. More than once have I amused myself and astonished others by asking certain tidy women who seemed to have much love for domestic cleanliness in dress if they had not come from such and such a town; and when, with a laugh, they answered me in the affirmative, and demanded to know how I had found that out, the reply would be —

"Well, only in Masston did they use such curtains stretched on thin brass rods across the window; and only in Hampton did men cultivate gardens with such earnestness and passionate love."

One day, being a couple of miles outside the little flat town called London in Ontario, I came on a cottage standing in a garden that roused in me much curiosity. I could not refrain from going to see the person who lived in it and learning, if possible, if the builder of that cottage and the maker of that garden had not once lived in Masston. The cottage had a wide porch in front, supplied with a settle on each side, and the walls were spread over with honeysuckle, whose branches were pinned against the walls in careful regularity.

"Good morning; do you come from Masston?" was my greeting to the solitary man who opened the door.

He was a spare built and somewhat timid fellow, not in the least like a man who would of his own accord get up from the place where he had been knocked down and renew the strife in which he had been worsted.

"Masston?" was his reply, "no, I did not come from

Masston; but I was born there, and so was my father and my grandfather."

" Did you know anyone in Masston?"

" Why, yes. I knew the Haydons and Mr. Buckle and old Sparrer—that was when I was a Dame Cumberladge's scholar; but I left Masston early and settled in 'Ampton after my father died. Won't you come in and sit down?" he said abruptly, but with evident cordiality.

Without asking me if I would take any refreshment he straightway went and brought a brown stone jug full of beer—of his own brewing—two clean pipes, and a tobacco pot with a leaden damper inside.

"This," I said, taking up the straight brown jug with a wide mouth, " is Masston ale, and that is a Masston tobacco pot."

" Yes, I follow my mother's way of brewing, and that tobacco pot belonged to my father; it is the only thing of his I have, except yonder pair of sugar-nippers, which I saw him make."

" Do you follow your father's trade?"

" Not exactly; he was a steel toy maker, I am a coachsmith," he said, with much mildness.

"That surely is a new name," I remarked; "used you not to be called a whitesmith?"

He did not know, he replied, in a voice which clearly said, " I am a solitary man, I know nothing, except to make springs, brew my own beer, and dig my own garden; and although I live more on the past than in the future, yet I do not lead a questioning life. I live on the things which come to me of their own accord."

I made myself as pleasant as I could. I spoke of cheerful things. I praised his garden, his cottage, the tobacco, and what appeared to be his way of life; but the more I talked the more silent he became, and a look came into his eyes which made him wear the expression of a man who had once been tired, and could never get a sufficiency of rest.

"I suppose you had to leave the Old Country," I said, leading up to my usual question, "like many others, because there was no work for you."

"No," he answered, with an animation that raised my spirits, and helped me to put my query point blank.

"Well, well," he began, "it is strange that it should be so pleasant to talk to a stranger, but it is like going back to early times to see one who knows the town where you were born when we meet in a strange land."

Here he took a long pull at the brown jug, and then, with some brightness coming into his somewhat careworn face, he told his story, which was something like as follows:—

"If you had asked me why I left Old England a little while after I got here, I could not have told you. I don't mean to say that I didn't know, but that I couldn't tell. I had no words in my mouth for the job. I had plenty of feelings, and plenty of hope, and plenty of disgust, but I could not have expressed myself well enough to make anybody understand either one or the other. What is very curious is, that after I had lived here for a couple of years and began to make the garden grow, I began to talk just as when I was a lad. I could not only speak plainly what my thoughts were, but new words came to me every day, just as naturally as the graining comes into oak; and I believe that curious welling up of words inside me is owing to nothing else than the fresh air and living among green things of your own growing, to say nothing of having plenty of work to do and as much play as you like.

"How I came to emigrate was something like this: You must know that when I was born and for some time after, the gardens in my native town were almost as many as the houses. Every householder had a garden, and our garden was famous for its gooseberries and black currants, cherries and pears, potatoes and spinach, and all the herbs. For many a year after the time when I as a young shaver was allowed to go into the garden and pull as many gooseberries as I liked, that old garden was the only thing that was a real pleasure to me to think about—it came into my dreams, it stuck to my fancy, and all the more that by the time I had grown up, the garden, somehow or other, had gone; yes, gone for ever, as clean as the days of my childhood had gone. It was eaten up by a brickfield first, then a thundering big manufactory was built upon it, and, last of all, the garden and the country round it was run through by a railway.

"That eating up of our garden was the fate of all the other gardens, and in less than fifteen years there was no garden to be seen, much less to walk in. Still less were there any blood-red, or bearded, or gold-skinned gooseberries to pick. The town became as famous for smoke and dirt and disease and accidents which maimed men, as it was once famous for its gooseberries and good beer.

"I, among many others, became a ruined man at the age of thirty. What the process of my ruin was, may I be damned if I know. If I had been the only one among them who became poor I should have said it was through my own fault; but all my neighbours got into the same mess. Not a week passed but somebody came to grief. There was an auction in every street at exactly the same hour every week, some of the neighbours being sold up for their rent. Men with ten children had to give up living in a decent house and to go into pigsties and huddle together; then they began to die. Some fell into low habits, others died with their eyes wide open. The women—God Almighty love them—took to tippling; then their big daughters ran away to other towns, and were never heard of again. We were all brought to horrible straits. Only the masters got rich, and the richer they became the poorer we became; and may I go to hell if it isn't true that when one of our neighbours had to sell up, and come down and go and live with thieves, it acted like a plague on everybody else. Everybody else, sooner or later, came down too. But the greatest blow was robbing us of our gardens. And when the gardens went, and were covered over with houses and shops, we, who had lived in the country all our lives felt as if we were being walled up alive."

"Do you really recollect all that?" I inquired; and my voice, against my will, sounded as if laden with tears.

"Recollect it!" he exclaimed, looking at me out of his large blue eyes, which had now for the first time, as it seemed, come into view, "no, I don't recollect it; it ain't recollection at all; it's something a tidy bit stronger than recollection. I don't recollect my heart beating yesterday. It was somewhere about that time," he proceeded to say, "that I got a fever. I was altogether thrown on my back. I had to sell all my tools and my clothes and my old father's watch and seals, and was as near going on the parish as hundreds of the old men and women of the town had gone already."

"What is the cause of this hatred of the Workhouse among you working people?" I inquired—not because I was altogether ignorant of many of those causes, but I wanted to hear this man's particular reason for reasons of my own. "Some of you fellows," I continued, "look upon the Workhouse as a disgrace."

"So it is."

"As a deadly insult—"

"So it is."

"To your existence; or as if it were not a place of refuge to which you have a right to fly, but a trap to catch and hold you, from which they will serve you up for somebody's dinner when the order comes."

Here there came into my host's mouth and nose and eyes the most abominable sneer I had ever seen mar a human face; it was not only visible to the eye—you could almost smell it. It wrinkled his forehead, buried his blue eyes out of sight, and crumpled his cheek bones.

"You seem to be a clever enough chap," he began to say at last, after regarding me through his wrinkles as a thing to be despised. "You go to an English Workhouse, the best on 'em, and try to read what is written on the faces of some of the men; they'll never tell you what they think or feel, because they can't—if they could, mark you, they wouldn't be in that Workhouse, and that's a nut you can try and crack whenever you like to try; but am I to tell you how I came to emigrate?"

"By all means; I am not going to let you off telling me that story, and then we can return to the Workhouse afterwards."

"Damn the Workhouse," he cried, fiercely, "let's have another jug of ale;" and up he got, and with much cheerfulness went and drew another quart of the wholesome brown beverage, of which we both partook with equal grace and thankfulness.

"While I was down in the fever," he continued, with a

new face, a new voice, and a simple gesture of his right hand, " the gooseberry gardens used to come into my mind as real as when I was a lad. I could smell the strawberries and the nettle-blossoms. I'm blessed if the taste of some of the black hearts and gold beards and jargonelles did not come into my mouth and make it water again. At last, when I was able to get up and walk about, I went straight to the spot where our old garden once grew, and when I found that I was no longer dreaming, but was then standing in a new dirty street and for gooseberry bushes there was nothing but long, dead, straight brick walls, and for sunshine falling on lettuces and onions, beans and apples, there was nothing but clouds of black smoke, and beastly mud, and broken bits of crockery, and brick ends, and pieces of dirty newspapers, I began to cry like a child.

"I got better, and soon got to work again. One day there came a letter from Canada, from an old shopmate. I heard it read, and two lines in that letter opened my eyes, and put new life into me. The two lines were these: 'We have got a splendid garden, and grow our own grapes as well as apples; and as for peaches, they are worth walking twenty miles to see.'

"I said nothing to anybody, but I made all sorts of inquiries, and I read more newspapers than ever I had read before in all my life, but I could never find anything about Canada in any one of them that gave me any light. But I started off at last, with a sort of tremble for my hope that I was going to get a garden of my own, and live among people who owned their own gardens. God knows I never dreamed the half of what I have found it. Here I have a garden twice as big as my old dad's; all my neighbours have gardens; and one of the blessings of having a garden of your own, and neighbours with their own plots of flowers and vegetables and fruits is, out here, that we can live—live together without talking or anything else, except being up early in the morning and taking in the breath of the sweetest things that grow. That was how I came to emigrate. I wanted a garden. Hundreds of folk have asked me what I have done after all by coming to Canada. 'You are still a working man,' they say, 'and you could be that in the Old Country, where the work is not so hard, nor the winter so long, nor everything so new that it tumbles to pieces for lack of years.'

"I just answer them," he said, with a hearty chuckle, "that I've got my own garden, and nobody can take it from me. All my neighbours have got their gardens, and nobody can take 'em from them; and we are all hearty and well, and if the winters are long they are not cold, and if they are cold the air is fresh, and there is plenty of fuel. Besides, the winters here are a wonderful time for rest and for good fellowship. All the time that the soft snow lies on the soil, men's hearts grow closer to one another, and get warm."

I believe that one of the best means of restoring hope in the breasts of those of our countrymen who are well-nigh past hope, who get drunk in order to forget their sorrows, is to give them a stake in the New Domains which we ourselves have called into existence. Nor am I sure that the time is far off when wholesome work of a novel kind will be begun in this our land, that shall make it increase in wealth, peace, and perhaps godliness; and if the beginning of that work must needs be attended with inconvenience to some, the fault will be largely due to those who thought too much of their own ease and comfort, and too little of the cheerless labours of those without whom no ease is possible and no comfort can last.

CHAPTER XX.

BOOKS AND LIBRARIES IN THE COLONIES.

How different is the taste of a book at sea to what it is on land. A favourite book in London is sent to Coventry on board ship; and although the good traveller does not put up with all kinds of companions, yet he welcomes nearly all who come in his way, if they come with courtesy. I have always gone abroad with plenty of books, and by means of books I have made more agreeable companions than by means of tobacco, wine, or court plaster, although these have frequently stood me in good stead and brought me in delightful contact with people whom it has been a joy to know. I have known many whose popularity was founded on nothing else than a pack of cards. A well-stored housewife has been known to do wonders, and so has a pair of pocket-scissors; a wax candle will make a man immortal under some circumstances, and so will a small bull's-eye lantern. These, however, are only appreciated in times of trial and emergency. Books, on the contrary, are for all times; they are never sea-sick. My own seafaring books have always been working books; one set devoted to the bibliography of Don Quixote, another set to the bibliography of Shakespeare, and the rest to the migrations of man and the acclimatization of plants and animals. Technical, as for the most part they all were, they were always looked at with great interest, and sometimes devoured with startling avidity, by fellow travellers. There is nothing like a long sea voyage for making new acquaintances with books and women.

"Can you lend me a book? I am tired of my own company and of that of others," said a large, self-complacent man of money to me one day, after we had been a fortnight at sea without exchanging a word.

I had a well-printed copy of Gulliver's Travels, richly bound, and offered it to him. He began to read, and stood reading for ten minutes. I left him and came back after a quarter of an hour's absence. He was still at it. He read through the little book without stopping. It made him think; it took him out of himself.

"Could you lend me another book by the same author?"

I happened to have with me Swift's "Aphorisms," another little volume of the size of Gulliver, but thicker, and gave him that. He had never read a word of Swift in his life, and he was astonished at his ignorance of one from whom he found he could get something good to drink.

On another occasion I lent Georges Sand's "Consuelo" to a large and handsome Scotchwoman with daughters, and much useless luggage in the form of closely-packed opinions and traditions, all of which became very heavy lumber before she finished the enchanting book. She read it with great delight; it changed her manners, it changed the tone of her voice, it made her a human being. She would never have read this book on shore; she would not of her own accord have had anything to say to me, and still less to the doctor of the ship, who was known to be a Roman Catholic, and very dangerous on account of his religious knowledge and the fascinating way he had of imparting it. And I think it is very likely if all, or nearly all, Scotch women could go to sea for a while and get away from their fierce and narrow, and sometimes shallow, beliefs and thoughts about the future, it would do them good. As for the Scotch minister, he is always so much at sea in a metaphorical sense that if he could make a long trip on a real sea it might do him good also. But I do not know. We once had one of these godly men on board a Cunard steamer coming home. He was very sick for the first three days, but he was able to preach on the "Sabbath," and he took for his text the words from the Revelations, "*There shall be no more sea!*" He spoke with great fervour, and looked forward to the time when he would be able to go about the world without passing through the perils and pains of the ocean, with real gratitude to the Giver of all good, and appealed to his hearers to come into a closer union with heaven, that they too might enjoy a future in which there should be no more sea! The idea produced much sadness in me, because I am never thoroughly happy except when I am at sea. I was, however, much struck with the handiness of the Scotch minister, who proved himself able for anything, while he was thoroughly persuaded that the drying up of the sea was a part of the heavenly blessedness of the future, for had he not been very sick in the Atlantic?

As a rule, I think people do not read much trash at sea. I once saw as many as seven copies of Kinglake's "Crimea" all being read at the same table on board the *Simla*. Books of travel are well thumbed, and Darwin's

"Naturalist's Voyage Round the World" was a constant favourite; so were the works of Charles Reade and Mr. Walter Besant. "The Earl and the Doctor" was always much wanted; so was "Harry Lorrequer" and "A Day's Ride," Borrow's "Bible in Spain," and "Lavengro," Halliburton, Sir Francis Head, "Noctes Ambrosianæ," Gœthe's "Faust," Mr. Ruskin's Lectures, Green's "Short History of England," Mr. John Morley's "Diderot," "The Ingoldsby Legends," Carlyle's "Miscellanies," Thackeray's "Esmond," Dickens' "Hard Times," Trollope's "Framley Parsonage," Sir Arthur Helps' works, Headley Vickers, Hood, Charles Lamb, Wordsworth, J. L. Motley's "Dutch Republic," and Prescott's Histories. In biographies, the favourites undoubtedly were the Duke of Wellington, Sydney Smith, Burke, Scott, Nelson, the Rev. Rowland Hill, Lord Lawrence, George Stephenson, and Macaulay. I never saw more than two or three at sea reading Shakespeare, and only one besides myself sticking to the "Don Quixote," a young fellow who would not have read it if he had not picked it up at sea; but when he once got hold of it, or it had got hold of him, he could not give it up. I never saw anyone reading a volume of sermons at sea or religious tracts; but a good selection of English plays was regarded as a godsend. French novels of all kinds were always on hand. I never saw a human being reading one of Mr. Henry James's novels, and the same may be said of Mr. W. D. Howell's, which is strange, for I see these authors constantly spoken of with high favour in English and American newspapers. And this has happened so often that I ask myself, Whence comes the difference between the discernment of the practical reader and the undiscernment of the critic? I suppose we never shall know the real merit of a novel through the Press until authors write their own criticisms!

The finest public library in any of the colonies is unquestionably at Melbourne, and it is very well used. Its founder was the late Sir Redmond Barry, one of the judges of the Supreme Court, whose private Saturday night dinners I remember with delight. For one thing, however much wine you drank and how late soever you stayed, you always came away sober from Sir Redmond's house. This cannot be said of all the houses where you dine in the colonies, nor for that matter in London either.

The Parliamentary Library in Brisbane is one of the best of its size that I have ever seen, with a catalogue which is the model catalogue of all catalogues.

The library in Lima was once very rich in patristic theology and reports of missionaries of the interior of Peru, in manuscript, all of which have been carried off by the victorious Chilenos. The library in Bogotá, although small, was excellent when I saw it, and rich in local histories.

What has become of all the old books, well-bound in full calf, printed on fine paper, and kept in good preservation, which often met us in many a lowly shop in London? The answer is that they have, like many of our Irish fellow-subjects, gone to New York. All the fine old books which once were ready to hand, and after being turned out of the big house where they had ceased to command any care, had taken refuge in Orange Street, the Haymarket, in the slums of Covent Garden, and the Strand, may now be seen well taken care of in clean and orderly shops in Nassau Street, Wall Street, or Cedar Street, New York. A great trade is done in old books in the States. There is no duty on old English books, and much attention is given to the business. You can pick up a " Sentimental Journey " one hundred years old, an original "Robinson Crusoe," a "Tristram Shandy" of 1759, in New York, but not for eighteenpence. Here you shall meet with no bargains; books which are bought in London by the cartload for the price of wastepaper are sold in the Empire City at their highest value, and sometimes beyond it. A folio Hume in Russia will fetch £10 a volume. Whole libraries are often transferred bodily from some broken-up old family house in Devonshire, Warwickshire, Yorkshire, Lancashire, and Berkshire to the United States. Nothing can compete with fine old English books in bestowing an air of distinguished antiquity on a new house. The people of the United States only pay a rubbishing price for rubbish, and buy their "Romola" for tenpence; " Daniel Deronda," " Middlemarch," tenpence; " Impressions of Theophrastus Such," fivepence; " The Spanish Gypsey," tenpence; the latest and best of all the English rubbish never costs them more than a shilling of our money. But although they will not, on principle, give more than twenty-five cents for Mr. W. Besant's last novel, they willingly pay twenty-five dollars for a prime old Burnet bound in full calf; a Clarendon, and even a Stackhouse has his price, and that not a low one. The stamp of age, the seal of authority, the fame which no newspaper reporter can tarnish, the name which is sacred to the unanimous worship of all respectable people always command the attention and respect of the rich well-to-do people of the United States. The money they have to spend on books they devote to the classical authors, bound in calf, and at least a century old, and pay no duty at the Custom House.

Lima was the great place for picking up prizes. Many

a rare old book have I rescued from the *pulperias*—the low grocers' shops—where the soldiers and the poor bought their lard and *chorizos*. In one of these dirty places I found the first Atlas of the world in five volumes, double elephant, bound in gold and vellum, and mounted with the Royal Arms of Spain. Among the treasures thus rescued were early volumes of Las Casas, Garcilasso's "Florida," Lacunza, and Mollino's valuable work on Chile. These with many others, had been sold for waste-paper by profligate priests, who had stolen them from the church libraries and the once great Convent of San Augustine. Many of the books in the Biblioteca Nacional were thus rescued from the *pulperias*. This speaks volumes.

Melbourne used to have some good old book shops. Dwight's at the top of Bourke Street was excellent, and oh, what tales some of the books could tell, if they could only speak. I once bought Mr. Ruskin's "Stones of Venice" at Jamaica. A book from Lord Elgin's library, with his name written in it, I picked up in Chuquisaca. I found no books in the West Indies except at Jamaica; the white ant is an awful book-worm in those latitudes. But French photographs were as thick as leaves in Hyde Park. Montevideo was great in old books, hidden away in fruit barrels, in all kinds of shops. In Spain, if it became known that you were hunting after books, lay-men and priests would look you up in your hotel and bring you bundles of them. I once exchanged Bowle's Annotations for a choice selection of rare editions of sixteenth century Cancioneros, a fine Calderon, and three of the naughty books which, say what we will of the times in which we live, cannot be printed now. But Spain has been literally swept of its books by American agents.

I suppose next to the books which people read and store in their houses, the houses they build are most expressive of their taste and way of life. In this I think the English colonies surpass the Americans. There are finer private edifices in the United States than in Australia, but as a rule the Australians are foremost in this kind of nest building. Outside the great towns in America, it is great fun to go and look at the house architecture of the oil and shoddy dry-goods and lumber aristocracy. You will not fail to come on a Balmoral Castle, a Shakespeare's house, many Queen Anne's houses, French chateaux, Swiss châlets, and often an Hotel de Ville in wood—all in wood, giving one the idea of a lot of children having amused themselves by means of an immense—I beg pardon—a great box of wooden blocks. On the other hand, real Americans live better in their own homes than any other colonial people. Their food is better and of greater variety, it is served with good taste and in ample abundance. The magnificence is sometimes overdone, and you seldom drink wine without being made aware of what it cost. This is a polite way of showing you attention. If you are informed that you have eaten a two hundred dollar dinner, or that a ten thousand dollar dinner was given in honour of your illustrious countryman, this must not be set down to so much bragging, but as a token of affection or regard. It is very colonial, but it is their way. It also not unfrequently happens that you learn that last night you dined with fifteen millions of dollars. At first this does not strike one as having any practical bearing on one's own happiness, but you must understand from it that you were for once in your life in the society of real men. The only houses in a world of unnecessary evils where during "fly time" you can sleep without being teased out

x

of your time and temper by mosquitoes, are American houses. You are shown to your bedroom—which to your anxious mind is always viewed with apprehension—and you notice with horror that your bed has no mosquito curtain.

The mosquito torment robs you of all repose. I would rather hear the sound of the last trump than the trumpet of a mosquito. But in the house of the good American the mosquito is not allowed to enter; and I think the people who can abolish the mosquito in the parlour, dining and bedroom can do anything—and this they have done. You get plenty of fresh air and good ventilation, but no mosquitoes inside your dwelling. Wire gauze is stretched across every window, and a gauze door is also provided for all the entrances, through which no bloody-minded mosquito can pass. You only hear the concert outside, the players can't get at you; and this, in a fly country, is a blessing above rubies. For the American mosquito is not like the Eastern brute, or the South American, or the South Sea Islander. The American mosquito is a very intelligent devil. He has not yet learnt how to leave off sounding his trumpet before indulging in his bloodthirsty habits, but he has learnt many cunning ways in laying hold of you, and also in making his escape from your onslaughts on his blood-gorged carcass, all of which has come from his living with an excitable, active, and ready-handed people. The American mosquito only cares for the blood of a high-tempered race—the quick, the alert, the knowing, the spry. This is the reason why there are so many intelligent mosquitoes in the United States. But he has been circumvented. It is a great triumph.

Of colonial hotels enough has been said; turnpikes and hotels never remain in my memory. But there is one hotel which I can never forget. I was one evening sitting in the smoking-room of Palmer House, Chicago, with an American railway king whose guest I was, when there came limping up to him a broken-down man, pale, emaciated, and looking much like a disreputable tailor, for his clothes did not fit him, and he was obviously starving.

Addressing my friend by his name, he said —

"I heard you were here. I was born in the same village as you."

"What's the trouble?" demanded my friend.

"There ain't no trouble. I've made this," was the answer, on which he handed in what seemed to me to be nothing else than a meaningless piece of wire tied in a knot.

"How much do you want for this?"

"I thought it might be worth a matter of twenty or thirty thousand dollars."

"Will you have some supper?"

"Yes."

On which my friend rose and took this disreputable-looking man into the dining-room and returned. He then explained to me this very remarkable invention, which was nothing else than a permanent soda water cork-fastener.

In an incredibly short space of time the disreputable-looking man rejoined us.

"Will you have a cigar?"

"Yes."

After a little while the conversation was resumed.

"I will give you twenty-five thousand dollars for this."

"You can have it."

"Do you want any money now?"

"You can give me ten dollars if you like."

Giving him a ten-dollar note, my friend said to him —

"See me at my office in the morning, at ten," and the inventor went away.

That incident could not have happened in any hotel in London. The waiters would not have allowed this disreputable-looking man to enter the smoking-room; nor do I believe that even the late Lord Shaftesbury, friend as he was of the working man, would have taken him in to supper, offered him a cigar, and given him £5,000 for a bit of wire the model of a permanent fastener of a soda water bottle. Nor does this inventor live or get born in London or in England; he is essentially an American. This man was by trade a compositor. He had fallen sick and lost his place, but he had not lost his manhood. He was not to be beaten. He was not going into the Workhouse, or going a-begging, or borrowing, or going into the Army, even if he had been strong enough for that. His mind was free; he had the whole world to make his pick in. What could he do for it, to save its time—to save even, if it might be nothing else its fine wire? Here was a man who had no fear of the world; on the contrary, he would do the world some service. He had also no fear of this railway king, rich as he was and powerful.

"I was born in the same village as you."

I can still hear his plaintive drawling voice after a lapse of sixteen years or more; and I wish I could hear, or hope to hear, a similar voice from the village where I was born.

This chapter—the last of these Recollections—was designed to be a roaming chapter on books and libraries, and we have roamed. I first met Thackeray at the opening of the Free Library in Manchester, some thirty-six years ago. There were two meetings, one in the morning and another at night. Dickens' speech was certainly the speech of the day, the leading idea of which was the " Manchester School," about which his fancy played with an exuberance which rose into much practical eloquence.

Thackeray was next called up, and was received with much enthusiasm by the great fashionable assembly; but, to the amazement and confusion of everybody, Mr. Thackeray could not get one leg before the other. He broke down as if he had done it on purpose; but this I am sure was not the case, for he caused much suffering and pain to many. He stayed for the evening meeting. Mark Lemon, Douglas Jerrold, Albert Smith, Sir Ed. Bulwer Lytton, and Dickens returned to town by the afternoon train. The principal speeches in the evening were made by Sir James Stephen, then Regius Professor of History at Cambridge, Dr. Robert Vaughan, Thackeray, Mr. John Bright, Richard Monckton Milnes, and the Bishop of Manchester. Thackeray's speech was delicious, and no doubt was relished all the more for the painful breakdown of the morning. The Bishop expressed his own thankfulness for this speech in what, for him, was a real human expression of downright gladness, an emotion to which Prince Lee must have been an almost total stranger. Mr. Bright's speech was tame to the last degree, and during its delivery Monckton Milnes, who sat next to Thackeray, gave way to much ostentatious yawning, which Thackeray rebuked by a no less ostentatious shaking of his fist in Milnes' face. When, many years afterwards, I reminded the late Lord Houghton of this incident, he pawed the air between us, trying to look as fierce as a bear as he exclaimed, "Oh, you were not born then!"

Lord Houghton was a master of subtle flatteries, and of all the men I ever knew the least known for his great goodness. An ordinary archbishop endowed with the little-known goodness of Lord Houghton would have been extolled to the skies for his holiness; and as I must draw the line of these Reminiscences somewhere, I will do it with an archbishop. It was once my very great delight to meet Archbishop Whately at dinner. Nearly all the guests were clergymen; but not for that did the Archbishop cease to pour out his stories, his learning, his wit, and his brilliant play upon words, while the laughter was simply glorious. As for me, I sat like a little Jew boy might have sat with his eyes wonder-stretched as he gazed on Moses balancing the two tables of stone in both hands as the law-giver came dancing down the side of the mountain.

The Rev. J. B. Marsden historian of the Puritans was there, and wished, as he said to me, to turn the Archbishop's visit to some good account, if only for the sake of the younger clergy who were present; but at the same time, not to break in too suddenly upon the fun that was going on, Marsden began —

"My lord, did you ever hear Sydney Smith preach?"

"No, I never did," said the Archbishop.

"I heard him once," said Marsden, thinking that he had now got the archiepiscopal fun pretty well collared; "and, my lord, there was not a single word of Gospel in the whole sermon, except the text."

"Ah! yes," exclaimed the Archbishop, in his magnificent voice. "'Ἐν ἀρχῇ ἦν ὁ λόγος.'"*

On which there was another explosion of gorgeous human joy, and Marsden was shut up.

These recollections, however, are not foreign, but domestic.

Post scriptum.—It is with great repugnance that I tell the two stories that follow, but I am assured by some friends on whose judgment I am accustomed to rely that information on what may happen to a man in the gold colonies is of much importance to people at home; there-

* "In the beginning was the Word," John i., 1.

fore I will tell these stories as briefly and clearly as is possible to me.

An Englishman, who had travelled much in South America, and made acquaintance with its animals, including the wool-bearing alpaca, was induced to go to Victoria to treat with its Government for the introduction into the colony of a flock of these valuable quadrupeds. New South Wales was already in possession of some of them, which the Government had bought from Mr. George Ledger, and it could not be borne that Victoria should be behind New South Wales in anything. Moreover, Victoria had shown great enterprise in the acclimatization of all sorts of birds, plants, animals, and fishes, including the sparrow, the rabbit, the thistle, and the grape, salmon and trout; and great enthusiasm was roused by the mere hope of the Victorians getting hold of the koodoo. The camel they had already, and the Angora goat. Alpaca wool was then worth four shillings and ninepence a pound, and the annual value of one alpaca was greater than the annual value of six merino sheep. Therefore the Victorian Government received the Englishman's proposal to bring a thousand alpacas from the Andes with marked alacrity, and the O'Shannassy Government of their own generous free will offered this Englishman fifty pounds sterling in cash and fifty acres of land of his own selecting for every alpaca that he should bring. It may be said here that Mr. Ledger, with wonderful pluck and skill, had marched his alpacas out of Bolivia to Buenos Ayres, from whence he shipped them to Sydney, at a time when to take alpacas out of Bolivia to a foreign land was a capital offence; so that had Mr. Ledger been caught by the Bolivian authorities at a convenient spot, he would inevitably have been shot. The Victorian Government, however, was dealing with a gentleman who was associated with Mr. GEORGE WILLIAMS of Chuquisaca, who had obtained the sole privilege to export a thousand alpacas from the Bolivian Government, and the Victorian Government was satisfied that they were dealing with responsible men. Within less than two years after the above contract had been made with the O'Shannassy Government, a flock of these alpacas was brought from the Andes across the desert of Atacama, and landed in Melbourne. But by this time the O'Shannassy Government was overthrown, and another Government, composed chiefly of sons of the soil, had taken its place. The O'Shannassy Government was composed for the most part of men of wealth and social distinction, with the one exception of Mr. Charles Gavan Duffy, now Sir Charles, who was Minister of Lands, and who, by his eloquence and mastery in Parliamentary debate, had made himself indispensable to the great squatter party then in power. The party that succeeded the O'Shannassy or squatter party was composed of men, for the most part, of lowly origin, whose daily occupations unfitted them for the cares and responsibilities of Government. They sneered at koodoos and camels, and as for alpacas, they would have none of them. They also refused to recognize the contract made by the previous Government; they even rejoiced at the opportunity of giving the "Gentlemanly Government," as it was jeeringly called by the proletariat, a slap in the face. This Government was speedily succeeded by another and another, but to this day that bill has not been paid. When Sir James M'Culloch—if that is the way his name is spelt—came into power, he offered to put on the estimates a sum of ten thousand pounds sterling to be given to the man who brought the first alpacas if he would go and bring another batch, but the man in question, in his folly and pride, refused to accept this offer until the first bill was paid. When at length he left the gold colony of Victoria to come home, they gave him a gold cup at a public dinner, which was presided over by Sir Charles Darling. Running round the marble pedestal on which the vase was mounted, is a gold ribbon, on which is engraved, "Presented to A. J. Duffield Esquire, to commemorate the landing in Melbourne of a flock of two hundred alpacas." This man, with several others, notably John Farmer and George Williams, went through four years of hard work and had spent much money in trying to do a great work, which was let and hindered solely by their having to deal with little men. If the alpaca could have been acclimatized in Victoria in 1862, beginning only with a flock of five hundred, the annual income from alpaca wool alone would now be more than ten million pounds sterling. But, alack, not only has much time and money been lost, but also the valuable experience which had been gained. This is one of the things that may happen to any man in the lands of the Golden Fleece.

The other is this :—

The colony of Queensland is rich in gold, but it is poor in men. It has hitherto been ruled by men of whom the best thing that can be said of them is that they may probably beget statesmen, but at present it is somewhat uncertain. Queensland is an off-shoot of the convict colony of New South Wales, whose laws and constitution it adopted when it set up in the Government business for itself. It has had a chequered history, young as it is, but it has a prolific soil. Many excellent men and women are to be found in Queensland, who have settled down to dressing and keeping its garden, which is full of excellent things. Into this garden it was proposed by an Englishman to introduce the theobroma cacao from Caracas, and the erythroxylon cuca from the Andes, about which the poet Cowley has sung in this manner—

> " Our *Varicocha* first this *Coca* sent,
> Endowed with leaves of wondrous Nourishment,
> Whose Juice succ'd in and to the Stomach tak'n,
> Long Hunger and long Labour can sustain;
> From which our faint and weary Bodies find
> More Succour, more they cheer the drooping Mind,
> Than can your *Bacchus* and your *Ceres* join'd.
> Three Leaves supply for six days march afford,
> The *Quitoita* with this Provision stor'd,
> Can pass the vast and cloudy *Andes* o'er."

whose praises Charles Kingsley has more accurately sounded, which many travellers have confirmed, and I can ratify from personal experience. But this poor enthusiast of an Englishman had bad luck with the Queensland weather, and all his seeds and suckers perished of cold and storm. Not wishing to return home without trying to do something that should recompense him for having gone to Queensland, he made the acquaintance of the official scavengers of Brisbane its capital, whose duty it was to carry the night soil out of the town and bury it nine miles away on a sewage farm. This method was crude and dangerous to the public health, and our enthusiast demonstrated to the official scavengers that the danger could be overcome; he also demonstrated that the garbage of the town could be handled in an economical way, and with no offence to anyone. The experiments were on a small scale, and the scavengers, whose cupidity had been excited, desired to see these things done on a scale of magnitude that would appeal to and impress a scavenger's mind. They paid all the necessary expenses in a liberal manner; they did everything without stint; they were illiterate men, but full of natural shrewdness and great kindness. One of the things required to make a perfect experiment on a large scale was the erection of a model of Gay-Lussac's Tower, but there was no one in Brisbane of sufficient skill to make it. It was however quite easy to demonstrate the suitability and fitness of the great chemist's invention to the purposes required by means of a large cast-iron pot, fitted with a goose neck of sufficiently ample proportions. When this was prepared and all things were ready to prove that garbage and all other filthiness of the town could be disposed of with ease and sweetness, two officers of H.M. Customs, aided by a police sergeant, entered the temporary laboratory of the sanitary enthusiast—without any warrant—and handcuffed him and took him to the gaol in Brisbane, where he had to remain in a loathsome cell, surrounded by many evil men and women who were drunk, dirty, and blaspheming, and was kept there for more than five hours, or until the Attorney-General could make out his warrant. The good-natured scavengers came and offered bail to any amount, which was refused, and this poor enthusiast, who had been dreaming of nothing but how to make Brisbane a sweet place to live in, was taken out of the filthy gaol in the town and driven at his own expense in a Hansom cab to a large handsome gaol five miles in the country, and kept there for fifteen days without any accusation having been brought against him all that time. It is true, and ought to be told, that some dear English women when they heard of this strange thing drove out to visit this new sort of prisoner, and they brought him fresh eggs and butter and diaper napkins and silver spoons and forks and knives with ivory handles; he also had as much Scotch whisky as he wanted, and two prisoners of the ordinary sort were told off to wait upon him. One was a Methodist preacher, who emptied the slops, made the bed, and swept out the room; the other was a saucy Chinaman, who knew how to make tea, cook chops and beefsteaks, and to scramble eggs. It should also be told that when the large-hearted JOHN DOUGLAS, C.B., came to know of where our sanitary enthusiast was lodging he became his bail, and the enthusiast was restored to liberty. After a delay of some three months the enthusiast was found conducting his own case in the Supreme Court of Brisbane before Mr. Justice Pring, the Attorney-General prosecuting, with whom was Mr. Sheridan. Mr. Virgil Power had been retained on behalf of the enthusiast, but that bright and able barrister was at the last moment sent up the country on Government business, and there was no time to instruct another. The trial lasted all day; the charge against the enthusiast was that of having in his possession an illicit still. The judge proved himself to be ignorant, cruel, and tyrannical, and the enthusiast, in the jargon of the junior bar, won his case, and so ended the monstrous trial of Regina *versus* Duffield.

It is a great delight to me to say that the jury were composed of Scotsmen, who were Presbyterians, but for whose common sense and courage I might now be writing stories or remembering dreams in Brisbane Gaol, Queensland.

Immediately after this high-handed, purely colonial proceeding I applied to the Queensland Government to be taken into its service, and I was appointed Government agent on board the *Hope* to go and fish for kanakas in the Archipelago of New Ireland, and I trust it may be allowed to me to say that I did do something before I returned home.

THE END.

INDEX.

A.

	PAGE
Aboriginal Australians	123
Actors	196
Agent, Government a farce	106
,, ,, Instructions of	108
Albupharagé, Reference to the sage	40
Alpaca, The	81
,, Story of the	311
American and atheist	46
Americans	vii, 212

Americans colonials still—I do not mean that Americans are subject to any superior state, nor do I call them " colonials " save to denote their inferiority in a spiritual sense 114

Ames Fisher, reference to	230
Amencaes, The hills of	64
Ammón, The South Sea canoe	97 n
Ancizar, M. reference to his " Peregrenaciones "	80
Angelis, Pedro de reference to his works	139
Army, An industrial proposed	xiii
Artola, Pleasant recollections of the family of	131
Asensio, Don José Maria	241
Ass, The Peruvian	73
Atacama, The desert of	133, 135
Australian art	122

	PAGE
Australian life, Facts of	115
Australia, references to	90, 176
Avellaneda's false " Don Quixote "	242
Azequias artificial water-courses	169

B.

Badulaque, Don Juan de Gorduro	24
Ballard, Mr. Queensland	209
Baranquilla	41
Barcelona, why Don Quixote went there	242
Barretto, Doña Isabel	63
Beads, Coloured glass	97, 98
Beggars in Canada and the States	259
Belgrano, Doña Juana	62
Birds, butterflies, and flowers	71
Black fellows, Australian	121, 122, 123
Blood revenge the only religion of South Sea Islanders	144
Blueskin Bay, New Zealand	128
Bogotá, Santa Fé de	37, 39
Bolivia	128, 140
Books, Old	302
Bouka, Solomon Islands	161
Bowen, the port of Queensland	121
Breakfast with murderers	137
Bribing God	142
Brisbane, reference to	92, 123, 180, 314
Brookfield, Charles Esq.	vii
Burns, Dr. his cruel Presbyterianism.	129

C.

Calama, a village in the desert of Atacama	138
Calancha Fray Antonio, reference to.	77
Calderon, reference to	181
Canada	251, 279
Canada, a colony *sui generis*	xi
Canchas Blancas	150
Caracas, capital of Venezuela	156-159
Carupano, Venezuela	155

INDEX. 319

	PAGE
Castellanos, Doña Anita Ysabel de	62
Castilla de Oro	173
Cervantes, reference to	178, 233, 235, 237, 242, 250
Charcas, Archbishop of	147
Cheyne, Dr.	40
Chile, The Republic of	182
Chinamen in Peru	75
Chocolate a Mexican word	242
Chorillos	74, 75
Chunyo, preserved potatoes	2
Chuquisaca, or Sucre, capital of Bolivia	128
Church, Romish in New World	53
Clarke, Col., Governor	170
Cobija, chief port of Bolivia	131
,, Preparations for leaving	132
Colonial office, its coldness justified	114
Colonies, The influence of on mother country	xii
Colonists, a notable unlikeness between Spanish and British	127
Consumption, Cure of	83 n
Convicts in West Australia	171
Coolies	164
Coolies, The need of in Queensland	113
Coral trees at Bouka	161
Cowley, Quotation from	314
Coxe, Bishop his opinions	228
Creole, Meaning of the word	218
Cuca, Erythroxylon	68, 69
,, ,, Story of	314
Culupo, an Indian post-house	132
Curaçoa, H.M.S., reference to	143

D.

Daroca, Castile	141, 231, 265
De Quincey, reference to	20, 63, 238
Desolation in mining towns	141
Diamond, H.M.S. reference to	142
" Disintegration " a cant word of the Colonial Institute	xii
Djolgute river, Valley of	178
Doctors, Some of bodies	281

	PAGE
Don Quixote, reference to	16, 49, 242
Drake, Sir Francis reference to	213
Dunedin	128-9
Dushenka, a Russian term of endearment	2
Dynamite	162

E.

Earthquake in Lima	56
,, at Solomon Islands	57
Emigrant, The British	203
Emigration to Canada	261
English, Influences of the in Peru	82
Epitaph, A curious	115
Espinosa, Colonel, reference to	59
,, ,, his "Diccionario para el Pueblo"	77

F.

Farms, Model	273
Federation of Australian Colonies not a national cry	93-116
Fierabras, The balsam of	16
Fishes, Strange in the Coral Sea	99
Flower stall, A curious in Lima	58
Frenchmen, Two suspicious-looking	150

G.

Garcellaso Inca, reference to his Commentaries	190
Gayangos, Don Pascual	241
Gentleman, A definition of	20
Good Friday in Lima	51
Government Agent, Duties of	106
Governors, Colonial	126
Griffith, Sir Samuel reference to	111
Groom, Mr. Speaker	209
Guano—also spelt Huano—a Quichuan word for dung	124
Guayra, La	156
Guayaquil, The river of	25, 28, 29, 65, 67
Guinea pigs, A stew of	139

INDEX.

H.

	PAGE
Haggard, Mr. Rider	216
Hale, Right Rev. Bishop reference to	171
Hare, Julius reference to	249
Hawkins, Rev. E. C. reference to	206
Hebrides, The New population products and climate of	85, 88
Hecla and Calumet, largest copper mine known	267
Hector, A Newfoundland dog	276
Hole, Captain	68
Houghton, The late Lord	309
Houses, American and other	305
Human beings, Traffic in	95
Hump, Don Tomas	65
Huxley, Mount in the Coral Sea	99

I.

Idea, A great	274
Immigration question, The	93
Independence, Declaration of	217
Indian of Peru and Bolivia	76, 78, 80, 81, 148
Industry of the Peruvian Indian	81
Infanticide, Unconscious	96
Inter-State Commerce Act	224
Inventor, An American	307
Irish in America	229
Islands, South Sea, Number of visited for slaves	95

J.

Jagaranda, The	72
Jaguar, Agility of	38
Jowett's translation of Plato	196

K.

Kanaka, a Polynesian word for labourer	111
Karl, The slave ship	97, 114
Kidnapping by British Colonists	89, 143
,, how it used to be done in the South Seas	104
Kingsley, Charles reference to	37
King of Bouka	161

L.

	PAGE
Labour Coloured question in Queensland	94
Labourers, Australian	175
„ Cowardly	176
La Guayra	156
Lake Superior, American side	267
Land grabbing in Queensland	92
Lap, a small animal of tender delicious flesh in Trinidad	163
Ledger, Mr. George	311
Libraries, Colonial	302
Life, Colonial very hard	175
Lighthouses, The morality of	116
Lima, the capital of Peru	51, 117
„ Early charities of	117
Lima, Founder of	119
Lost in the desert of Atacama	134

M.

Mackay, Awful mortality among slaves at	111, 112
Macuchimina, Territory of	67
Magdalena river, The	37
Magellan, Straits of in Spanish *Magellanes*, in Portuguese *Magālhaes*	185
Magellan scenery	186
Man hunting	145
Maoris	128
Markham, Capt. A. H., reference to	144
Marsden, The Rev. J. B.	310
Marigold Rose	278
McIlwraith, Sir Thomas, his schemes, etc.	93, 96, 113
Melbourne, Victoria	118, 119, 123
„ The possible founder of. John Fawkner is the recognized historical father of Victoria, but was preceded by Batman	119
Mellon, Mrs. Alfred	197
Mescanti, a *posta* in the desert of Atacama	136
Meyra, Don Alvaro Meñdano de	63
Miners of Lake Superior	268
Monkeys	72

	PAGE
Montevideo	184
Moors, reference to the . . .	141, 265
More, Sir Thomas quotation from Hugh Latimer	43
Mosquito, The Yankee	306
Moseley's *Challenger* Notes reference to . .	43, 162
Mud, A definition of	29
Mugwump, A dissatisfied Republican . .	227
Murderers, Contact with	32, 137
Murders in the South Seas	89

N.

Napoleon the First, reference to . . .	211
Nature in the Coral Sea	99
„ „ desert of Atacama . . .	135
Negro, A handsome	160
„ „ learned	219
Negroes in various countries	162
„ Petition of	224
Newfoundland dog, A fine	276
New Ireland	98
„ „ Productions and climate of . .	100
„ „ Natives of	101
"Noticias Secretas," reference to . . .	110

O.

Ocllo Mama	80
Old foes with a new face	110
Osa el Señor, reference to	131
O'Shannassy, The late Sir John reference to. .	144

P.

Pachacamac	80
Pally Ally, or pale ale	139
Pampero, A biting wind	184
Paradise, A real	273
Patagonia, Natives of	185
Patteson, Bishop Explanation of his murder . .	143-4
Paterson, William and his bubbles . . .	275
Peru, Climate and diseases of . . .	82

	PAGE
Peruvian Coast, The	70
Philosophical Institute, A tribute to Edinburgh	249
Philip III. of Spain, Petition to	84
Phœnicians in Old Castile	232
Physiognomy of mining and other towns	141
Planters, Main blame of Sugar	113
Piracy, American	212
Plato, Dialogues of reference to	197
Potatoes, Preserved	2
Potosi, or Potosee—The value of silver taken from these mines has been considerably more than £300,000,000 in the course of 342 years	84, 139, 140, 167
Prayer, How to make a long Presbyterian	207
Presbyterians of Australia, a proud and powerful sect	125
,, ,, St. Louis, Missouri.	220
Priest, The Spanish Peruvian exactions of	80
,, Roman Catholic, in Australia	204
Pring, The late Mr. Justice	316
Publishers, American	215
Pulperias, or grocers' shops	304
Puntas Arenas Magellan Straits	185
Puquios, post-house	150

Q.

Queensland Government, reference to	145
Queensland, Land-grabbing in	92
Quiñones, Don Felipé	232
Quindio Mountains	38
Quipos, or Quippus, A Quichuan word signifying a knot	194
Quiros, Captain his petition to Philip III. of Spain	84
Quito, Distance of from Guayaquil	29
Quixote, Don reference to	233

R.

Railway, Great Trans-Continental of Australia	94
,, from La Guayra to Caracas	160
Reading, Methods of	21, 22
Recruitor, The on a slaver	104 *n*

	PAGE
Redhill Reformatory.	254
Religion, The of fashionable women	14
„ and morals in the Colonies.	195
Relique of the religious press of Peru	52
Remittance, Appointed Conductor of	148
„ Story of the robbery of.	148
„ Gold and silver.	154
River, A tropical	30
Rosario, The Cruise of H.M.S. reference to.	143

S.

Sacrament, The Holy allusions to	14, 15, 17, 52
Salvado, priest and hero	170
Samaria, Women of reference to	23
Sandstorm in Peru.	71
Saya y Manto	62
Sea, The Coral	99
Secretaries of State British, coldness of explained	114
Sermons, On	205
Servants, Domestic in Australia	174
Ship Canal, Panama reference to	75, 116
Sinners, English 3,661 in Western Australia.	171
Skipper, How I locked up a.	130
Skippers, Kidnapping fate of many.	114
Slaves, Price of on sugar plantations.	96
Slavery in Peru	78
" Slavery," " slaver," and " slaves ".	96
Slaves, Mortality among	112
Smith, Dr. Archibald	83 *n*
„ Rev. Sydney.	310
Snowstorm, A theatrical	42
South Sea Islands, Early mention of.	84
Spanish Colonists, Humanity of	117
Spain	231, 264
„ History of, how to be written.	198
Spanish early reformers	244
Spectacles trick	111
Spiritualist, Confessions of a.	47, 49
"Spirit and Form," reference to	206

	PAGE
Spring, Job a Canadian colonist	253
Stars, Beauty of in the desert	135
Sterne, allusions to	12, 13
Stevenson, Mr. Louis reference to	212
Stephenson's, H. H. cricket team	xiii
Stowe, Mrs. H. Beecher	214
Strong, Rev. Dr.	228
Suez Canal, Incident in the	176
Sugar Company, The Great Australian	95
Sugar, Importance of growing in Queensland	113
Superior, Lake	267
Supreme Court, Brisbane	316

T.

Tattooing in New Ireland	100
,, ,, New Zealand	128
Tennyson, allusions to	xiii, 3, 8, 9
Thackeray, The late Mr.	308
,, Letters of	viii
Theatre, Importance of the	200
Thirst, Real and imaginary	135
Tierra del Fuego	185
" Trade " rubbish	97, 109
Travellers of literary distinction, reference to	114
,, ,, ,, ,, their mistakes	118
Trinidad	155, 163
Tumbara, Native name of New Ireland	99

U.

United States, The	211
Uruguay	184
Utopia, Canadian	274

V.

Valparaiso	187
Victoria, Australia	118, 119, 125
Vieyra, Rev. Padre de	166
Virgin de Pilar	243

	PAGE
Viracqocha Inca, Sayings of	193
Voyage in prospect	196

W.

Walters, The late Rev. Charles	254, 271
War, A new kind of	35
Water, Storage of	169
Wesleyan Chapel, A handsome	119
Whately, The late Archbishop	310
Wilson, Don Patricio	40
Williams, Mr. George Chuquisaca	312
Wiseman, Sir W., referencé to	143
Women, Peruvian	60, 61, 63
,, Aboriginal, of Queensland	122
,, Slaves in Queensland	96
Woman, A shining	164
,, The poor English Emigrant	177
Woolgar, Miss, reference to	197

Y.

Yncas, same as Incas	190

Z.

Zaragosa	242, 248
Zealand, New	128

www.ingramcontent.com/pod-product-compliance
Lightning Source LLC
Chambersburg PA
CBHW030006240426
43672CB00007B/843